THE NATURE OF
DESPOTISM

THE NATURE OF
DESPOTISM

From Caligula to Mugabe, the Making of Tyrants

Tom Ambrose

NEW
HOLLAND

For Justine and Poppea

Published in 2008 by New Holland Publishers (UK) Ltd
London · Cape Town · Sydney · Auckland

www.newhollandpublishers.com

Garfield House, 86–88 Edgware Road, London W2 2EA, United Kingdom
80 McKenzie Street, Cape Town 8001, South Africa
Unit 1, 66 Gibbes Street, Chatswood, NSW 2067, Australia
218 Lake Road, Northcote, Auckland, New Zealand

10 9 8 7 6 5 4 3 2 1

ISBN 978 1 84773 070 1

Publishing Director: Rosemary Wilkinson
Editors: Kate Parker; Julia Shone; Aruna Vasudevan
Design and Cover design: Peter Crump
Production: Melanie Dowland

Front cover image: © Corbis

Reproduction by Pica Digital Pte. Ltd., Singapore
Printed and bound in India by Replika Press

Power is not a means, it is an end. One does not establish a dictatorship in order to safeguard a revolution; one makes the revolution in order to establish the dictatorship.

— George Orwell, 1984

Contents

INTRODUCTION

Who is the Despot?

With his colourful uniforms and spurious military decoration General Augusto Pinochet of Chile (1915–2006; in power 1974–1990) certainly looked the part of a typical Latin American despot. For 16 years his disdainful gaze looked down on a country that he claimed to have rescued from the socialist chaos of President Salvador Allende (1908–1973; President 1970–1973). In typical despotic fashion, Pinochet, on seizing power in September 1973, immediately closed down the Parliament, suspended the constitution, banned all political and trade union activity and imposed strict controls over the media. Over the following years more than 3,000 supporters of the Allende regime were killed and thousands of others were arrested and tortured or forced into exile. Pinochet pursued a policy of wholesale privatisation in Chile which led to the destruction of national industry and agriculture. With unemployment rising to over 30 per cent, the gap between the rich and poor widened dramatically but the resulting mass protests in 1983 were swiftly repressed by Pinochet. Finally, in 1988, under international pressure Pinochet agreed to hold a referendum on the Presidency. Much to his surprise and dismay, the people had developed the courage to reject him and he won only 44 per cent of the vote. In March 1998 Pinochet resigned from the army but sought immunity from his crimes by becoming a senator. Later that year, while visiting London, Pinochet was arrested by the British police on a warrant issued by the Spanish authorities investigating the death in Chile of one of their citizens. Allowed to return home he was threatened with being brought to trial for his crimes but was eventually released on the grounds of age and diminished responsibility.

What remains highly significant about the Pinochet affair was that it proved that the world had changed and that the international community was now prepared to take action against a despot anywhere in the world. Proof of this intent has been the arrest in 2006 and ongoing trial for alleged war crimes of Charles Taylor of Liberia (b.1948; President 1997–2003) at the UN-backed Special Court in The Hague. Taylor has been accused of supporting and encouraging rebel atrocities in Sierra Leone and his trial marks the first time that a former African head of state has faced such censure. Taylor's trial has proved a distinct turning point in the world's attitude towards crimes against humanity, with the New York-based Human Rights Watch (HRW) declaring that it 'sends a strong signal that no one is above the law.' For it is now just possible that the age of the despot may be coming to an end and even the most brutal and ruthless tyrant will soon be called to account. For who today would like to be described as a despot? It may seem extraordinary, but at the time of the Byzantine Empire it was a highly desirable title implying high status and great honour. Only the emperor himself and close members of his family were allowed to use the term; the heir to the imperial throne, the crown prince of Byzantium, was traditionally given the title of Despot of the Morea, the area that comprises the present-day Greek Peloponnese. Yet over the centuries, the word despot became pejorative – the title given to kings, tyrants and later dictators who had abused their power and subjected their people to a rule of cruelty and injustice. In pre-modern times, the difference between a strong king and a bloody despot was often marginal. Neither could be deposed, because they claimed to rule in the name of God, and both depended on violence to impose their will. What, then, differentiates them? Surely it must be the use of cruelty for its own sake, a perverted enjoyment in inflicting pain that rulers like Caligula (AD 12–41; Roman Emperor AD 37–41) and Ivan the Terrible (1530–1584; Tsar of Russia 1547–1584) made notorious. Nor need the cruelty be personal; as witnessed in the 20th century, it can be imposed dispassionately, leading to the misery and deaths of millions.

If this distinction holds true, then many of the great rulers in history cannot be condemned as despots, despite their ruthless grasp on power. A man such as Alexander the Great (356–323 BC; King of Macedonia 336–323 BC), for example, appeared to be far too busy conquering the world to bother with inflicting unnecessary pain. Some writers have sought to portray Alexander as a bloodthirsty megalomaniac who should be ranked alongside Joseph Stalin (1879–1953; ruler of Soviet Union 1924–1953) and Adolf Hitler (1889–1945; dictator of Nazi Germany 1933–1945), but his cruelties do not even begin to compare to the crimes of these two monstrous 20th-century dictators. Others have suggested that Alexander was a charismatic, humanistic missionary, determined to unify the races of the known world.

A similar problem arises when considering Julius Caesar (100–44 BC). Certainly, he infuriated the Roman Senate by having himself appointed dictator for life in the winter of 45 BC. Although he did not impose a cruel reign on Rome, he gave signs of the self-aggrandisement that was to characterize all later despots. He outraged convention by ordering a statue of himself to be placed in one of the oldest and most revered temples in Rome, and then went even further by changing the month known as Quintilis in the Roman calendar to Julius, his own name. So scandalized were the leading senators, and so keen their commitment to the Roman Republic, that they assassinated him before he could use his armies to gain total control. That Caesar had introduced a series of much-needed reforms counted for little when compared to the threat he posed to Roman democracy.

At the time of the Renaissance, the term 'enlightened despot' came into use, describing kings and rulers who applied the principles of the Enlightenment through their administration, encouraging intellectual freedom and reform, but demanding total obedience from their people in return. The Enlightenment, an intellectual movement of the 17th and 18th centuries which discussed ideas concerning God, reason, nature, and man, put forward new radical political theories questioning the authoritarian state and advocating social organisation based on individual liberty and rights. A typical example of an 'enlightened despot' was Frederick the Great (1712–1786; King of Prussia 1740–1786), whose military successes and domestic reforms propelled Prussia from a rural backwater into a leading European nation. Although very much the absolute ruler, Frederick followed the strict principle that he was the 'first servant of the state'. As such, he claimed to exercise power not for personal gain, but in the best interests of Prussia as a whole – yet woe betide anyone who disagreed with him.

More despotic and far less enlightened was the rule of Louis XIV (1638–1715; King of France 1643–1715), also known as the 'Sun King', who gave traditional monarchy a bad name by withdrawing his entire administration to Versailles and reviving religious intolerance in France. Yet the Sun King captured the spirit of the age; the royalty and aristocracy of Europe adopted the language and customs of France, and admired his prodigious passion for order and love of beauty. Louis was little concerned with the wellbeing of the French people; but although his armies committed atrocities, there was no resort to slavery, mass deportations or genocide.

A later French ruler who gives us even greater problems with the definition of despotism is Napoleon Bonaparte (1769–1821; Emperor of France 1804–1815). There is no doubt that he was an enlightened ruler, but he also had despotic tendencies – although he never resorted to extremes of cruelty to enforce his will. As he once said, 'The true conquests, the only ones that leave no regret, are those that have been wrested from ignorance.' But he alone would later dictate what news and knowledge were permissible in France. His definition of what education should be, '... to impart the same knowledge and the same principals to all individuals living in the same society, in order to create a single, uniform body, informed with one and the same understanding, and working for the common good on the basis of uniformity of views…' could just as well have been said by totalitarians such as Benito Mussolini (1883–1945; Italian dictator 1922–1943) or Hitler. A champion of egalitarianism, Napoleon was convinced that a person should have the chance to rise on the basis of ability alone. Nevertheless, he crushed anyone who defied him. Perhaps his greatest despotic crime was to involve France and most of Europe in needless wars for his own benefit, which resulted in the deaths of ten of millions. In this he was very like Hitler, and made the identical mistake of invading Russia – but unlike Hitler, he refused to commit suicide when all was lost.

The 20th century saw the rise of the modern totalitarian despot, who combined the growing appeal of nationalism with that of a new political ideology to bind the people to his wishes. This had the most appalling consequences for the people of Europe. In the past, a despot's injustices and cruelties affected a relatively small group – mainly his potential rivals. Now, they could bring misery and terror to millions. Former British prime minister Winston Churchill's warning that these men heralded a new dark age 'made more sinister, and perhaps more protracted, by the lights of perverted science' proved prophetically true. Yet the defeat of the totalitarian dictators and the fall of Communism have produced a ray of hope: at least future despots may pay a high price for their crimes by being made the subject of international justice. In recent years, Slobodan Milošević (1941–2006; President of Serbia 1989–1997; President of Yugoslavia 1997–2000) had been brought to trial on war crimes charges when he was found dead in his cell at the detention centre at The Hague. Facing charges of genocide, crimes against humanity, grave breaches of the Geneva Conventions and violations of the laws or customs of war, Milošević's trial proved that tyrants would now be held accountable for their actions. The trial of Charles Taylor also serves as a stark comment that such behaviour is becoming increasingly unacceptable in the modern world.

The recent elections in Zimbabwe have also proved that tyrannical rule will not be accepted indefinitely by an oppressed public. Taking control of Zimbabwe in 1980 on a wave of popular support, Robert Mugabe (b.1924; Executive President from 1987) promised to bring peace and reconciliation to a country divided after decades of colonial rule and a bitter civil war. However, Mugabe merely tightened his grip on power and carried out a brutal suppression of any opposition to his government. Amid allegations of intimidation and torture, Mugabe has been able to stifle any political opposition but growing discontent over Zimbabwe's failing economy has threatened his authority and left him vulnerable. The much disputed results of the March 2008 elections have declared that a run-off will take place between

Mugabe and opposition leader Morgan Tsvangirai of the Movement for Democratic Change party. Although a date has not yet been set for the run-off and there have been reports of intimidation of voters by Mugabe's Zanu-PF party, Mugabe's position is undoubtedly becoming increasingly untenable.

Yet most despots have evaded the vengeance of the people, and have died either in their beds or in comfortable exile. Nicolae Ceausescu (1918–1989; President of Romania 1974–1989) and Saddam Hussein (1937–2006; President of Iraq 1979–2003) are rare examples of tyrants who have met a violent, if arguably justified, end.

Perhaps the only real defence against despotism is a constant wariness and suspicion of the powerful individual, and the recognition that tyranny can come not only from the left or right, but also from religious fundamentalism and excessive bureaucracy. It would be reassuring to believe that those who struck down the aspiring despot Julius Caesar on 15 March 44 BC were acting in the cause of democracy past, present and future.

CHAPTER 1

The Coming of the Despot

On the evening of 9 April 2003 a column of American Marines drove to Firdos Square in the centre of Baghdad, Iraq and began attacking a gigantic statue of Saddam Hussein that had stood for years as an embodiment of Saddam's despotic rule over the Iraqi people. As film crews recorded the event for posterity, a soldier climbed onto the statue's shoulder and prophetically placed a noose around its neck, followed by an American flag over its face. The crowd that had gathered were then encouraged by their self-proclaimed liberators to drag the statue to the ground. When it refused to budge, a heavy armoured vehicle appeared which, with steel chains, dragged it in a series of juddering moves from its pedestal. As the statue crashed to the ground the crowd surged forward, dancing in exultation and beating the fallen idol with their shoes in a gesture of contempt. That day the latest of the long line of despots who, throughout history, have ruled their people with ruthlessness, cruelty and contempt had symbolically fallen.

Perhaps despots like Hussein have always been with us, and were already present when small groups of 20 or 30 people first began crossing the land bridge out of Africa 2,000 generations ago; these wandering groups of hunter-gatherers depended for their very survival on the presence and leadership of strong and intelligent individuals. Such men were essential both to the success of hunting expeditions and to ensure a co-ordinated defence against rival bands. What they had in common was the innate ability to provide strategic leadership when it was needed, to be able to assess a situation and then produce a winning solution for their group. Naturally they would have enjoyed high status among their companions, and would have sought or demanded power and recognition in return for leadership. Then, as these groups settled and the first primitive agriculture began, the function of the leader changed. A more sophisticated form of leadership was required; as permanent houses were built, domesticated animals were reared and crops planted, the settled group had to be ready for attack.

These tribal cultures saw everything in their environment as animate and believed every object in nature to possess a soul or spirit. Each animal, hill or mountain, each forest and garden, every body of water, especially medicinal streams and springs, had its own deity. Only a fine line separated people from the surrounding spirit world. This deep belief led early people to fear the fickleness and whim of the spirits controlling natural disasters even more than they feared attack from other humans. Archaeology has revealed that at this stage of social development, magic-working shamans appeared to placate the gods and ensure a safe harvest. Soon the first priest-kings emerged, enjoying the same god-like status as the later pharaohs of Egypt.

With the establishment of settled communities came a proliferation of possessions; disparity of wealth produced inequality, which in turn provoked envy. This, according to the 20th century French philosopher René Girard, led inevitably to violence. Those without food began attacking wealthier settlements, which, in turn, sought to defend themselves under the command of the most aggressive and capable individuals. Such disputes became the first recognizable wars in history, and the leaders the first kings; they used specialist soldiers and established primitive administrations to collect rewards from their people, in return for protection and conquest. These early leaders were essentially men of action, strongly motivated, their decisions uncompromised by doubt or debate. What they offered the people was simple affirmation, an irrational belief in some idea or concept of which they were the sole administrator and that could not be questioned – on peril of death.

The invention of the plough 5,000 years ago dramatically improved the efficiency of agriculture. More advanced and much wealthier societies appeared in the river valleys of Mesopotamia. Kingship itself was now more sophisticated and more assertive. Vast monuments celebrating the might and charisma of great rulers were erected, and human sacrifice became increasingly popular as a form of tribute to powerful and ruthless individuals. Ceremony and ritual were the mystical ingredients that kings relied on to emphasise their importance. Military parades and displays were used to encourage loyalty to the ruler much as Hitler would use the Nuremburg Rallies to assert his own charisma and the Nazi control of Germany in the 20th century. Across the world, the cult of the powerful individual was now paramount; it is still visible in awe-inspiring structures such as the pyramids of Egypt and, later, the towering ziggurats (temple towers) of Mexico and Peru. Yet the power of these despotic kings remained inextricably linked with religion, which combined their terrestrial power with the threat of the supernatural. Their allies were the priests and soothsayers, who were even more important in maintaining control over the people than armed soldiers. God and ruler were now one, with the king wrapped in a protective cloak of mysticism. Power was exercised with unwavering ruthlessness against anyone who challenged the royal prerogative; the imposition of suffering became the accepted means of doing so. Little wonder that the concept of freedom, if it had ever existed, had disappeared, and would not re-emerge until the rise of the Classical Greek civilization, around 1200 BC.

Despotic rulers recognized early on that the suppression of individual liberties must be accompanied by the suppression of public opinion. As the first Emperor of China, Qin Shi Huang (259–210 BC; reigned 221–210 BC), stated in the 3rd century BC, 'The way to organize a country well is to have no free speech... therefore one does not rely on intelligent and thoughtful men. The ruler makes the people single-minded and therefore they will not scheme for selfish profit', a sentiment that would certainly have found resonance with a modern tyrant such as Stalin. It is perhaps ironic that the only surviving expression of individuality from Qin Shi Huang's China is on the faces of the thousands of statues in his huge terracotta army, which has endowed these humble soldiers with an immortality denied them in life.

Appropriately it was the Greeks who produced the first recorded treatises on the importance of civil freedom and its abuse by despots or tyrants, as they called them. Greek society had seen a group of nobles gain ascendancy over the king, but rather than abolish the role altogether, they astutely retained him as the titular head who continued to perform a series of limited functions. In some ways this resembled a modern constitutional monarchy, but it was controlled by a small number of aristocrats rather than by a democratic assembly. Around 594 BC, one of their number, Solon (c.630–560 BC), was made *archon*, the new executive head of Athens. He was given wide-ranging powers to act impartially and without allegiance to any particular group. Rather like Qin Shi Huang, he introduced a new standard of weights and measures, essential for free trade of goods; he reorganized the coinage, and ordered that all laws be recorded on pillars and displayed in the centre of the city. Solon's reforms created the first open political arena in which the public could participate until Peisistratus seized the support of the poorer sections of Athenian society, 30 years later. Tyrannical in nature and without any legitimacy, Peisistratus ignored the laws and the constitution and ended public involvement in the public arena. Eventually he was driven from power, and in around 510 BC Cleisthenes (c.570–508 BC) reintroduced a primitive form of democracy that was fully developed 50 years later by the most illustrious of the early Greek democrats, Pericles (c.495–429 BC). From then on, all political decisions were taken by the 'Council of the Five Hundred', a people's court, and the people's assembly, the *Ekklesia*. This fundamental advance protected the people against future despots and it gave even the poorer members of society access to political office, with daily allowances for members of both the council and courts. This system became the model for all the democratic

constitutions that followed, and was the yardstick used by Plato (428/427–348/347
BC) and Aristotle (384–322 BC) in their works on political philosophy.

Yet despots continued to arise. Among them was Theydon of Argos who, in the
manner of later despots such as Genghis Khan of Mongolia (1162–1227; in power
1206–1227) or Hitler, offered the people military glory in place of civil freedom and
established the first standing army in Greece. Aristotle states that his military successes altered his character, transforming him from an honest king into a harsh tyrant.
Significantly, all the early tyrants were, like Theydon, able and successful military leaders; like King Leonidas of Sparta (d.480 BC; reigned c.490–480 BC), whose stand
against the Persians at Thermopylae was to be immortalized, they maintained a rigid
control over their people. Each one devoted much of their national resources to
creating and maintaining a powerful army, much as Hitler did in Germany in the
1930s. Although the Greeks considered such men an unpleasant necessity in war, they
criticized them for their greed and oppression in times of peace. The greatest philosophers and historians of the age, Plato, Xenephon and Aristotle, all produced works
that questioned the inevitability of the rise of such tyrants, and sought to define the
rights and obligations needed to maintain a free people. Each studied the past tyrants
in great detail, comparing them to each other and debating the circumstances of their
rise, achievements and fall. All were unanimous in their condemnation of tyranny,
while recognizing that it was the result of the new prosperity enjoyed by maritime
states such as Athens. This had led to the need for a powerful ruler who could bring
control and authority to increasingly chaotic and greedy societies. According to Plato,
prosperity would lead inevitably to corruption, as rulers became 'masters and
enemies instead of allies of the people; hating and being hated, plotting and being
plotted against, they'll lead their lives far more afraid of the enemies within than those
without'. With rich money-lenders oppressing the people, a 'deliverer' was needed;
this led to the rise of the tyrant, who promised to protect the people but instead
sowed mistrust among them, 'for a tyranny will not be overthrown until some people
trust each other'. Although he conceded that some tyrants exercised their power
benignly or achieved military glory for the state, they all, without exception, shared
one cardinal and unforgivable sin: they had seized power, and then refused to relinquish it when the people so desired. Furthermore, their own will had become the
one and only law in force. This was to be the defining characteristic of authoritarian rulers throughout history, from Charles I of Great Britain and Ireland (1600–1649;
reigned 1625–1649) to Napoleon Bonaparte.

Yet supreme power does not bring peace or contentment. Plato gives a powerful description of a typical tyrant, 'hemmed in by a ring of warders, all of them his

enemies', and racked by fear and loathing of his subjects. Such a man lives as a near-recluse, unable to enjoy the simple pleasures of the world and compelled to bribe and flatter the worst of men, thinking himself rich in worldly possessions but in reality a moral pauper. These views were shared by the great majority of Plato's Athenian contemporaries and produced an acute awareness of the need to preserve the freedom of the people. Anyone suspected of tyrannical ambitions was held in contempt, and often became a target for violence. Even those who had delivered the people from tyranny by rebelling, such as Harmodius and Aristogeiton, came under suspicion. So seriously was the issue taken that, in the 4th century BC, Timoleon of Corinth killed his own brother for saying that he was considering seizing power. Such men were honoured as heroes by their fellow citizens, despite the fact that the Athenian state bore little resemblance to a modern democracy. As the statesman Pericles admitted, the harsh rule of Athens over its subject states was little better than the injustice imposed on the city by the tyrant Peisistratus.

This fundamental Greek hatred of tyranny and respect for civil freedom was passed on to the Romans. The politician and philosopher Cicero (106–43 BC) wrote later that 'no animal more hateful can be perceived or more justly detested than the tyrant; he wears a human shape but in character is worse than the most savage beasts'. Cicero would have the opportunity to put his theoretical hatred of tyranny into action when he became involved in the plot to assassinate Julius Caesar for overthrowing the Republic in 44 BC. Cicero had been much influenced by the earlier Greek historian Herodotus (c.484–420 BC), who had given a telling description of the paranoid nature of the tyrant when he wrote 'pay him moderate respect and he is angry because your respect is not enough; give him profound homage and he is again offended because, as he says, you just fawn on him like a lapdog'. One has only to recall the dangers of dealing with Idi Amin (1924–2003; president of Uganda 1971–1979) or Ivan the Terrible of Russia to realize the accuracy of Herodotus' words. Judging the right degree of sycophancy when dealing with a despot has always been dangerous, but in some instances it can be farcical; one notorious example is the occasion on which Stalin's audience continued applauding a speech at ludicrous length, because each member was terrified of showing disloyalty by being the first to stop clapping.

The Romans' fear of tyranny and desire for freedom became enshrined in their belief in and respect for the Republic. Established at the overthrow of the Tarquin monarchy, this form of democracy was the Romans' ideal of what government should be, something to be defended at all costs against would-be tyrants. It flourished until Julius Caesar's heir, Octavian, defeated Mark Antony and Cleopatra at Actium in 31

BC. Although Octavian paid lip service to the Republic, he was awarded the new title of Augustus by the senate, followed by the role of consular for life. This amounted to the *de facto* overthrow of the Republic and the establishment of Octavian as sole ruler of Rome, so paving the way for the despotic emperors that were to follow him. At first there was little sign of tyranny from the new emperor – although anyone seeking to overthrow him, or to restore the Republic, was dealt with firmly. The same policy was pursued by Augustus's successors; only those who presented a threat to the emperor suffered persecution. Much harsher measures were introduced when Tiberius (42 BC–AD 37; Roman Emperor AD 14–37) came to power in AD 14. The rights of the remaining democratic assemblies were removed and handed over to the more malleable senate. More insidiously, Tiberius reformed the law of treason, *lex maiestatis*, that had formerly applied only to acts of crime against the state, and made it apply to any words or conduct – even looks or gestures – that could be interpreted as hostile to the emperor. In essence, this was the origin of several laws that would later be used by despots to protect themselves against conspiracy and stamp out any form of opposition. Tiberius was also the first known ruler to use state funds to provide rewards for informers, thus creating the professional spy system that would characterize every successive authoritarian regime until the present day.

Elsewhere in the world there was no such earnest questioning of the principles of despotism, or any attempt to define the meaning of freedom. Little attention appears to have been paid to these issues in Asian and Far Eastern society. Here, despots were accepted as a necessary evil; contemporary Indian and Chinese philosophers and historians agreed that kingship must involve some degree of tyranny, and that a ruler should only be condemned if he resorted to excessive cruelty. Therefore a harsh ruler such as Qin Shi Huang, who unified China between 221 and 210 BC and established the first police state in history, largely escaped criticism in his lifetime. That he killed Confucian scholars and ordered most of the books in China to be destroyed carried less weight with his contemporaries than his undoubted achievements in unifying the vast country, introducing a common currency and establishing a reliable system of weights and measures. Unlike in Classical Greece, Eastern despots such as Qin Shi Huang were, if not accepted as gods, at least accorded the status of the gods' representatives on earth. This cloak of royal divinity would remain popular with kings for centuries, enabling the supporters of authoritarian monarchs such as Charles I of Great Britain and Louis XVI of France (1754–1793; reigned 1774–1792) to claim their deaths as martyrdom. True despots also found it useful to claim semi-mythical status; 8th century caliph of Baghdad, Harun al-Rashid, 14th century Mongol ruler of Samarkland, Tamerlane,

Genghis Khan, and Ivan the Terrible were all transformed by superstition from ordinary (if brutal) historical figures into demons of the imagination, whose very names were used to scare children.

Such men ruled by fear supplemented by superstition; the exercise of cruelty added to their myth. Yet the great majority of early despots appear to have been more concerned with conquest and subjugation than with cruelty for its own sake. Even the vengeful Roman army that obliterated Carthage spared the majority of its inhabitants, preferring to make them into useful slaves. Again, when the Romans took Jerusalem they killed most of its defending soldiers, but spared the rest of the Jews so that they could resume paying taxes to Rome. Such largesse was impossible for the Mongol despots who overran Asia and Eastern Europe 600 years after the fall of the Roman Empire. Tamerlane and Genghis Khan controlled vast horse-mounted armies that were constantly on the move; they could not afford the luxury of holding captives taken in battle, as they had nowhere to imprison them. It was therefore perfectly logical to kill all prisoners immediately so that the Mongol horde could move on. Their reputation for ruthless cruelty had the advantage of encouraging the swift surrender of besieged towns, whose inhabitants would have known in advance what fate awaited them if they resisted. The same tactic was successfully used by the Crusaders, and by Ivan the Terrible when he besieged the city of Novgorod in Russia. As late as the 17th century, Oliver Cromwell, a religious bigot who flirted with despotism as the Lord Protector of England, Scotland and Ireland, slaughtered all the inhabitants of the town of Drogheda as a warning to other Irish garrisons of what to expect if they did not capitulate. However, no one excelled more at this tactic than Vlad the Impaler of Walachia (c.1431–1476; reigned 1456–1462 and 1476), whose very name became inseparable from one of the most exquisitely painful methods of execution ever devised – a metal stake driven into the anus which exited through the shoulder; yet even Vlad's eye-watering brutality appears to have been used less for his personal enjoyment than as an unforgettable warning to his Turkish opponents to surrender or suffer the inevitable consequences. That Ivan the Terrible was, as a child, fascinated by the legend of Vlad is not surprising, given his own struggle to free Russia from foreign occupiers by using similarly ruthless and brutal tactics.

In spite of their spectacular reputations for inflicting cruelty, despots such as Vlad and Ivan differed more in degree than in kind from their contemporaries. Throughout Europe, every king fully understood that he could only retain his throne by the use of the most rigorous discipline. Any sign of weakness could provoke a coup by one or more of his nobles, as happened to both Edward II (1284–1327; reigned 1307–1327) and Richard II (1367–1400; reigned 1377–1399) of England. Nor was such practical ruthlessness confined to Europe; in the 14th century the Indian ruler of Delhi, Muhammad bin Tughluq, responded to an attempt to overthrow him by driving the entire population of the city out into the countryside and off to a distant part of his domain. A blind man who refused the order to move was dragged by horse over a hundred miles across country, with the result that only a leg reached the final destination. Stories of brutal despots are common throughout this period, but it should be remembered that such men were seeking to unify and expand their countries, and that their efforts were frequently frustrated and obstructed by their self-seeking nobles. For this reason, Ivan the Terrible reserved his most brutal methods for his own boyar nobles, the Russian aristocrats who sought to preserve their power and influence as well as to retain the obscurantist customs of old Russia. It is significant that Ivan the Terrible and, 400 years later, the Turkish dictator Mustafa Kemal Atatürk (1881–1938; President 1923–1938), both would-be modernizers of an archaic society, ordered all beards to be shaved off as a symbolic rejection of the old system and as a mark of compliance with the new. This need for visual conformity is a frequent characteristic of despotic regimes, whether it be shaven heads, Mao Tse-tung's (1893–1976; in power 1949–1976) collarless jacket in China or the black pyjamas decreed as the universal uniform in Pol Pot's (1925–1998; Prime Minister 1976–1979) Cambodia.

As Ancient Greece had developed a great culture in spite of its petty tyrants, so the arts flourished in Renaissance Italy at a time when it was dominated by authoritarian and often despotic regimes, ruled by aristocratic dynasties such as the Medici in Florence, the Visconti and Sforza in Milan and the Este in Ferrara. Unlike the 20th-century dictators who rigidly controlled their national culture, the Renaissance dukes and princes encouraged freedom of expression. It was during this period that the Florentine diplomat Niccolò Machiavelli (1469–1527) wrote his two great works on the exercise of power, *The Prince* (1513, published 1532) and the *Discourses* (1518). These books were the most significant contribution to the discussion of freedom and despotism since Classical times. As a creature of the Renaissance himself, Machiavelli believed firmly in the Humanistic celebration of the individual and was accused of being an apologist for the excesses of 15th-century Italian despotic tyrants like Cesare Borgia and Lorenzo de Medici. In reality, he recognized the benefits of having a strong ruler at times of uncertainty, although he abhorred the loss of personal freedom that it often entailed. Machiavelli became convinced that the Italian city-states, currently under threat from French or Spanish invasion, needed strong and ruthless leaders to survive. The lesson of history is that proven tyrants are more effective in times of danger; people should realize that short-term despotism is the price that must be paid for the restoration of long-term freedom under a republican system. However, despotism does not necessarily have to mean tyranny; the 'good prince' of Machiavelli's book is quite capable of governing honestly and fairly. The danger, as Machiavelli sees it, is that the ruler is tempted to make his office hereditary, so breaking the bond of trust with his people. The result must then be an oppressive society in which the individual cannot achieve self-fulfilment – only free people can accomplish great things. For Machiavelli, tyranny is based on armed violence, and this oppression destroys the complex system of checks and balances that a free society demands. Finally, in an idea that was far ahead of his time, Machiavelli suggested that true civic liberty also depends on some degree of social or economic equality to prevent social and political strife. Ironically, this potentially radical concept was ignored for centuries by critics who preferred to depict Machiavelli as a cynical supporter of unbridled despotism, rather than as an important champion of civic freedom.

Machiavelli was writing at a time when Italy in general and Tuscany in particular were divided into numerous small states, each with a prosperous economy and constantly in dispute with each other. Generally the petty despots who ruled them did so without excessive cruelty or injustice, in spite of the constant threat of rebellion. Produce and labour were the ruler's to command, but if they demanded too great a share of either then the nobles, upon whom they depended for both support and survival, would rebel and attempt to overthrow them. For this reason Machiavelli advised rulers to divert their energies from internal intrigues to foreign adventures: provoke a dispute with a neighbouring state, he said, then send your own warlords off to fight and loot there; when they return, share the booty with them. This was sound advice for all future tyrants. It had already been demonstrated at the time of the Crusades, when northern Europe's more insecure monarchs had welcomed the long march to the Holy Land as a wonderful distraction for their more aggressive and ambitious nobles. Even in our own time, involvement in a foreign military venture has been used by despots to head off discontent and subversion at home. Iraqi dictator Saddam Hussein's enthusiasm for his 10-year war against Iran might well have helped him stay in power in Iraq, simply because the war helped kill off the more fanatical elements in both countries. Eight years later Hussein attempted to repeat the operation by annexing neighbouring Kuwait, one of the wealthiest oil states in the world. This miscalculation, and the inevitable defeat by the Allied Coalition, (made up of 34 countries, including the United States and the United Kingdom) began the series of misjudgements and military disasters that led to his eventual overthrow.

It was 300 years after the death of Machiavelli before the next attempt to define and analyze despotism was made. It came when the 18th-century philosophers Voltaire, Rousseau and disciples of the Enlightenment became concerned with the growing absolutism of the French monarchy under Louis XIV and his successors. Such philosophers argued that the people possessed certain inalienable natural rights that any king had a moral duty to respect and protect. By consistently ignoring these obligations, the French monarchy had become little more than a well-mannered tyranny and the king himself a conventional despot. The power of their argument was persuasive, fuelling popular discontent among the emergent middle classes and exacerbating a growing national distaste for the economic corruption and inefficiency of the Bourbon regime. When the great famine of 1788 devastated the French peasantry, the common people were roused to action; the ensuing Revolution shocked Europe and changed the political scene forever. The English radical Tom Paine wrote from Paris after the fall of the Bastille, 'The French rebel against a mild and lawful monarch, with more fury, outrage, and insult, than any people has been known to rise against the most illegal usurper, or the most sanguinary tyrant.' Paine went on to describe how such discrete tyranny can spread from the person of the king like a cancer through the whole body of society. 'Every office and department has its despotism, founded upon custom and usage. Every place has its Bastille, and every Bastille its despot. The original hereditary despotism resident in the person of the king, divides and sub-divides itself into a thousand shapes and forms... proceeding on through an endless labyrinth of officials till the source of it is scarcely perceptible and there is no mode of redress.' Paine's description of how a despot can poison the entire fabric of a society could have applied equally well to 1930s Soviet Russia under Stalin. Yet Paine's suggested cure was to prove far more damaging for France than the disease itself. While the old regime under the monarchy may have been moribund and unjust, the new revolutionary government proved to be far more violently despotic, condoning massacres of innocent people, the seizure of private property on a vast scale and the crushing of the individual spirit. Soon the high-minded philosophy of the revolutionaries had been abandoned; France descended into bloody tyranny controlled by Maximilien Robespierre and his Jacobins, with informers and spies everywhere and guillotines to execute the aristocracy and any enemies of the new state erected throughout the land. Louis XVI, the despot of Versailles, had been exchanged for the brutal tyranny of the Committee of Public Safety in Paris, with its summary trials and instant executions. Again, it is one of the great ironies of history that it took the absolutist rule of Napoleon Bonaparte to restore safety and justice to the ordinary citizens of France.

Although neither a bloody nor an unjust tyrant, Napoleon has often been described as an 'enlightened despot', as he applied the principles of the Enlightenment through a fundamental change in the administration of French society. After the bickering and factionalism of the self-proclaimed revolutionary democrats, Napoleon's reforms proved extraordinarily effective. He encouraged religious tolerance, and at first allowed freedom of the press and speech while maintaining his complete authority at all times. Opposition to his rule was minimal; his whirlwind military progress across Europe and progressive social legislation provided France with a new purpose after the strife and disappointments of recent years. Internally, he strengthened the administration by creating a strong centralized government and abolishing the myriad local administrations. Education was now funded by the state, and government careers were thrown open to all those with talent. For the first time in history, France was administered as a single unit. In 1804, he introduced the Code Napoleon that remains the single legal system for French law, based on the principle of equality before the law. Curiously, some of his reforms were retrograde, for the Code deprived women of much of their newfound social equality; once more, they were subject to the approval of a man before they could work or take a public role in society.

The price that the French paid for this new efficiency was the total repression of political liberty and the banning of any opposition to their leader's benign despotism. Napoleon was the word and the words were Napoleon's. Ahead of his time, he recognised the need to gain and maintain public favour, and to shape public opinion by controlling the media. To ensure obedience he required every newspaper and book publisher, printer and even bookseller to swear an oath of allegiance to him personally, effectively placing the entire French media under state control.

The horrors of the French Revolution and the threat of Napoleon were not lost on the remaining European monarchies. They became acutely aware of the dangers of defending the 'divine right of kings' in a fast-changing and increasingly industrialized society. But the principles that drove the French Revolution remained undimmed, fuelling a continued assault on old-fashioned and repressive regimes. This quest for freedom coincided with a growing sense of nationalism in Italy, Hungary, Ireland and, eventually, Germany. Significantly, it was the last great struggle between rival European monarchies in 1914 and the outbreak of the First World War that was to lead directly to the rise of the most oppressive and sophisticated despots in history. When the war ended in 1918, the soldiers on both sides of the conflict felt themselves abused and betrayed by their own establishments. The Germans, Russians and Italians in particular were convinced that they had been used as mere cannon fodder in a war that arguably was little more than a dispute between various branches of the European elite. Russian Communism, German Nazism and Italian Fascism were the direct result of this anger and discontent, making the ordinary people of Europe ideal material for a takeover by a new breed of violent radicalism. Nor did the post-war bourgeois governments that emerged throughout Europe (apart from Russia where the Communists were already fighting for control), appear to offer anything better to the disgruntled masses.

The political predicament of the ordinary citizen has been closely analyzed by the French political philosopher Georges Sorel (1847–1922), founder of Revolutionary Syndicalism. His book, *Reflections on Violence* (1908), argued that the growing bureaucratization of modern society in general, and the cowardice of the middle classes in particular, impeded the emergence of a new and more dynamic society. Nations had, according to Sorel, become effete and decadent; violence was now needed to destroy democracy and materialism and to save the world from a return to barbarism. To those returning from the battlefield to a bankrupt society that offered them little more than unemployment in return for the sacrifice they had made, this was a powerful message – one that both Hitler in Germany and Mussolini in Italy were to exploit in the following decades. It is not surprising that many of their first converts were angry and disillusioned ex-soldiers, supported by their families.

At a time when democratic ethics were utilitarian and materialistic, Mussolini's call to decisive action, on the basis of high ideals and an appeal to comradeship, had a strong appeal. One old Italian socialist said admiringly of Mussolini before his rise to power, 'This man stands out clearly in a world of shadowy figures.' Mussolini appeared, like his fellow despot Hitler, to be the right man for the time; and they both experienced a meteoric rise to power on a wave of huge public support. In both cases, their early successes were followed by a fatal compulsion to overreach themselves with an ambition that would cancel out all previous gains. This tendency had been identified by Plato 2,000 years earlier, when he had written that it was consistent with the nature of a tyrant that he could never be satisfied with his current gains and would always greedily seek more because he was driven by uncontrolled desires. Plato's prediction proved uncannily correct in the case of Hitler and Mussolini, and both were defeated because they were not satisfied by their early successes. Once Hitler had conquered France, there was only Britain still opposing him. Had he then offered Winston Churchill more generous terms, ones that the British government could have forced Churchill to accept, Hitler could perhaps have consolidated his other European conquests and concentrated on developing an even stronger and greater German empire. That, in turn, would have bought time to resist the potential threat of the United States to his ambitions. Instead, he chose to invade Russia with the familiar and inevitable consequences that Napoleon had experienced a century earlier.

Hitler's fascist ally Mussolini made a similar tactical mistake in abandoning the early caution he had shown. When Britain and France declared war on Germany for invading Poland in 1939, Mussolini remained neutral; but once France was defeated his greed for the spoils of victory got the better of him – and he disastrously threw in his lot with Hitler. The more wily Spanish dictator, Francisco Franco (1892–1975; head of government of Spain 1939–1975), kept his country neutral, thereby saving his regime from the devastating defeat suffered by Mussolini's Italy.

Nevertheless, it will always remain a mystery that so many people, even the most disillusioned, were politically seduced by the promises of Hitler, Mussolini and Stalin. One explanation may be that social ethics had changed fundamentally. The traditional sense of duty, stoicism, hard work and integrity, all part of the Protestant work ethic that had been encouraged in the mid 18th to 19th centuries during the Industrial Revolution, had waned. In their place had arisen beliefs originating in the United States that encouraged self-expression and the need for personal achievement. The inevitable consequence was the abandonment of traditional religion, and the search for a strong individual who stood out from the crowd and who could change society. Such a person would rely on personal charisma rather than traditional moral values for success, and would also need the support of a personality cult. Books such as Orison Marden's *Masterful Personality*, published in 1921, encouraged people to perceive themselves as dramatic personalities, and the cult of personality began to replace the cult of character. This change in social aspiration coincided with the growth of the cinema; the images of screen actors acquired an almost god-like importance with the masses. This cult of personality soon worked its way into the politics of the early 20th century, and was embraced by despots throughout the world from Mussolini in Italy to Kim Jong-Il, leader of North Korea since 1994. Today, it pervades the media of every democracy – although democratic politicians have become wary of embracing it too closely. Actors, footballers and TV personalities depend on such exposure for success. The cult of Princess Diana, ex-wife of Prince Charles, heir to the British throne, gave a disturbing insight into how powerful mass adulation can be, and is perhaps a demonstration of how easy it was for Hitler, Stalin, Mao and others to manipulate their captive audiences.

CHAPTER 2

A Terrible Childhood

When the late Saddam Hussein was just a few months old, his mother abandoned both her son and her home, in a village near the town of Tikrit, in Iraq, and went off to live with a new man in a different village. As Hussein's father had already disappeared, the only person left to look after the baby was his uncle, a brutal ex-soldier named Talfah Khairallah. In 1942, when Hussein was five, Talfah became involved in an attempted uprising against the British occupying force, and was arrested. Abandoned for the second time, Hussein was taken by neighbours back to his mother. She had remarried and found the child an embarrassment. Hussein's new stepfather took an instant dislike to him and treated him with cruel hostility, barely allowing him into the house and often beating him with a stick. These were traumatizing experiences, but Hussein did not fall into despair. Rather, he vowed that as an adult, he would never again submit to anyone. Hussein became a loner, rejected by his family and shunned by the other boys in the village. The effects of this trauma were soon apparent in his own anti-social behaviour: he took to carrying an iron bar for defence, and amused himself by heating it in a fire until it was red hot, then stabbing passing animals with it. Denied an education by his stepfather, Hussein began stealing from neighbours until he was caught, at which point he was sent to a juvenile detention centre. While still in his teens, Hussein committed his first political murder, assassinating a supporter of the Communist leader General Abdul Karim Kassem (1914–1963), who also happened to be his own brother-in-law. That this child should grow up to become a cruel and heartless despot, unable to trust even his closest associates and living a violent life spent intimidating others, is hardly surprising.

The miserable and brutalized childhood that Saddam Hussein endured has been the common experience of many tyrants throughout history. It is seen by psychologists such as Alice Miller, author of *The Drama of the Gifted Child* (1981), as the greatest single factor in the making of a despot. She has found that children who have suffered severe abuse at the hands of their fathers are often helpless pawns, powerless to defend themselves. The shame and humiliation that they endure deeply affects their character in adulthood, fuelling a bitter determination for revenge and quest for power. In the case of a political despot, the real enemy is his cruel or neglectful parent, but the symbolical target becomes one or more groups within society. These are his scapegoats.

In the ancient world, the childhood humiliation and deprivation suffered by the Roman Emperors Caligula and Nero (AD 37–68; Roman Emperor AD 54–68) were reflected in their later acts of cruelty. The precedent for their tyranny had been established by the Emperor Tiberius, who had extinguished the political rights of the people by removing legislative power from the popular assemblies and transferring it to the Senate. Tiberius's revision of the *lex maiestatis* to include any words, looks or gestures that could be interpreted as hostile to the person of the emperor, coupled with an act by which the State rewarded anyone who informed on fellow citizens, became the greatest instrument of despotism under the Roman Empire. At a stroke, Tiberius had created a whole new class of informers, the *delatores*, who acted as government spies. Among the first victims of this regime were the young Caligula's mother and brothers, who were arrested in AD 29 on suspicion of treason and were brutally tortured before being left to starve to death. Although granted his life, the young Caligula received a punishment for his father's supposed treachery that was far more corrupting and insidious. Each day he was required to dance attendance on Tiberius at his court on the Isle of Capri, where a group of young boys, his 'minnows', entertained the ageing Emperor with a variety of sexual pleasures, including pretending to nibble his genitals as he swam. The Roman historian Suetonius (c.AD 69–140), who would later catalogue Caligula's atrocities in great detail, wrote, 'While he remained on that island, many insidious artifices were practised, to extort from him complaints against Tiberius, but by his circumspection he avoided falling into the snare.'

This life of danger and insecurity, in which he could lose Tiberius's favour at any moment and suffer a similar fate to the rest of his family, contributed to Caligula's own brutal and revengeful actions when he became emperor himself. His treatment of the Roman senators was particularly perverse, intended to humiliate as well as punish them for supposed misdemeanours. Under his orders, any father and son suspected of disloyalty was arrested and then executed in the other's presence while the emperor looked on. Caligula's nephew Nero suffered similar childhood terror and insecurity; he once claimed that his earliest memory was of being torn screaming from his mother Agrippina's arms as she was dragged away by soldiers to be sent off alone into exile and disgrace. In his most formative years, Nero, too, was without a mother, but when Agrippina was allowed to return, she kept Nero under a tight reign, knowing that he would be a useful card to play at court. She was a dominant woman, described by Suetonius as 'masculine'. She gained more power at court than any woman had before her. Although forbidden to enter the Senate, Agrippina had a special door built at the rear through which she could watch and listen to the debates. Yet her imprisonment when Nero was still a child had meant social disgrace and economic deprivation and it condemned Nero to a loveless childhood. He was raised by slaves in near poverty on a farm owned by an aunt, and she begrudged him the barest necessities. Little wonder that in his adult life Nero indulged in extravagant excess, compensating himself for this childhood neglect.

To add to the boy's humiliation, Nero's mother was accused of sexual misconduct: she was alleged to have slept with her own brother, also the Emperor Caligula's male lover, a situation that was further complicated by Agrippina having once been Caligula's mistress. Social humiliation resulting from a parent's sexual misdemeanours is particularly distressing to a child. The first emperor of China, Qin Shi Huang, also suffered it two centuries earlier when his mother was similarly disgraced after it was revealed that she had behaved like a common whore, and that her many lovers included a brothel entertainer who had posed as a eunuch. Such disgrace and loss of face in Chinese society had a profound effect on the young Qin. His later career can be seen as a determined attempt to revenge himself on the conservative and hypocritical behaviour of the Chinese court by destroying many of its long-cherished traditions. The most obvious example of this was an action that shocked the feudal establishment of the time; he decided to abolish the long established title of king, in favour of that of emperor or in Chinese *huangdi*. He also launched a fundamental attack on a centuries-old courtly tradition by banning the posthumous names by which former kings were known after their death. Future generations, he decided, would refer to him simply as the First Emperor and his successors as the Second Emperor, the Third Emperor and so on, for the next ten thousand generations. To reinforce the atmosphere of radical change at his court he ordered that black, traditionally associated with water and change, should become the new official Imperial colour. Those families that had held power under the previous regime were now ignored and replaced by just three new officers of state, the Gongs; Cheng Xiang, was the equivalent of a modern prime minister, Tai Wei, the war minister and Yu Shi Dai Fu, the general administrator, providing support for the prime minister In theory, the three Gongs would exert checks on each other, while final power remained concentrated in the hands of the emperor. Below the Gongs there were nine Qing whose responsibilities included caring for the palace, the royal family, and the emperor. Faced with the possibility of a backlash from the dispossessed aristocracy, Qin imposed harsh laws and severe punishments on any dissenters and particularly on the many traditional Confucian scholars who opposed him. In return the Confucians began preaching against the new Emperor's dangerous reforms, so provoking his wrath that not only were their books destroyed on imperial orders but 400 of the most vociferous scholars were burned alive in a barbarous *auto-da-fé*.

Danger and uncertainty also haunted the childhood of the Walachian despot Vlad Tepes. Destined to be the dominant figure in his small nation's struggle for independence from the Ottoman Turks, his early life could hardly have been more insecure. Vlad was born in the fortress city of Sighisoara in Transylvania. In 1431, his father, the claimant to the Walachian throne was summoned to Nuremberg by Sigismund, the Holy Roman Emperor. There he was made a member of the Order of the Dragon, an unusual honour that required him and his successors to defend Christianity against the Turks. Life was made all the more difficult for the young Vlad when his father, against the spirit of his oath, proceeded to sign a treaty of obedience to the Turkish Sultan – pledging his sons, the six-year-old Vlad and his brother Radu, as hostages for his good faith. Powerless to protest, the boys were taken to the Turkish city of Adrianople. For the next six years the two boys were held in a state of the greatest danger and insecurity at the Sultan's court and they lived in constant fear of summary execution in the event that their father, as expected, should rebel against his Turkish overlords. At the start of his captivity, Vlad's misery was exacerbated by the conditions he was kept in, locked in an underground dungeon with little food. In contrast, his brother Radu, who was a handsome boy, converted to Islam and became one of the Sultan's favourites. For Vlad, this was a double betrayal: not only had his father handed him over to the enemy without a fight, but his brother had also changed sides. These events were instrumental in forming Vlad Tepes's vengeful character in later life; it was this that fuelled his obsession with dispensing punishment of the utmost cruelty to anyone he suspected of disloyalty.

An even greater humiliation was suffered in childhood by the young Ivan the Terrible. When Vasily III (1479–1533; Tsar of Russia 1505–1533) died unexpectedly in February 1533, his young and inexperienced wife, also Ivan's mother, became Grand Princess, with sole responsibility for ruling Russia. Within five years, she had also died in mysterious circumstances, leaving her vulnerable young son in the care of a council composed of boyar nobles, notorious for their dissent and treachery. Too young to intervene, Ivan could only watch as Prince Obolensky, his late mother's lover, was arrested and thrown into a dungeon where he starved to death. Anyone who had cared for the young prince in his infancy met a similar fate. Without his mother's protection, Ivan was left quite alone and unprotected at the dangerous

Russian court. He only had a younger brother, a deaf-mute, for company. Control of the council now lay in the hands of two powerful boyars, the Shuisky brothers, who used their position to enrich themselves and their favourites at the expense of the young Tsar. It was their personal treatment of Ivan that was to breed in him a hatred for boyars, in general, and the Shuiskys, in particular. The brothers displayed their contempt for Ivan with flagrant rudeness and disrespect for him in front of the entire court. Their behaviour had a devastating effect on Ivan, whose grandfather had suffered similar ritual humiliation years earlier at the hands of the Crimean Tatars. Each year, that Russian prince was obliged to travel to the Khan's court and humiliate himself by falling on his knees and feeding the Khan's favourite horse with oats from his own cap. His grandson now endured similar humiliation, this time not at the hands of foreigners but by members of his own court; and yet he was powerless to challenge them. Ivan released his frustration in wanton acts of petty cruelty, such as throwing live animals from the top of the towers of his palace and laughing as they were dashed to pieces on the rocks below. When told the story of Vlad the Impaler, he appears to have recognized a fellow sufferer and adopted the Walachian despot as a role model. At the same time, Ivan resolved to make the boyars pay dearly for their arrogance and lack of respect.

What despots like Ivan the Terrible, Vlad, Caligula and Nero endured as children was a cruel and unfair abuse of adult power, without any compensatory experience of love, respect and affection. This in turn led to their own addiction to power, a desire to control the unfortunate societies over which they ruled just as their persecutors had once exercised control over them. This perverse phenomenon has been well researched by Alice Miller in *The Untouched Key* (1990): if a child experiences constant harassment by a brutalizing authority, 'what it does in its relationship with others is to replay early parental relationships or scenarios as dramas involving the exercise of power'. Put simply, if parental authority is experienced as punitive, then the child will come to believe that it is 'normal' for power to be used in a repressive, negative and punitive manner. The unconscious conviction is that love and cruelty are the same thing, so leading to sadism, which manifests itself in vicious aggression against any person or group defined as being threatening or evil. Or in the case of a despot, anyone who dares to oppose his will.

Evidence of this type of behaviour is especially apparent in more recent despots, because their early lives are far better documented than those in the ancient or pre-modern world. None has received deeper analysis than that of Adolf Hitler, whose early abuse was fundamental to the evolution of his perverse character. Hitler's father, Alois Hitler, a minor customs official in the Austrian town of Linz, was described by his neighbours as being 'strict, exacting, pedantic, a most unapproachable figure'. Like many Germans of his era, Hitler's father was obsessed with uniforms and insisted on having his picture taken whenever he wore one – an obsession that his son inherited. This was a comparatively harmless peccadillo to that of the beatings that he handed out to his wife and young Adolf when drunk. Unfortunately, his behaviour was all too common among German fathers at the time. Alice Miller believes that by meting out these punishments, a parent such as Alois Hitler was seeking to regain the power he had lost to his own father in childhood when he too was beaten. As she puts it succinctly, 'To beat one's child is to avoid beating oneself. Therefore beating, whether psychological beating or actual beating… is a never-ending task.' But Alois's ill-repressed violence may well have been aggravated by a suspicion that he, a notorious anti-Semite, was the product of a relationship between his mother and a Jewish man. Some historians have speculated that Hitler's onslaught against the Jews was fuelled by a personal desire to remove this suspected taint of Semitism. His revenge was the 'Final Solution', an attempt to wipe out the entire Jewish population of Germany and the occupied countries of Eastern Europe. It could also be argued that without a son of his own to beat, Hitler was symbolically beating an entire race of people instead.

What often redeems children in seemingly hopeless circumstances such as that of Hitler's is the love of a mother, or of someone close, to whom they can confide their misery. In Hitler's case, his mother Karla did not appear to make herself available or to show enough love to compensate for his father's extreme hostility. Perhaps she was too frightened of Alois to show open affection towards her son. The Hitlers must have been an exceptionally loveless family: when Hitler's younger brother died, neither parent attended the funeral. Eleven-year-old Hitler was the only mourner. In the rural Catholic society of the time, this caused much gossip, as did the lack of a tombstone for the dead child.

The absence of a caring mother can have a devastating effect on a child's emotional development. A recent study of battered and maltreated children has revealed that the ones who grow up 'normal' always have someone who showed them genuine affection in their early lives – perhaps a teacher, neighbour or sibling. Such a person has been described by Alice Miller as a 'helping witness', someone who could prove to the child that he or she was not entirely alone. Unfortunately, young Adolf Hitler was totally isolated in his misery. He was unable to question the correctness of his father's decisions, in much the same way that he would later deny the German people a right to question his own dictates. As any sign of disobedience provoked a beating from Alois, so any dissent by a German citizen would invite arrest, torture and often murder.

Between the ages of five and sixteen, Hitler attended five different schools as his father moved restlessly from one bureaucratic job to another. One night, rather than endure yet another beating, Hitler took off his clothes and attempted to escape through a barred window. His father caught him in the act, and called his mother to mock his nakedness as he crouched in the middle of the room. It was at that moment, Hitler later recalled, that he resolved never to cry again when his father whipped him. The brutality continued: Alois allowed no conversation in the house when he was present and he never called his son by name, but whistled for him like a dog. After years of such treatment Hitler, was all but morally dead. As Miller also points out:

> To combat cruelty the person must first be able to perceive it as such.
> When someone has been exposed throughout childhood to nothing but
> harshness, coldness, coercion and the rigid wielding power... when any
> sign of softness, tenderness, creativity or vitality is scorned, then the person
> against whom the violence is directed accepts it as perfectly justified.

Unfortunately for the peoples of Eastern Europe, Hitler's personal quest for revenge after his terrible childhood experiences coincided with that of the majority of the German people who were looking for a scapegoat – a social group to blame for defeat in the First World War (1914–1918) and the humiliating post-war reparations that had to be paid to the victorious Allies. At the end of the 19th century, there may have been millions of Alois Hitlers throughout Germany, tyrannizing their children to become a vengeful generation that would easily be seduced by what National Socialism (Nazism) had to offer. Alice Miller is convinced of this, claiming that Alois's behaviour was not uncommon, and that millions of children suffered a similar fate at the hands of abusive and dictatorial fathers. This argument is supported by the many educational treatises published at the time, in which children are looked upon more as wild and wilful animals that must be tamed than as naturally spirited young people. In these works, invariably German, fathers are repeatedly warned that sparing the rod will spoil the child and that wilfulness and disobedience must be beaten out them. One of the doyens of this school of German pedagogy, J. G. Kruger, in his book *Gedanken von der Erziehung der Kinder* (*Some Thoughts on the Education of Children*) published in 1752, instructed his readers that 'the blows you administer should not be merely playful ones, but should convince him you are the master... if he has seen that he is vanquished the first time and has been obliged to humble himself before you, this will rob him of his courage to rebel anew.'

That these draconian principles were acted upon was confirmed after the Second World War (1939–1945), in an analysis of the childhood of all leading members of Hitler's Third Reich. The survey revealed that every single one had been subjected to an unusually strict and rigid upbringing, based on Kruger's harsh principles. When Hitler arrived on the political scene claiming to know, just like father, what was good and right for the German people, they rushed to obey his commands with almost childish servility and 'Father' or 'Leader' (Führer) Hitler was infallible in all matters related to the national interest. It is astonishing even today to read Nazi leader Hermann Göring's (1893–1946) emotional response to his meetings with Hitler. 'Every time I am in his presence, my heart stands still... Often I could not eat anything again until midnight because before then I should have vomited in my agitation.' This was no girlish ingénue writing of a romantic passion, but one of the leading air aces of the First World War.

In spite of this sentimentality, men such as Göring became ruthless implementers of Nazi tyranny, obeying the Führer's directives without question. Among them was Rudolf Höss (1900–1947), the infamous commandant of the Auschwitz concentration camp, who presided over the extermination of over 1.5 million human beings. Under interrogation by his captors, Höss confirmed that he had been brought up in a strict and fervently religious atmosphere, and at one time seemed destined for the priesthood. Throughout his childhood it was impressed upon him 'in forceful terms' that he must obey the commands of his parents, teachers and priests at all times without question. Nothing, he was told, should distract him from doing his duty. Shown no affection by his parents, he sought friendship with animals. His SS boss, Heinrich Himmler (1900–1945), must have endured a similar childhood, for he once criticized his interrogator angrily for enjoying shooting as a hobby. 'How can you find pleasure,' he exclaimed, 'in shooting from behind cover at poor creatures grazing on the edge of a wood, defenceless and unsuspecting? It's really just murder. Nature is so marvellously beautiful and every animal has a right to live.' This may seem an astonishing sentiment from a man who presided over the torture and murder of millions of his fellow human beings but the Jews were reduced in many German minds to beings that were less than human – 'vermin', diseased things that needed to be exterminated.

Although the social and political situation of Hitler's childhood was in many ways peculiar to Germany at the time, other future despots in quite different societies also endured misery, brutality and humiliation as they grew up. One of the other great tyrants of the 20th century, Joseph Stalin, experienced a childhood uncannily similar to that of Hitler. Born 10 years earlier in 1879, he grew up in a small town in

Georgia, as an illegitimate son with a drunken step-father who humiliated him by beating him unmercifully in the presence of his ineffectual mother. As in Hitler's case, there was no one to protect Stalin or to offer witness. Stalin's hatred of his step-father must have been intense; it is even claimed that in 1906 he tried to hire an axe-man to kill him in the town of Telavi. In addition to this, Stalin had to endure constant bad health, the legacy of which would dog him throughout his adult life. An attack of smallpox at the age of seven left him with a heavily scarred face and the village nickname 'Poxy'. Worse was to come, however. Soon after, he was run over by a carriage; the subsequent blood poisoning left him with a withered shoulder that would preclude him from serving in the First World War. Some writers have suggested that the injury was not an accident, but the result of a particularly heavy beating by his father. Apparently, untreated fractures of the type he suffered are common in battered children. They hold out their left arm to ward off the stick in the parent's right hand. In Stalin's case he was left with an arm three inches shorter than his right arm and he frequently needed a brace to support it. Bad luck struck again five years later when he was run over a second time. His leg was badly damaged, an injury that gave him a permanent ungainly walk. Some biographers have speculated that this accumulation of injuries meant that for the rest of his life, Stalin was never free of pain, and thus developed a bitter and cynical animosity towards others; which, in turn, led to his irritable and sadistic nature. As a young man Stalin must have been an unprepossessing sight, short in stature with a pock-marked face, one arm three inches shorter than the other and with webbed toes on both feet. Moreover, he had to bear the stigma of illegitimacy: his mother Ekaterina Geladze was a poor servant girl who had become pregnant by her master. He married her off to the local cobbler, who was yet another child- and wife-beating drunk. Mocked by the local community in Gori, Stalin endured daily misery as a near-outcast, the only respite being his mother's occasional signs of affection and the relative prosperity of the family home. Family life, as they then knew it, ended abruptly when his step-father abandoned them and went off to live in another village. Reduced to poverty, his mother was said to have become half-mad with worry, and was seen wandering through the streets of Gori with dishevelled hair, praying, singing and muttering to herself. Her behaviour bred in Stalin a rigid determination never to give way to adversity. Throughout his life, he was never once seen to cry or display his true emotions in public; he adopted instead a smiling mask of confidence.

For a poor boy in Georgia, the only path to an education was via a religious seminary. Stalin entered the Tiflis Seminary in 1892, where he established himself as a tough loner who had learnt to look after himself. As a school friend, Joseph Iremashvili, later recalled, 'He sneered at the misfortunes or joys of others and was lacking in compassion for animals or people. He enjoyed scaring other boys. To Stalin, friendship meant the submission of others to his domineering will.' The historian Alan Bullock wrote in his book *Hitler and Stalin: Parallel Lives* (1991), 'The experience of the first half of his life, living on the margins of society, often in the company of thieves and other low-lifes... left psychological handicaps from which he was never to free himself. He emerged as a rough, coarse, and difficult person whose original motivation as a revolutionary was coloured far more by hatred and resentment than by idealism.'

Like Idi Amin of Uganda, Stalin came from a minority that was looked down upon as deeply provincial by the Russian elite; yet, in the 12th century, Georgia had outshone the then more primitive western Russia, both culturally and militarily. All his life, Stalin remained fascinated by Georgian history. His own political career was to have a striking resemblance to that of ruthless medieval Georgian kings, who did not hesitate to destroy potential rivals, even those who had served them well. One of his inspirations was King David IV, who took the throne in 1089, after an Arab Islamic occupation that had lasted from the 7th to the 9th centuries. A formidable warrior, he drove the Seljuk Turks out of Tbilisi and turned his country into one of the wealthiest in the region, initiating vast projects that earned him the name of 'David the Builder.' Only the reign of his granddaughter, Queen Tamar, who extended Georgia's borders to the Caspian, could be compared to his. This golden age of Georgia had a further appeal to Stalin, the compulsive reader, for King David IV was also a gifted writer and author of the classic work the *Hymns of Repentance*. The tradition of military kings who also encouraged the arts continued for over 200 years with a later monarch, George V, driving the barbarians back over the Caucasus Mountains in 1320, much as Stalin would do to the German invaders in 1942. Again George V's reign was characterised by a magnificent secular art and culture, philosophical discussion and a series of political innovations that included religious and ethnic tolerance. Another Georgian characteristic was to manifest itself in Stalin: a readiness to take offence and a cold determination to avenge any insult. Yet, he also possessed great cunning and patience, combined with a frightening ability to apparently read an opponent's mind at will. He remained constantly alert to potential attack, and dealt with his growing paranoia by striking first. For this reason, millions of innocent suspects would be arrested, tortured, murdered or exiled or, as sometimes happened, suddenly and mysteriously released – all at the whim of the despot.

A miserable childhood was also the lot of the Italian despot Benito Mussolini, who considered his school years the bitterest of his life; although his sufferings appear relatively minor compared to the brutality suffered by his two contemporaries, Hitler and Stalin. Mussolini did not take to the Salesian school at Faenza, where he was sent at the age of nine as he found the moral atmosphere and constant surveillance inimical to his natural rebelliousness. He was also lonely, his only friend being a thick-skulled boy, on whose head Mussolini claimed he had broken bricks. There was humiliation too, for he was forced to sit with the non-fee paying children, even though his parents had agreed to pay fees, so advertising the poverty of his family. In his second year at the school, he demonstrated his future organisational abilities by leading a strike of pupils against the bad food, before stabbing another boy and being immediately expelled. That the school then sued his family for back fees only added to his sense of humiliation and outrage.

The fourth member of this quartet of 20th-century despots, Mao Tse-tung, was severely beaten as a child, and developed a life-long resentment of his father. Mao once described him to the 20th-century American journalist Edgar Snow as 'a hot-tempered man who frequently beat my brothers and me. He gave us no money whatsoever and only meagre food.' What appeared to have outraged Mao far more than the beatings, however, was his father's lack of charity to the poor, which may well have sparked his own concern for the poor of rural China. The humiliation experienced by other despots was also present in Mao's childhood, albeit in a milder form: his father used him as a debt collector, sending him round the local village to collect money for the chickens and eggs he had sold. The future ruler of China found this demeaning and embarrassing, but not as damaging as his father's insistence that he receive only a minimal education – appropriate to a man who would spend the rest of his life working in the fields. Such treatment provoked both anger and contempt in the child. 'I learned to hate him,' Mao later told Snow. But unlike Hitler and Stalin, Mao had been able to strike back at his despotic father by organizing the whole family to stand up against him and present a united front. This ability to organize would stand him in good stead in his political career. Throughout his life, Mao constantly referred to how this childhood battle with his father had influenced his later actions. As Alice Miller points out, a child that has experienced authority as frustrating and debilitating, will, as an adult, use it in punitive and retaliatory acts. In the case of a political despot, it is used to enslave a whole society to his will. In this sense, power is a poison that eventually overwhelms even an idealist such as Mao.

Other tyrants who have shared the experience of suffering at the hands of a drunken and violent father include Nicolae Ceausescu of Romania. He had the additional humiliation of public mockery, as his father periodically abandoned the small family farm and wandered off to Bucharest in search of drink and prostitutes, leaving his family penniless. Like Stalin, Ceausescu suffered from an obvious physical defect, in his case a debilitating stutter that he managed to overcome during his rise to power in the Romanian Communist Party. As in all other cases of childhood misery, the humiliation he suffered in front of the local community appears to have been as damaging as the violence itself. In such circumstances, the hatred of the bullying father is transferred to the witnesses of the child's shame, and he comes to hate the community as a whole. This is particularly apparent in the case of Idi Amin, the murderous despot of Uganda, who was brought up by a single Nubian mother in a village near the town of Jinja. As members of a minority tribe, both mother and child were treated with contempt by the dominant Bantu Kakway community. Amin's family was also Muslim in what was a largely Christian society, and was thus excluded from the local tribal customs and rituals. Amin's mother did not appear to offer him the love that could have compensated for the poverty and rejection he endured. This became so intolerable that at the age of only nine, Amin left his mother and wandered off to live on his own, never to contact her again. Moving from village to village, he survived as a petty thief, stealing food and cigarettes from houses. Nearly dead of starvation he eventually found a British army post that took him in and gave him work in the kitchen, thus initiating the most bizarre military career in British army history: Idi Amin progressed from dishwasher to Field Marshall.

A more curious example of childhood humiliation is that of François 'Papa Doc' Duvalier (1907–1971), the despotic ruler of Haiti for almost two decades. When he was still a young child, Duvalier's mother was declared insane and incarcerated in a mental asylum in Port au Prince. As a result, Duvalier developed a deep and unusual sense of shame, exacerbated by the upbringing he received from an aunt in deprived circumstances. In the voodoo-dominated society of Haiti of the time, mental illness carried a magical stigma; it certainly caused Duvalier to withdraw into himself and to shun the company of other children. Quiet and well educated, he gave no hint in his youth of what he would do once he came to power. Yet like Hitler, he wrote an ideological tract that expressed in detail his unambiguous hatred for mulattoes, the Catholic Church and foreigners in general; like the Führer, he wasted no time in putting his repressive theories into action when elected president of Haiti in 1957. Small, bespectacled and dressed in the cut-down clothes of his grandfather, Duvalier must have appeared a strange and possibly pathetic sight on the streets of Port au Prince. He maintained the sartorial style of a shabby bureaucrat for the rest of his life, projecting the image of a quiet country doctor throughout his entire despotic and bloodthirsty rule of Haiti.

The modest yet oddly sinister appearance of Duvalier was in complete contrast to that of the Libyan despot Muammar Gaddafi (b.1942; President of Libya from

1977), whose flamboyant clothes continue to surprise. His childhood trauma was not the result of deprivation or brutality, but the sudden death of many of those close to him at the hands of occupying colonial armies. Both his uncle and grand-father were killed by Mussolini's troops in the 1930s and his father was imprisoned by the Italians before being hunted down and thrown into jail by the British. Deprived of male contact in his early years, Gaddafi took refuge in the beliefs of Islam and a growing commitment to the cause of Libyan independence. As his Bedouin family were too poor to pay for Gaddafi's education, the local community clubbed together to pay for his fees at a local Islamic school. Humiliated to receive this public charity, by the age of 15 the young man resolved to overthrow the ruling monarchy and make himself sole ruler of Libya.

Although terrible childhood experiences appear to be the norm for many of the world's worst despots of the 20th century, there are always exceptions to any rule. Some appear to have enjoyed perfectly normal, prosperous and even contented childhoods. Pol Pot, responsible for the Killing Fields of Cambodia, for example, was brought up in tranquillity on his father's large estate and was given a good education. Family life was normal, and he had the benefit of an attractive and influential sister, Roeung, who was a royal mistress. Like Stalin, he was exposed at a young age to the certainty of religion, spending a year as a novice monk at the Buddhist temple of Wat Bottum Vaddei, near the gilded royal palaces of Phnom Penh.

However, in his adolescence a strange event occurred. Within the palace walls, Roeung was living as a royal concubine to the elderly King Monivong. At the age of 15, the boy was still deemed a child, and was allowed to visit his sister in the harem. According to Keng Vannsak, a contemporary of Pol Pot who later became his political mentor in Paris, the harem women would indulge in sex play with him, stopping just short of intercourse. It was certainly an unusual experience for an adolescent, and may have in some way led to the sense of frustration combined with an almost total lack of emotion that he displayed in later life.

CHAPTER 3

Murderous Revenge

When Idi Amin seized power in Uganda on 25 January 1971, he moved fast to revenge himself on the country that had rejected and reviled him as a child. Every member of his predecessor Milton Obote's (1924–2005; President 1966–1971 and 1980–1985) administration was seized and immediately executed by firing squad. Next, he ordered the arrest of many of the country's skilled professionals, including lawyers, clergymen, teachers and even doctors. Their crimes, it appeared, were to have received the education that Amin himself had been denied and to have prospered in a society that had rejected him. In fact, it was only the occupying British forces who had treated him with any kind of respect and had shown him the path out of the poverty and unhappiness that he had experienced as a child. The catalogue of horrors he inflicted on his victims in those first days of rule is as appalling and as primitive as anything perpetrated by the Nazis or even Ivan the Terrible. The Chief Justice of the Ugandan High Court, Benedicto Kiwanuka (1922–1972), was dragged off to prison where his arms and legs were severed and his genitals cut off and stuffed into his mouth before his tormentors set him alight. Frank Kalimuzo, vice chancellor of Makere University, was arrested the same day and was never seen alive again. He had sat passively throughout the night, listening to himself being denounced on Ugandan radio while he waited for his killers to arrive. Most of the condemned were taken first to the palace of the Kabaka, the ex-King of Uganda, in Kampala, where Amin enjoyed watching them squirm and plead for mercy while they were tortured and tormented. Then, in an African reprise of Stalin's bloody assault on the Red Army, Amin had most of the senior officers in the Ugandan army arrested and shot. It was soon apparent that no one well-educated or in a senior position in Uganda was safe. With their senior officials dead or having fled the country, the ordinary civil servants struggled to maintain the rapidly collapsing Ugandan economy and administration. Then, they too came under assault from Amin, the lucky ones dismissed from their posts, others shot, together with many police officers. The only authority left was the army, now led by its junior officers.

To celebrate the first anniversary of his coup, Amin struck again, ordering 503 prisoners to be massacred at Mutakula Prison in Kampala. By the following March it is estimated that over 30,000 Ugandans had been killed by the new regime. Most nights, a beaming Amin would appear on the state-controlled television, reassuring the people in his avuncular manner that all was going well and that any deaths they may have heard about were either the result of accidents or border clashes with Tanzanian troops, and were being thoroughly investigated by the Ugandan security forces. Amin abandoned formal speeches to the people in favour of spontaneous harangues delivered with his customary clownish good humour. The true horror masked by this joviality was revealed when the Tanzanian army eventually invaded Uganda and overthrew his despotic regime. In the basement of Amin's headquarters, the troops found a bloodstained drainage gulley where prisoners had been forced to lie down before being shot, so that their blood would drain away without staining the floor. It was a simple procedure; the next person to be executed would carry the corpse of his predecessor to a pile outside, then return and climb down to take his place in the gulley. The sheer horror of this sordid procedure reflects the hatred that Amin had nurtured against Ugandan society. Given the nature of African tribal massacres that would later be seen in the Congo and Rwanda, it was not surprising that he used his minority group, the Nubians, to wreak revenge on the traditionally more numerous and powerful tribes, and on the Asian community that played an important role in the Ugandan economy, who he expelled from Uganda in September 1972. When interviewed in Saudi Arabia after he was deposed, Amin was asked if he felt any remorse for what he had done in Uganda. 'No,' he replied. 'Only nostalgia.'

Yet Amin's brutality was nothing new in Uganda; his draconian methods of control would have been familiar to past inhabitants. Buganda, as the country was known in the 19th century, was first visited by Europeans, when the English explorer John Hanning Speke arrived there in 1859 seeking the source of the Nile. Then ruler King Mutesa (c.1838–1884; King of Buganda 1856–1884) punished the slightest infringement of his elaborate rules of conduct by instant death at the hands of his bodyguards. Court officials had to attend him at specified times on pain of death, and those who failed to salute him in the correct manner or whose clothes were worn incorrectly were also instantly executed. Revealing a glimpse of naked ankle showed disrespect at Mutesa's court, and was a capital offence. Extreme caution was always necessary in the presence of the king, for to inadvertently touch his throne or his clothes, or even cast a glance in the direction of any of his wives, earned the same punishment. Every member of his court moved carefully for fear of instant death which awaited any page who walked instead of ran to deliver a message, for example. Items from outside the country were forbidden to anyone other than members of the royal family. Those found in possession of beads or brass wire died immediately. During his time at Mutesa's court, Speke watched in fascinated horror as people were executed daily for trivial offences. One of the worst examples that Speke witnessed was a young woman who had run away from her husband and taken shelter for a few days with a decrepit old man. Both were brought before Mutesa, who ordered that they be fed and kept alive as long as possible while they were systematically dismembered and fed to vultures. On another occasion, Speke presented Mutesa with some carbines. The king loaded one of them, then passed it to a page and told him to test its power by shooting a bystander, which the page instantly did. Later, as they walked together, Mutesa noticed a woman who had received the punishment of being tied to a tree. Taking the carbine from Speke, he shot her dead on the spot. Speke observed that this behaviour was not unusual in a country where it was the custom to burn alive the brothers of a new king when he came to the throne.

Such barbarities carried out by ruthless despots were also common in other parts of Africa, as an earlier explorer, Henry Fynn, recalled. While present at the court of the Zulu king Shaka (c.1787–1828; ruled 1816–1828), he noticed that the slightest, almost imperceptible movement of the king's finger would indicate someone who must be instantly despatched. On his first day at the court, Fynn witnessed the execution of 10 men; on a subsequent day, 60 boys under the age of 12 were killed before Shaka had breakfasted. The method of execution in Zululand was by a sudden twist of the neck, but anyone accused of witchcraft was hung upside down from a tree by the feet and slowly burnt to death. Occasionally, in the technique made notorious by Vlad the Impaler, a victim had a stake driven through the anus and was left to a lingering death. Throughout his time at Shaka's court, Fynn witnessed with growing horror such daily atrocities as the massacre of 500 women for supposed witchcraft. The brutality appeared universal throughout the Zulu kingdom. Shaka's mother Nandi also had the authority to order executions, and every village chief was permitted to kill any of his own people. One of the most bizarre events that Fynn observed was the mourning ceremony that followed Nandi's death. A crowd of 8,000 people were assembled and ordered not to eat or drink, but to weep. Those who failed to produce tears, or were found trying to drink at the nearby river, were beaten to death by the others. By the following afternoon, Fynn calculated that 7,000 people had perished in this manner while Shaka and his chiefs were throwing themselves about in wild displays of grief. Yet the horror did not end there. Shaka then ordered the execution of one of his aunts, who Nandi had disliked, and warriors were sent out to execute all those who had not come to express sorrow. In a last brutal gesture, all women found to be pregnant within a year of Nandi's death were executed, along with their husbands.

When seen in the context of Uganda's bloody past, the despotism of Amin seems a little more explicable; he was merely reviving a savage tradition that had been suppressed under the British colonial rule from 1896 to1962. What is most shocking about this tyranny is the sheer arbitrariness of it: death is dispensed on a whim and no one knows who will be the next victim of the despot's sudden and irrational anger. Such circumstances recall the short but bloody rule of the Roman Emperor Caligula 2,000 years earlier, when Roman patricians lived in fear of his sudden mood swings and random punishments. Indeed, Caligula may well have taken his revenge on Tiberius for the humiliation he received at the emperor's hands. In one account of the death of the 77-year-old emperor in AD 37, Caligula, thinking Tiberius to be dead, drew the imperial signet ring off his finger and was greeted as the new emperor by the crowd. But then it was announced that Tiberius had recovered, and was asking for food. Caligula was terrified of Tiberius's revenge, and ordered Naevius Cordus Sertorius Macro, commander of the Praetorian Guard, to go into the emperor's bedroom and smother him with a cushion.

Right from the start of his reign, Caligula behaved with disturbing perversity; when visiting a Roman legion stationed on the Rhine, he decided to have it decimated on the spot for having rebelled against his father, Germanicus (c.16 BC–AD 19), 24 years earlier. The brutal custom of decimation was an accepted Roman tradition. The soldiers were drawn up on parade, then ordered to draw lots to decide the one in 10 men who would be clubbed to death by their colleagues. But as anger spread through the ranks and the soldiers appeared about to mutiny, Caligula, a notorious coward in spite of his brutality, beat a hasty retreat back to Rome. It was the randomness of his decision, in this as in many other aspects of his rule, that came to shock the Romans, together with his seemingly pointless cruelties.

Back in Rome, the emperor soon found easier victims – wealthy Roman citizens whom he accused of treason in order to seize their assets. He was said to have quickly frittered away the 27 million gold pieces he inherited from Tiberius. But even this was as nothing compared to the cruelties that he inflicted on those who had crossed him in his youth, or who now criticized his behaviour. Much of his anger was directed at the Senate, some of whose members were arbitrarily arrested, then subjected to torture and a slow agonizing death for supposed disloyalty. His innate sadism was clear as he forced parents to witness their children's executions while he sat watching them, making jokes. He indulged in macabre wit, ordering a writer to be burnt to death for writing something ambiguous, or having people beaten to within an inch of their lives, then allowing them to recover to prolong the suffering.

With Caligula's sadism went a need to shock and humiliate – payback for the misery of his own fraught childhood on Capri. The humiliation he had suffered there was repaid with interest on those who had failed to protect him or his family from the tyranny and sexual perversions of Tiberius. His contempt for what passed as Roman morality was exhibited when he decided to open a brothel in his own palace. The first customers were his terrified senators, who were summoned with their wives to attend him there. After dinner he took each wife in turn into his private bedroom, leaving her humiliated husband to sit with the others in silence. Returning to the room he would then recount in great detail the sexual acts he had performed. Behaviour like this was insufferable; it became inevitable that the once-popular Caligula would be assassinated. Delivery from his tyranny came in January, AD 41, when members of the Praetorian Guard stabbed him to death in the corridor of his palace. Ironically, their leader was Cassius Chaerea, an officer who Caligula had mocked for effeminacy before the whole court.

When Vlad the Impaler was at last released and returned to Walachia as king in 1448, the quest for revenge on his childhood tormentors fuelled a bitter campaign against his Turkish overlords. Matters were not helped by his now Muslim brother Radu's decision to remain at the Sultan's court. On arrival in Walachia, Vlad discovered that his father had been assassinated a year earlier, buried alive by his own rebellious boyar nobles. Before this, the same fate had been meted out to his eldest brother; other boyars had burnt out his eyes with hot stakes before also burying him alive. Vlad's subsequent attack on boyar power was perhaps then inevitable, as was that of his disciple, Ivan the Terrible, a century later. Although he was ruler of Walachia for just seven years, Vlad's demonic energy was such that he became one of the most notorious rulers in Eastern European history. His onslaught on his Turkish enemies was only equalled by the revenge he took on his own treacherous boyars. The historical documents that remain, portray Vlad as a psychopathic tyrant, while at the same time praising him as a national hero, forced to use ruthless methods against a pitiless foe. Tales of Vlad's exploits against the Ottomans circulated throughout Christian Europe in the 15th century, earning him both fear and respect. They were mostly written in German and illustrated with woodcuts that depicted the despot committing atrocities.

Most were produced when Vlad was still in his prime, using the newly invented printing press, and are perhaps the first example in Europe of the media promoting the personality cult of a despot. These publications, based on true, if elaborated, exploits such as *The Frightening and Truly Extraordinary Story of a Wicked Blood-drinking Tyrant Called Prince Dracula*, published in Austria in 1463, became the inspiration for the Victorian horror stories of Count Dracula, such as Bram Stoker's famous but completely fictitious account of a blood-sucking vampire. The only connection between Vlad and Dracula is that Vlad's father was known as Dracul. Turkish chronicles, not surprisingly, emphasize the unreasonable cruelties that Vlad inflicted on his enemies, especially during the battles of 1461–1462. By contrast, the Romanian oral narratives, still preserved in the villages near the ruins of Vlad's fortress on the Arges River, describe him as a hero who defended his homeland against the Turks at a time when every other principality in the region had succumbed to Ottoman rule.

Some Russian documents took the same line, and these stories about Vlad the hero king are what appear to have inspired the young Ivan the Terrible to emulate the Walachian despot. There are striking similarities between them; both came to deal ruthlessly with arrogant boyar nobles, and each had to deal with the constant threat of invasion from hostile nations. The difference with Ivan was his firm conviction that he was on earth to do God's work, and to rule Russia by divine right. 'I am subject to no one except Christ, son of God,' he stated unequivocally. As such he had no need to justify his campaign of revenge on the boyars, nor the slaughter of anyone who dared to flout his will. Such a person was obstructing the will of God – a heretic who must be destroyed. Ivan even came to believe that using violence against dissenters was his sacred duty, and that cruelty itself had a purifying effect on the recipients. This was a uniquely Russian concept of kingship, and would have been inconceivable anywhere else in Europe – other than in Spain, perhaps, at the height of the Holy Inquisition. Ivan's interpretation of his role as Tsar may well have been accepted because of the unusually pious nature of Russian people; they may have shared his unshakeable conviction that the Tsar had God-given right to punish transgressors of his will. In a letter to his childhood friend and closest adviser, Prince Andrei Kurbsky (1528–1583), Ivan affirms this belief with breathtaking simplicity: 'If you are so righteous and pious… why do you not permit yourself to accept suffering from me, your master, and so inherit the crown of life?'

Putting theory into practice, he ordered the city of Novgorod be destroyed in January 1570 on the mere suspicion that its governors were planning to hand it over to Poland. When they refused to open the gates to his army, Ivan ordered walls to be built around the city, thus preventing anyone's escape. On each day of the siege, his troops killed between 500 and 1,000 of the defenders and captured many more, who were brutally tortured and then killed in the presence of Ivan and his son. Not surprisingly, the city finally surrendered; but not before over 20,000 of its inhabitants had died from starvation or at the hands of the besieging soldiers.

On the whole, the Russian people appeared more impressed than horrified by their Tsar's harsh methods. When he secretly left Moscow at Christmas 1564, announcing his intention to abdicate, there was a popular outcry. After a month of negotiations Ivan finally agreed to come back, on condition that his actions in dealing with his supposed enemies be fully condoned by the people. Armed with this supreme power, Ivan returned in triumph to Moscow and set about teaching the boyars a bitter lesson. Soon the men who had poisoned his childhood were being subjected to his implacable revenge. Arrested on the least suspicion or on the word of the many informers that thronged his court, they were subjected to the most appalling cruelties. It should be remembered that this was the age of the artist Hiëronymus Bosch (c.1450–1516), whose paintings reflect the contemporary obsession with guilt and torture. One ex-favourite suspected of disloyalty was impaled on a stake, where he lingered for 15 hours. When the victim's mother came to pray for her dying son, Ivan encouraged 100 men of his artillery to rape her in turn. Even when she was dead, he continued the defilement by ordering her remains be fed to his hunting dogs. This was intense sadism, carried out with such crazed dedication as to be almost unique in the long history of despotism. Although Ivan claimed that he was cleansing the world of sinners, the protracted methods he used and the deep personal interest he took in the mechanics of death suggest that his motivation was the simple indulgence of sadistic urges.

Although Joseph Stalin was never personally involved in the act of murder as Ivan had been, he was nevertheless responsible for the death of millions of innocent Russians. These people were executed, worked to death in the gulags of the 1930s or simply died of starvation as a result of Stalin's disastrous economic policies. Without exception, his victims died because of the Russian despot's paranoia – the result of his own early insecurity. Stalin was suspicious of everyone, particularly his closest advisers, and was constantly looking for an opportunity to strike first. Even when in a position of supreme power, with every potential rival either dead or in prison, he remained consumed by suspicion. When his old comrade Sergei Kirov (1886–1934) was murdered by a lone assassin in October 1943, Stalin seized the opportunity to force the Supreme Soviet to ratify the so-called 'Kirov Law'. With his customary paranoia Stalin had become convinced that Kirov was a threat to him. While Stalin was prepared to sacrifice principle for expediency, Kirov remained a consistent old style Bolshevik, who had enthusiastically pursued the class war against the kulak landowners. By 1933, however, it was evident that the Bolshevik victory was complete and a relaxation of the Soviet dictatorship was in order, in line with ortho-dox Marxist belief. That year there began to be talk of the 'Kirov line' as an alternative to Stalin's rigid control. Although Stalin did not openly condemn this more liberal line, he became increasingly wary in the year preceding the XVIIth Congress, held in February 1934. Stalin's fears appeared justified when it became known that some senior delegates had approached Kirov with the suggestion that he agree to become the new General Secretary. Kirov refused outright, not wanting to split the party, but this did not stop 289 of the 1,966 delegates present voting against Stalin. From that moment Kirov was a doomed man. The Leningrad NKVD now began combing the police files in search of an assassin. Finally they found a disgruntled man, Nikolayev, who was prepared to carry out the execution. One of Stalin's most reliable biogra-phers, Robert Conquest, is convinced that Stalin gave the order to kill Kirov. The death of the second most prominent man in the Soviet Union became his means of destroying the thousands of Communist party members who he suspected might oppose or plot against him in the future. The first to go were the late Kirov's own supporters, those 100 or so delegates who had applauded him at the last Party confer-ence. All were denounced as enemies of the people, arrested and either executed or sent to the gulags. With the Kirov Law, Stalin had defined the power of the despot in the modern state; his example was soon followed by Hitler in Nazi Germany. Now both tyrannies had a law that violated the basic concept of justice, making it possi-ble for suspected dissidents to be executed without trial if it was deemed necessary for the defence of the state. From now on anyone who even questioned authority in either Soviet Russia or Nazi Germany knew that they risked conviction and summary execution. For the despots that ruled these societies, the revenge on the communities that had shunned them as children was almost complete.

Revenge, however, is not always equated with death. In the case of the Libyan despot Muammar Gaddafi it involved the imposition of extreme religious morality on what he considered to be the rich and decadent society that had forced him to grow up in poverty and humiliation. In September 1969, the 27-year-old Gaddafi was among a group of army officers who seized power in Tripoli. The elderly King Idris (1890–1983; King of Libya 1951–1969) was deposed with a minimum of violence and sent into exile; with American assistance, Gaddafi became sole ruler of the oil-rich state. From the start, he condemned Israel and announced that from now on Libya would be governed by the rules of the Koran. At once, the relatively liberal society was subjected to harsh laws, according to which thieves had their hands cut off and women were stoned to death for adultery. Alcohol was banned and all nightclubs, casinos and brothels shut down. Gaddafi took a keen personal involvement in their closure, often accompanying the troops when they arrived to board up the doors. At Tripoli's leading tourist nightspot, the Bowdlerina Theatre, he even marched on stage mid-performance brandishing a gun, and fired several shots into the ceiling as terrified visitors scrambled for the exits. 'This cesspit of Western depravity is now officially closed,' he shouted. The only religion now tolerated in Libya was Islam; as the Turks had done after the fall of Constantinople, Gaddafi turned all churches and synagogues into mosques. The familiar restrictions of despotism came into force: the press was censored, political activity banned, worker's unions disbanded. Long hair for men was banned, and women's skirt lengths were checked in the street by state-sponsored mullahs. For his Praetorian Guard, Gaddafi selected members of his own Bedouin tribe, whose loyalty he could rely on, supplemented by the obligatory secret police trained in the latest interrogation techniques by the Egyptians. A classic police state emerged, although without the extreme torture and murder usually associated with such regimes. An exception was the public execution in February 1984 of a group of university students, who had demonstrated against excessive government control.

Bolstered by money from oil, much as Hugo Chávez (b.1954; president of Venezuela from 1998) would later be, Gaddafi indulged his vanity by constantly appearing on the international stage attended by a bodyguard of Libyan paramilitaries. His revenge on the West for its decadence was far more serious. He sponsored the Black September terrorist group that massacred the Israeli athletes at the Munich Olympics in 1972, and funded numerous skyjackings by Palestinian groups. He then supplied Idi Amin with military aircraft that were destroyed by the Israelis at Entebbe, Uganda. These aggressive activities against Western interests ceased abruptly in 1986, when the United States sent 18 F-III warplanes from Britain to bomb his palace in Tripoli, narrowly missing him and killing his adopted daughter. The attack produced a change of heart in Gaddafi; his support for terrorism waned as he realized total control of his own country still left him vulnerable to attack by international forces. It was the same lesson that Slobodan Miloševic would learn, to his cost, a decade later.

CHAPTER 4

The Imperative of Cruelty

Accounts of the barbarities of Vlad, Ivan, Pol Pot or Idi Amin give rise to some fascinating questions: were they driven to excess by some innate compulsion such as an enjoyment of cruelty for its own sake? Or were they acting merely to retain power, by demonstrating a capacity for ruthlessness? Certainly it is likely that 20th-century tyrants such as Hitler and Stalin never killed anyone personally, and kept well away from the deaths and misery that resulted from their inhuman policies. It is reported that Hitler enjoyed a film showing the von Stauffenberg bomb plot leaders being hanged on piano wire, but it is arguable that even this was directed more at a satisfaction at watching traitors getting their just deserts than pure sadism. Nor did the Führer take much interest in the fate of the millions murdered in the concentration camps; this, like much else in the Nazi regime, he left to highly efficient assistants such as Heinrich Himmler and Reinhard Heydrich (1904–1942) – men who had the stomach for witnessing human misery at close quarters. Although reportedly given to occasional bouts of furious rage, Hitler never displayed a capacity for personal violence; he kept his distance from the horrors of the extermination camps, much as he did from the dangers of the battlefield. His absence from the Front seems at odds with his much publicized reputation for bravery in the First World War, when he won an Iron Cross in the trenches. When pictured in military uniform, Hitler never quite appears convincing, and his grasp of military strategy was proved to be particularly inept by events. His order to General von Paulus to hold Stalingrad at all costs is only the most obvious example of his addiction to theatrical gestures at the expense of military common sense. Hitler's refusal to allow General von Paulus to effect a retreat in the face of overwhelming Russian opposition finally led to a surrender to the Russians at Stalingrad in January 1943, with 91,000 German soldiers taken prisoner. This stunning defeat ensured that Germany's manpower was severely depleted and left the country vulnerable to the Russian advance which followed. Hitler always addressed the German people in dramatic language, but when, as the Russians entered Berlin, the opportunity finally came for a grand Wagnerian end to his regime, he was found wanting. Instead of leading his few remaining troops against the Russian invaders, he chose to stay hidden, committing suicide in his own protective bunker.

Equally shy of frontline action and personal involvement in cruelty was Stalin, who was as careful as Hitler to keep well away from the battlefront as the Germans advanced across Russia in 1942. Even when the German army was clearly beaten after Stalingrad, the great Russian hero remained wary of getting too close to the action – despite the increasing popularity of the victorious General Zhukov (1896–1974), who began to challenge his own standing with the Russian people. While personally brutal as a young man, Stalin kept the exercise of his mature cruelty at arms' length, leaving the dirty work to others. Driven by his obsessive paranoia, he sent millions to their death while reserving his personal aggression for bullying sessions with his own officials and colleagues. Many have written accounts of having to endure his malevolent threats as he became drunk each evening, taunted his companions with heavy-handed humour and forced them to perform before him like lap dogs. To despots like Stalin, Hitler or Mao Tse-tung, living people were merely the actors in their own personal fantasies – or, more accurately, human toys to be used in a power game and, when appropriate, simply thrown away. In China it was particularly easy to ignore the individual; Chinese societies had done so since the time of the first emperor. Mao inherited this tradition and imposed his will without the personal animosity or the enjoyment of cruelty that his regime inevitably involved. In Communist China, as in contemporary North Korea under Kim Jong-Il, the individual did not exist other than as an unquestioning component of the all-powerful State. In this context, the infliction of suffering is not a conscious process, as this would endow the victims with more significance than they deserve. The same is true of other totalitarian regimes of the 20th century; the millions worked to death in the gulags or driven to death in the concentration camps were of total insignificance to their persecutors. There is no better demonstration of this than the industrial processes of the Nazi gas chamber and crematorium, devised to dispose of people like household rubbish.

The atrocities of a much earlier despot were thoroughly recorded by Suetonius, who was a constant presence at Caligula's court and witnessed the macabre events that took place there. In his work *De Vita Caesarum*, (Lives of the Caesars), Suetonius's conclusions leave little doubt that he considered Caligula a dangerous pathological sadist who enjoyed watching torture and execution for its own sake:

> He evinced the savage barbarity of his temper chiefly by the following
> indications. When flesh was only to be had at a high price for feeding his

wild beasts reserved for the spectacles... After disfiguring many persons
of honourable rank, by branding them in the face with hot irons, he
condemned them to the mines, to work in repairing the highways, or
to fight with wild beasts... He compelled parents to be present at the
execution of their sons; and to one who excused himself on account of
indisposition, he sent his own litter... He burned alive, in the centre of
the arena of the amphitheatre, the writer of a farce, for some witty verse,
which had a double meaning.

Much of this sadism was performed live in front of the emperor as a form of after-dinner entertainment, under express orders that the torturers prolong the suffering of the victims as long as possible – or suffer a similar fate themselves. Caligula was said to have enjoyed the spectacle of human suffering in much the same manner as a more recent despot, François 'Papa Doc' Duvalier of Haiti, who had a torture chamber constructed in the basement of his palace in Port au Prince, much as others would order a swimming pool. It was painted rust brown to disguise the inevitable bloodstains, and had peepholes drilled in the walls through which the president could watch his victims' sufferings. Another with similar appetites was José Gaspar Rodriguez Francia (1766–1840; dictator of Paraguay 1814–1840) in the early 19th century, who took delight in listening to his torturers' reports of how their victims had shrieked and pleaded for mercy. He ordered the weekly executions in the capital city of Asuncion to be carried out in front of the Presidential Palace, where a single bench was placed to seat the victim. Watching from a window, Francia would then hand the execution squad just three miserly bullets to do the job. If the soldiers missed (a frequent occurrence given the poor marksmanship of the Paraguayan army) or merely wounded the victim, he would then be finished off with a bayonet. As a final gesture of contempt, the corpse was then left in the sun for a whole day under Francia's window, like some macabre trophy.

All this was as nothing compared to Caligula's manic sadism. The emperor's cruelties appear to have had no political purpose whatsoever; they were carried out solely for the purposes of enjoyment. There are numerous accounts by Suetonius of his shocking depravity, including an insight into Caligula's mind when, after one bout of sadistic excess, he lamented that it was a pity that Rome itself did not have a single neck so that he could cut it off. This was a dangerous sentiment for any ruler to profess, and it became inevitable that the Emperor's increasingly wild and dangerous behaviour would bring about his own destruction. What political purpose could possibly be served by arresting three elderly senators in the middle of the night and having them brought to the palace? As the terrified men sat in the palace theatre contemplating their imminent execution, Caligula suddenly burst onto the stage in a long cloak and began performing an impromptu song and dance act; then dismissed the senators with a cheery wave of the hand. It was as if he had decided to indulge his perverted sense of humour by terrifying those he relied on most. To many in Roman society, the emperor was already doomed. Even at a time when excessive cruelty was the accepted norm, Caligula's brief four-year reign stands out – not for the sufferings he inflicted on the Roman people as a whole, but for the intense persecution and fear that he visited on his own patrician class. The source of this compulsive but inevitably self-destructive sadism must have been the terror and insecurity he endured when a virtual prisoner of Tiberius on Capri, where he was subject to the whims of the perverted emperor much as he later subjected the Roman aristocracy to his own capricious cruelties.

If accounts of Caligula's barbarities suggest a macabre sense of humour, there was nothing amusing about Vlad the Impaler's atrocities almost 1,500 years later, and whereas Caligula was said to have been a physically attractive man, Vlad Tepes was certainly not. A Papal legate to Buda (now Budapest) in 1466 described the Walachian king as 'short, stocky and of a cold and terrible appearance, with an aquiline nose, swollen nostrils and a thin and reddish face in which very long eyelashes framed large wide-open green eyes… his face and chin were shaven but for a long moustache.' This is a description of the archetypical Gothic despot of the period, and conjures up the familiar pallid image of evil that gave birth to the legend of Dracula. Accounts of his reign provide a match between his appearance and his performance as a cruel and ruthless despot.

So appalling are the catalogues of his sadism that it is often hard to give them credence; many, of German origin, are clearly works of Christian propaganda designed to make the Muslim invader think twice before invading. By a strange coincidence, many are stored in the cathedral at Lambach in Austria where Hitler sang as a boy in the choir. Most describe Vlad's trademark practice of impaling his enemies, but others mention his second favourite practice of immolating whole towns and their citizens if they failed to surrender – again, a warning to anyone contemplating resistance to his besieging armies. The most dramatic incident, described in great detail and with predictable relish by the Greek historian Chalkondyles in his work, *The Proofs of Histories*, concerns a valley that had been devastated by Vlad's army. As Turkish troops rode through Carpathia in June 1462, they discovered a nightmarish scene:

> The Sultan's army came across a field with stakes, about three kilometres long and one kilometre wide. And there were large stakes on which they could see the impaled bodies of men, women, and children, about twenty thousand of them, as they said; quite a spectacle for the Turks and the Sultan himself! The Sultan, in wonder, kept saying that he could not conquer the country of a man who could do such terrible and unnatural things, and put his power and his subjects to such use. He also used to say that this man who did such things would be worthy of more. And the other Turks, seeing so many people impaled, were scared out of their wits. There were babies clinging to their mothers on the stakes, and birds had made nests in their breasts.

The numbers reported killed are impossible to believe given the laborious method of execution, but the propaganda contributed to the myth of Vlad's implacable cruelty on a grand scale. It also served to warn the citizens of Walachia of what they could expect if they ever attempted to ally themselves with their former masters, the Turks. Yet there is no doubt that Vlad was a true sadist who enjoyed killing and watching the infliction of pain for its own sake. There are credible reports that he occasionally participated in executions himself; one describes him stabbing a mistress to death. Other eyewitnesses report him torturing and impaling birds and mice. The question of why he used such a dramatic, inefficient method of execution has persisted to this day; some speculate that it had sexual implications, and was a metaphorical substitute for his own suspected impotency. Certainly he was known to have murdered another of his mistresses for declaring that she was pregnant, perhaps because he knew that he could not be the father of the child. Research has shown that his most bitter atrocities were reserved for women rather than men, making him unique in the annals of despotism. His obsession with punishing pregnancy increases the suspicion that he was impotent; wives and mistresses who confessed their condition were frequently strangled, sawn in half or merely buried alive.

Vlad's sexual problems may well have originated when, as a prisoner at the court of Mehmet II (1429–1481; Ottoman sultan 1451–1481), he suffered the depredations of the Sultan's violent homosexuality. Guilt and humiliation may have led to the development of similar tastes that were sublimated into cruelty and revenge. In his struggle against the Turks, Vlad used ruthless tactics that involved retreating to lure the enemy forward and then suddenly attacking again, coupled with a scorched-earth policy, burning down his own villages and poisoning wells, to deny the Turks supplies. In one example, he drove plague victims into the enemy camp to spread disease: an early example of germ warfare. Nor were his tactics confined to the Turks alone. One of his earliest actions was to even scores with the nobles of the city of Târgoviste for having betrayed his father and brother. In the spring of 1457, he invited them and their families to an Easter feast. After the meal, the guests were seized by soldiers and forcibly marched 50 miles (80 km) to the site of the Castle of Poenari, where they were used as labourers to build a new fortress. Any survivors on its completion five months later were impaled. This hallmark of Vlad's cruelty invariably caused excruciating pain for hours, even days, and his executioners were expert at prolonging the agony. But he had other, equally gruesome ways of disposing of his opponents. A German pamphlet published in Nuremberg in 1488 gives a list:

> Some were buried naked up to the navel and then shot at with arrows and others were roasted or flayed alive. Once he ordered a large pot to be made and then boards containing holes to be fastened over it. Through these holes the prisoners' heads were shoved, so holding them fast. The pot was then filled with water and a big fire lit underneath so that the people cried pitiably as they were boiled to death. Mothers nursing babies were impaled together so that the children kicked convulsively at their mothers' breasts until dead. Christians, Jews and heathens were impaled sideways and left lying on the floor like dying frogs.

While it is impossible to verify these accounts, there is no doubt that Vlad meted out his punishments with unusual relish; there are three or more independent sources, indicating a large measure of veracity. Another story tells how he dispensed his own particular brand of charity to the sick and poor of Walachia by inviting them all to a feast in the town of Târgoviste, where a lavish meal had been prepared for them. At midnight Vlad appeared, like Dracula himself, and asked if there was anything else they desired, adding, 'Would you like to be free of cares forever?' When his audience shouted their agreement he ordered the hall to be boarded up and set on fire. None escaped the flames. By way of explanation, Vlad told his boyars that these poor people would no longer be a burden to themselves or others; he had simply removed poverty from Walachia at a stroke. Even foreigners did not appear to escape his wrath. Two Turkish ambassadors removed their hats in his presence, but retained the felt caps underneath, saying that they could not possibly remove them – not even for the Sultan. Vlad had the offending caps nailed firmly to their heads.

The most infamous atrocity of all took place in the town of Brasov when, in 1459, the local merchants ignored his threats and continued to withhold their taxes. Vlad led an assault on the town, setting it alight and impaling many of its inhabitants on the nearby Timpa Hill. The scene has been immortalized in an especially gruesome woodcut that appeared as the frontispiece to a pamphlet printed in Nuremberg in 1499. It depicts Vlad enjoying a meal surrounded by his impaled victims, as his henchmen continue hacking off limbs of other victims alongside his table. Although the story may have been embellished by mythmakers over time, the destruction of Brasov is a historical fact, which enhanced Vlad's reputation as a man capable of terrible revenge. Yet for all his atrocities, Vlad Tepes is still regarded by some Romanians as a true patriot, who saved Walachia from the Turks and held the frontline against Islam at a time when it threatened to overrun eastern and central Europe.

Ivan the Terrible was similarly restored to the status of national hero by the Russians following the October Revolution of 1917. Stalin, in particular, seized upon Ivan's patriotism to boost his own image with the Russian people, and encouraged a film to be made of Ivan's life and achievements. The result was the celebrated filmmaker Sergei Eisenstein's great two-part biographical film released throughout Russia at the start of the Second World War. If Ivan shared Vlad's patriotism, he also had identical tastes in sadism; he delighted in torturing and dismembering live animals and throwing cats and dogs from the Kremlin walls before progressing to more mature cruelties. A terrible example was set to the young Ivan by his guardians, the Shuisky brothers, who had Ivan's loyal friend Fyodor Mishurin skinned alive and left on public display in Moscow. Ivan's revenge when he came to power was to have Prince Andrew Shuisky, the more dominant of the two, thrown into a pit where he was torn to pieces by starving dogs. In his later persecution of the boyar nobles, he was often present at their torture, taking his turn with the red-hot pincers. He carried a heavy metal-pointed staff that he used to batter anyone who offended him – the same staff that he later used to kill his eldest son, delivering a blow on the head during an argument. No one was safe from his anger. His treasurer was boiled alive in a cauldron. A councillor suspected of disloyalty was hung upside down; Ivan joined his companions in hacking pieces from the suspended body. In a gesture of brutal humour, worthy of Emperor Caligula himself, he had earlier ordered the Archbishop of Novgorod to be sewn into a bearskin and then hunted to death by hounds.

Driven by a crazed obsession with religion that produced occasional bouts of remorse, he continued his reign of terror at home while successfully freeing Russia from foreign incursion by its equally violent neighbours; the result of both was a gradual slide into famine and poverty. At the beginning of his reign a rare English visitor, Hugh Chancellor, described the countryside around Moscow as being 'well replenished with small villages filled with people. The ground is well stored with corn... you will meet each morning seven or eight hundred sleds coming and going to Moscow.' But over the years, Ivan's policies of constant warfare with heavy taxation and forced military levies resulted in a severe decline. Peasants were driven off their land; Ivan's personal bodyguard, the *Oprichniki*, soon reduced much of Russia to a wasteland. Around the town of Novgorod, over 97 per cent of the land was abandoned; by 1585 the area was so depopulated that there was not enough manpower to continue the war against the Baltic state of Livonia.

Unlike the monarchs of Western Europe in the 16th century, the Tsar of Russia was not subject to any moral laws governing his behaviour, nor did the ideas of Humanism that drove both the Renaissance, the Reformation and the Counter-Reformation have much effect. Ivan the Terrible existed in a moral vacuum with only the teachings of the Orthodox Church to provide a check on his behaviour. His friends were few, his wives did not appear to survive long, and the passage of time did little to soften his attitudes; he appears to have become even more cruel and paranoid as his reign progressed. The German traveller Daniel von Bruchau was shocked to witness Ivan in such a paroxysm of fury one day that he began foaming at the mouth like a horse.

Given that his appalling reputation had already spread throughout Europe, it is astonishing to find that Ivan once made advances to Queen Elizabeth I of England (1533–1603; reigned 1558–1603), suggesting that if either were overthrown they could take refuge in the other's country. With her customary diplomatic skill, Elizabeth appears to have agreed in principle to the proposal, while avoiding any commitment to a formal treaty. When Ivan later proposed marriage, Elizabeth showed no outward surprise at the prospect (an intimate union with a man who had just brutally murdered his own son), but quickly suggested that her niece Lady Mary Hastings, the daughter of the Earl of Huntingdon, would make a far more suitable bride. On being informed of her good luck, Lady Mary immediately took to her bed; she was saved from a fate literally worse than death by the repentant Queen. Ivan was informed by the British envoy that Lady Mary's attractions may have been somewhat overstated, and that on closer consideration she was in poor health, and her complexion very poor indeed.

The atrocities visited by Ivan the Terrible on the Russian people, intense as they were, were at least limited by logistical difficulties. Russia in the 16th century was a vast country with a sparse population, and torture and executions had to be carried out by hand. No such logistical considerations stopped Adolf Hitler from implementing his campaign of terror and mass murder. As the American historian

Daniel Jonah Goldhagen has written in his book *Hitler's Willing Executioners* (1996), 'In the long annals of human barbarism, the cruelties practised by Germans on Jews during the Nazi period stand out by their scope, variety, inventiveness, and above all, by their wantonness.'

Not only did the Germans imprison their victims in the most barbarous conditions, they also visited the most appalling personal cruelty on them, using both their hands and the latest modern technology. One physician at Auschwitz, Heinz Thilo, described the camp as the anus of the world through which the excremental Jews were voided. Victims were humiliated before death in a manner comparable to the crazed violence meted out by Ivan the Terrible; Jews were tormented and used as playthings, just as Nero ordered Christians to be mauled to death by wild animals. 'For us,' Hitler told Nazi leader Martin Bormann in February 1945, 'this has been an essential process of disinfection which we have prosecuted to its ultimate limit and without which we ourselves should have been asphyxiated and destroyed.' Hitler's belief that the Jews were a threat to Germany and had to be destroyed is comparable to Ivan's conviction that he was doing God's work by cleansing Russia of evil.

To rid his country of undesirable elements was also the intention of Cambodian despot Pol Pot when he came to power in 1975. Pot utilized the national Khmer tradition of absolute submission to the supreme leader to put into practice a programme of national and ethical cleansing. Pol Pot was unique in the history of Marxist Communism in actually attempting the full and consistent implementation of the ideals of Karl Marx (1818–1883) who had predicted that there must not only be a radical redistribution of wealth in society, but also a fundamental change in human nature, inaugurating a new brotherhood of man. As a keen student of Marx, Pol Pot convinced himself that an industrialized society and urban living were incompatible with the evolution of an ideal Communist society in Cambodia; so, he concluded, the people must leave the towns and industry must be abolished. When the Khmer Rouge seized power in April 1975 he ordered an immediate mass evacuation of Phnom Penh and the other Cambodian cities. Whatever the appalling human cost of this policy, Pol Pot could at least be said to be sincere; he may even have done future generations a favour, by demonstrating the basic absurdity of following Marxism to its logical conclusion. The Killing Fields of Cambodia led not to a modern Utopia but to a living hell that has been described as 'a grotesque monument to egalitarianism'. In Pol Pot's Brave New World, all the familiar mechanisms of tyranny were soon in place as the police drove the people out of the cities and into the countryside. Those considered a threat to the new regime were arrested and taken to prisons, such as the infamous Tuol Sleng, where they were tortured into making confessions. In a new refinement of cruelty, prisoners were prevented from committing suicide so that they could live to confess before being executed. Such fictitious admissions of guilt were not dictated, but had to be handwritten to add to their supposed validity. Interrogations could be stopped, intensified or interrupted at the whim of the interrogator, and could be obtained by any means possible. One survivor recalls being beaten and tortured daily for 26 days on end. Victims often died in the process, but if they did so before confessing the interrogator himself might be suspected of sabotaging the process. As more people were arrested, obtaining handwritten confessions became too slow; tape-recorded or dictated admissions became acceptable instead. As in German concentration camps, few in the country were unaware of what was going on. A man living near the Tuol Sleng prison ·recalled hearing continuous screaming at night when the rest of Phnom Penh was silent; the cries were often so loud that they could be heard more than half a mile away. In another parallel with Nazi efficiency, everything that happened in the prisons was rigorously documented, as testified by the photographs of every prisoner admitted.

Out in the Killing Fields, the living and working conditions were equally brutal. People were forced to work a 12 to 14-hour day on a single bowl of watery soup; children were separated from their parents and taken to work in groups together, or forced to become child soldiers. Anyone who did not work hard enough risked execution and, as in other similar regimes, those who could be recognized as educated, or wore spectacles, were at the greatest risk. Any demonstration of family loyalty – for example, when relatives were led away – invited immediate reprisal. There were no explanations, no exceptions to the rule. All were killed without mercy. In these pointless massacres in field and prison, over one-third of the Cambodian population perished before the Vietnamese army finally invaded, driving out Pot and the Khmer Rouge and ending the bloody nightmare.

Such wholesale cruelty is fortunately rare. But even a dictator who was accepted by the Western democracies as an unpleasant necessity in the fight against international Communism was capable of the most appalling savagery. When serving as the commander of the Spanish army in Morocco, General Francisco Franco was responsible for many small-scale atrocities in local villages, including the decapitation of prisoners and the exhibition of severed heads as trophies. Dictator General Primo de Rivera (1870–1930; dictator of Spain 1923–1930), on visiting Morocco in 1926, was appalled to find his guard of honour awaiting inspection with human heads stuck on their bayonets. During the Spanish Civil War (1936–1939), even Mussolini's Italian troops serving with Franco's forces were appalled by the brutality of the Spanish soldiers. Count Ciano (1903–1944), the Italian foreign minister, appealed to Franco to show moderation in his reprisals against Republicans, because this unrestrained brutality could only increase the duration of the war. Ciano later appealed to Franco again, suggesting he slow down the mass executions taking place in Malaga to limit the international outcry. The Basques in the north of Spain finally surrendered; but to the Italians' shock, Franco immediately began executing the prisoners. The commander of the Italian troops reminded him that the Basques had been offered terms, and pointed out that Italian honour was at stake. Franco simply ignored him. For every political assassination that Mussolini ordered, Franco carried out 10,000. As late as 1940 his prisons still held hundreds of thousands of political prisoners, who were being executed as fast as they could be 'tried'. The scale of it even shocked the SS leader Heinrich Himmler, who thought that most of them should have been rehabilitated rather than executed. Not counting those killed in the fighting, the total number of executions carried out by Franco during and after the Spanish Civil War was approximately 2 million men and women. As a proportion of the Spanish population, this is far more than even the millions murdered by Stalin in Russia. Political executions continued throughout Franco's dictatorship, and although he was never personally accused of sadism, there is no doubt that torturers and murderers flourished. Just a couple of months before his death in 1975, Franco signed his last execution order – this time for five of his remaining political opponents.

CHAPTER 5

The Need for a Support Group

Every despot needs a body of ruthless men to carry out his orders. In most cases the dirty work is done by a military elite, or, in a modern state, by the secret police. These people also provide the despot with a loyal and dedicated bodyguard to protect him against insurrection and deter any rivals for power. In turn, the support group relies on a network of spies and informers to identify their master's opponents. In some cases almost the entire population colludes in spying on each other, as happened in Nazi Germany, so that there is little need for professionals to become involved.

Writing when Renaissance Italy was ruled by petty if artistically enlightened tyrants, Niccolò Machiavelli suggested that the more successful the despot, the more people sought to protect him and were willing to inform on his enemies. Machiavelli also considered that it took little for a tyrannical regime to take power in a society that was already accustomed to violence. This was the position in Uganda when Idi Amin seized power from the previous dictator, Milton Obote.

A despot's supporters have needed either to share a commitment to their leader's beliefs, no matter how absurd or fanatical, or to be so bereft of moral sense as to be able to obey the most criminal orders without question. Their reward is the share of the spoils and an enjoyment of the often-considerable power delegated by the leader. The problem for the despot is that men capable of doing his bidding efficiently are also the ones most likely to overthrow him and seize power themselves. Successful military commanders are particular dangerous in this context, as Napoleon demonstrated when he seized power from the clique that ran the French Republic. For this reason, one of Stalin's greatest worries at the end of the Second World War in 1945 was the tremendous popularity of his most successful commander, General Zhukov.

Men capable of carrying out the despot's dirty work are present in every society – the misfits, the petty criminals, the psychopaths, the alienated. They float to the surface during times of revolution or social upheaval and are present in even the most apparently liberal countries. For example, the modern Greek republic is seemingly untroubled by political fanaticism and famous for its people's sybaritic attitude to life. Yet even here, criminals and sadists were lurking. In April 1967, a group of

army officers seized power in Athens, declared martial law and threw known socialists into jail. The coup was given some respectability when King Constantine II
(b.1940; King of Greece 1964–1973) agreed to support it, a decision that was to cost
him his throne when democracy was eventually restored. What most shocked international observers was the speed with which the country plunged into full-scale
despotism. Within a few months, under the puppet Prime Minister, George
Papadopoulos, the whole panoply of a police state was in place; the press was
censored, undesirables excluded from office and educational textbooks rewritten in
an attempt to blacken the name of the country's long-standing democracy. Popular
music was banned in favour of military marches; thousands were arrested and held
captive on the remoter Greek islands. And along with the suppression of information came the emergence of an unsuspected group of sadists and torturers, ready and
willing to do the dirty work of the regime by persecuting political prisoners and
torturing students and other activists for information. They were the ESA secret
police, who had received special training to prepare them psychologically for the
task. Prisoners were taken initially to Athen's version of Moscow's Lubianka Prison,
a large building on Vassilissis Sofias Avenue in the centre of the city. There, the
human rights organisation Amnesty International claimed, over 2,000 people were
tortured during the seven years that the Junta ruled Greece before its collapse in
November 1974. The conclusion must be that if appalling things could happen in a
liberal political democracy like modern Greece then they could, given the right
circumstances, happen anywhere in the Western world.

    ESA, which enjoyed such power in Greece, was typical of the special police forces
that despots have used to terrorize their opponents into submission. Such groups are
bound together by mutual responsibility for the crimes they commit. Early forms of
secret police existed under the tyrannies of ancient Greece, and were used by the
Roman emperors and by Muslim caliphates. Even such an admired sovereign as
Queen Elizabeth I of England allowed her advisor Sir Francis Walsingham's agents
to seize, torture and have executed suspected Roman Catholics and their priests in
order to keep her sovereignty secure. As self-proclaimed emperor of France,
Napoleon established a highly effective secret service organized by Joseph Fouché
(c.1758–1820); Prince von Metternich (1773–1859) relied on another in Austria.
But these organizations were essentially intelligence services, more concerned with
gathering information than in terrorizing people. Not until the 20th century did the
first modern secret police service, fully equipped with judiciary powers of arrest, trial
and punishment emerge. This was the CHEKA of Soviet Russia, an organization
that took over the work of the old Tsarist Okhrana police. Many of the Okhrana

agents simply transferred their allegiances to the new regime, and began working for the very people they had once persecuted.

In the Roman Empire, the duties of suppressing dissent and protecting the emperor were the responsibility of the Praetorian Guard, founded by Augustus Caesar soon after he came to power in 27 BC. Evolving from the sovereign's personal bodyguard, rather like the Household Cavalry in contemporary Britain, it came to fulfil the function of a secret police force within the city of Rome. Significantly, many of its members abandoned their military uniforms in favour of civilian clothes, for this enabled them to blend inconspicuously into the crowd, gathering information and keeping watch on potential leaders of dissent. Far better paid than the ordinary Roman soldier, the Praetorians became increasingly influential. Under their commander, Lucius Aelius Sejanus, they demonstrated their newfound importance by ruthlessly assassinating all Emperor Tiberius's potential rivals and political opponents. This savage act made the Praetorians the crucial power in Rome, and the new kingmakers of the Empire, a role they performed in AD 41 by making sure that Claudius was elected to the throne.

From then on, every emperor had to remain on good terms with his Praetorian Guard by guaranteeing them a share of the imperial spoils and offering lucrative positions when they retired. At worst, the emperor was at risk of having to placate them or face being overthrown. During the civil war that followed the death of Nero in AD 69, the Guard was decisive in determining who should be the next emperor; then, as Rome declined further, the Praetorians revolved around increasingly weak emperors until finally backing the wrong candidate, the usurper Maxentius, who was roundly defeated at the Battle of Milvian Bridge by Constantine in AD 312. The new emperor's first move was to abolish the Praetorian Guard altogether, stating that it had become little more than an unreliable and treacherous body of men.

The lesson from Ancient Rome was that despots should never become totally dependent on any single group within their body of supporters. The only way to ensure this is by the frequent use of purges, and the immediate rooting out of anyone suspected of disloyalty. This was certainly the tactic adopted and implemented rigorously by Stalin, who carried out constant purges of his secret police and administration. This culminated in the near destruction of the Russian senior officer corps in the late 1930s. A similar fear of disloyalty had also driven one of his predecessors, Ivan the Terrible, to ensure that none of his closest aides were drawn from the boyar class that had terrorized him as a child. Instead, he chose his advisers from the lower levels of Russian society, knowing that their elevation would make them personally loyal to their benefactor. Even then, he appeared reluctant to rely on his fellow Russians alone; he enlisted over 6,000 men from other countries into his service, at a time when Russia had little contact with the rest of Europe. This corps of reliable foreigners was similar to the contemporary regiments of Janissaries retained by the Turkish Sultan. These were Christian children captured in battle and trained as royal bodyguards to have fanatical loyalty for the person of the Sultan alone.

This reliance on foreigners may well have been a wise precaution by Ivan, for Russia – unlike the western European countries of his time – had no orders of chivalry, and by implication a non-existent or limited code of honour. As a consequence there were few rules of ethical behaviour among the aristocracy; oaths of loyalty were worthless. For this reason Ivan decided to create his own band of native defenders, the Oprichniki, brutal fanatics loyal to no one but himself. Using this horde of heavily armed horseman, Ivan inflicted a reign of terror on any individual or group in Russia that offered the slightest dissent. In the dead of night the Oprichniki, mounted on black horses and dressed entirely in black, descended on their victims. The choice of colour was significant. Black has often been associated with despotism; the first emperor of China, Qin Shi Huang, also used it for his flags and banners. Ivan realized, as Hitler would five centuries later, that the sight of a ruthless body of men dressed in a black uniform inspires terror in the population. Whereas the Nazi SS wore a double lightning flash as a badge, the Oprichnki's emblem was a broom and dog's head combined. This symbolized their mission to sweep treachery out of Russia with the utmost ferocity. Given complete licence by their master, the Oprichniki went about their business with the utmost zeal – raping, torturing, robbing and impaling, often without reference to the Tsar. Ivan even built a palace for them in Moscow, where he would often attend the daily torture and execution of the prisoners held in its dungeons. Then, in a periodic bout of piety and remorse, Ivan did symbolic penance by founding a religious order dedicated to the Oprichniki and insisted that every member join it.

Given their almost total freedom, the Oprichniki became over-zealous, robbing and plundering the entire country. As a result, the Russian economy went into a sharp decline. There were scarcely enough taxes to maintain the defences against the Tartars and other barbarians; Russia became so damaged that, in 1572, Ivan, with typical impulsiveness, suddenly abolished the Oprichniki altogether, replacing them with more disparate bands of equally ruthless men. The exact reasons why are unknown. He may have been prompted by the decisive victory of Russian forces over the Crimean Tartars and their Turkish allies outside Moscow, which freed Russia from the threat of further invasion. The mistake the Oprichniki had unwittingly made was to be too successful for their own good, so becoming a threat to the Tsar and a danger to the state. As a punishment for their past transgressions, Ivan seized the newly acquired estates of the leading Oprichniki and gave them back to their original owners. To emphasis their disgrace, the very mention of the word Oprichniki was banned; and in a move that presaged Stalin's infamous purges of the 1930s, half of the band's successful commanders were eliminated. Among the first to die was a Prince Vorotynsky, along with his wife, sons and entire household. Death was delivered by slow roasting over a small fire, a fiendish method of execution suggested by Ivan himself. The reason given in this particular case was a typical manifestation of Ivan's paranoia – Vorotynsky was accused of having paid witches to cast a spell over him.

Appropriately, given his own reliance on a secret police, Stalin praised the work of the Oprichniki in harrying the moribund aristocracy of old Russia and its role in transforming the country into a centralized state. Stalin's own Oprichniki was the infamous NKVD, later the KGB, which had evolved from the CHEKA under Lenin. In the early days of the Revolution, when the Reds' hold on the country was tenuous, the CHEKA was essential for fighting the White Russians, stamping out dissent and imposing the edicts of the new government. NKVD activities were not confined to Soviet Russia alone; during the Spanish Civil War, a group of its agents set up a secret camp in Spain to deal with opponents of Stalin found fighting for the Republic. Later, other agents organized the assassination of Stalin's most dangerous rival, Leon Trotsky (1879–1940), in Mexico City. Less spectacularly, the NKVD carried out the day-to-day business of arresting and torturing suspects, often shooting their victims out of hand at the Lubianka Prison in Moscow, or transporting them to Siberia to rot in the gulags. The Soviet penal colony system was enormous, numbering over 2,000 labour camps scattered across 13 time zones. These brutal places were emblematic of Stalin's Russia in the same way that the Nazi death camps symbolized the true horror of Hitler's Germany. One camp alone, established to build the Belamor Canal in Siberia, held over 250,000 prisoners, all working without machinery in the bitter cold and in the most appalling conditions. The novelist Alexander Solzhenitsyn, a victim himself, described the Soviet gulags as '…inhabited by a population of slaves who made up some 10 per cent of the total Soviet work force and who could literally be worked to death.'

Stalin was the ideal overseer for this murderous organization; his corrosive paranoia guaranteed it a constant stream of new victims. Outside the camps, the numbers eliminated exceeded those of the SS and the Gestapo combined. On a single day in 1938, Stalin and his sycophant minister Vyacheslav Molotov (1890–1986) personally sanctioned the execution of over 3,000 prisoners held by the NKVD. This was at the height of the infamous show trials era of the 1930s, when even a humble factory worker could be arrested for poor productivity. The three main trials began in 1936 and ended in 1938, during which time some of the most senior Communist Party leaders were charged with conspiring with Western powers to assassinate Stalin and other Soviet leaders and planning to bring about the collapse of the Soviet Union and restoration of capitalism. Sixteen members of the so-called 'Trotskyite-Zinovievite Terrorist Centre' appeared in court in August 1936. The chief defendants were Gregory Zinoviev (no relation) and Lev Kamenev, who were accused of plotting the assassination of Sergei Kirov and of Stalin himself. Inevitably all 16 defendants were convicted of the charges and executed. The second trial, which took place in January 1937, was of 17 lesser figures, including Karl Radek, Yuri Piatakov and Grigory Sokolnikov. Thirteen of the defendants were found guilty and immediately shot, while the remainder soon perished in Siberian labour camps. The last trial, known as The Trial of the Twenty-One, was of those who were alleged to be members of the so-called 'Rightist and Trotskyite Group'. Among them were Nikolai Bukharin, former head of the Communist International, Alexei Rykov, former Prime Minister, Christian Rakovsky, Nikolai Krestinsky and Genrikh Yagoda – all were convicted and executed. The most remarkable aspect of these trials was that they were held in open court and Western observers who attended were convinced that the accused had received a fair hearing. The confessions of the accused appeared genuine and there was no evidence that the prisoners had been either tortured or drugged. It is now known that the confessions were given only after great psychological pressure, as well as actual physical torture, had been applied to the defendants. Prisoners had suffered repeated beatings, simulated drownings, sleep deprivation and had been made to stand for hours on end. Yet the most effective pressure to confess resulted from threats to arrest and execute the prisoners' families. Stalin's perfidy was also revealed as Zinoviev and Kamenev had demanded, as a condition for their 'confessions', that their lives and that of their families would be spared. This was agreed during a personal meeting with Stalin but the despot's word proved worthless as, not only were the defendants summarily shot, but their relatives were arrested and executed too.

The terror extended from the bottom to the top of Soviet society, but the closer to the seat of power a man was located, the more danger he was in. Of the 2,000 delegates who attended the main 'advisory' conference of the Soviet Union in the period 1936-1938, only 24 had escaped arrest and execution by the start of the Second World War. But this was as nothing to the 2 million Russian citizens exterminated in this period by the NKVD under Stalin's direct or indirect orders. A comparison of the Russian people's fate under Stalin and the oppression they had endured at the hands of the last Tsar makes astonishing reading. In the last year of Tsar Nicholas II's reign, there were approximately 170,000 people in Russia's jails and camps. In 1938, at the height of Stalin's despotic rule, the figure had grown to 16 million – a 10th of the entire population.

When the Second World War ended in 1945, Stalin ensured that Communist regimes came to power in Poland, Bulgaria, Hungary, Romania, Albania, Czechoslovakia and East Germany. Each country had a secret police system that was based upon and co-operated with the Russian KBG. The name had changed, but the tactics remained the same, and were intended to enforce Communist party orthodoxy throughout Eastern Europe. Among the most infamous and certainly the most insidious was the STASI of the German Democratic Republic. State documents released in 1989, after the fall of the Berlin Wall and the return to democracy, reveal how thoroughly the organization suppressed opposition to party rule. At the height of its power there were about 100,000 people working directly or indirectly for the STASI, keeping detailed files on an estimated 6 million people. Many kept their identity secret from their neighbours while using phone taps, bugging devices and video cameras to spy on them. Even fellow-members of the STASI spied on each other. Their work was aided by the huge number of people – including church ministers, teachers and housewives – who passed on unsolicited information and rumours about their neighbours, fellow workers, or even their relatives. Just as repressive, but less thorough than the STASI was the Romanian Securitate, a well-funded organization that was powerful enough to take on the army after the revolt against President Nicolae Ceausescu in late December 1989. Hundreds, possibly thousands, of people died in the streets of Bucharest and other Romanian cities before the battle was finally won, and the remnants of Securitate were captured and imprisoned by the new democratic Council of National Salvation. At the height of its power, the Securitate had been responsible for guarding the internal security of the Ceausescu regime and suppressing any unrest, disturbance or dissident group that dared challenge the despot's rule. Again, the secret files released after Ceausescu's fall reveal that there were almost 2 million Romanians listed as possible suspects, with 700,000 of their fellow-citizens regularly informing on them. Romanian telephones were routinely bugged and the calls taped. It has even been estimated that, at the height of Ceausescu's regime, as many as one in three Romanian citizens were either Securitate agents or acting as their informers. Yet in spite of this comprehensive repression, spontaneous outbursts of discontent with Ceausescu's cult of personality and economic mismanagement still occurred throughout his rule.

Any manifestation of dissent would have been difficult while Hitler presided over Nazi Germany. Repressive as the secret police organizations were in Eastern Europe, they lacked the murderous fanaticism that had characterized Hitler's own Praetorian

Guard – the Schutzstaffel or SS, formed in 1925, and its secret police department, the
Gestapo. The SS saw themselves as a military elite. From the beginning, members
revelled in their notoriety, their distinctive black uniforms, their austere camaraderie
and their unique *esprit de corps*. Wagnerian-style ceremonies were held at their gothic headquarters, the Wewelsburg Castle in Westphalia, where they celebrated their
blood alliance as dedicated disciples of the Führer and swore to obey him unques-
tioningly. While mass murderers have generally kept their business low-key, the SS
were shockingly open and flamboyant, taking visible pride in carrying out the most
appalling atrocities and murdering unarmed civilians. They found their ideal
commander in the mild-looking, bespectacled but utterly ruthless Heinrich
Himmler. Perhaps, what is most astonishing about Himmler and the SS is not the
extent of their crimes but the sanctimonious and almost weary acceptance with
which they approached their self-appointed task. As Himmler told his storm troopers in the occupied Polish city of Poznan in 1943:

> 'Most of you must know what it means when 100 corpses are lying side by
> side, or 500, or 1,000. To have stuck it out and at the same time – apart
> from exceptions caused by human weakness – to have remained decent
> fellows; that is what has made us hard. This is a page of glory in our history
> which has never been written.'

The lack of insight revealed in Himmler's words and the terrible events that
followed have been characterized by psychologists as a classic example of 'mass
group regression'. In such cases, a self-appointed group dehumanizes its perceived
enemies, transforming them into inanimate targets for destruction – whether it be
Jews in 1930s Germany or workers at the New York World Trade Center in
September 2001. So enthused by their self-imposed task were the members of the
SS that Hitler had no need to be suspicious or wary of them, as Stalin was of the
NKVD. These men considered themselves on a mission from God (or Wotan, the
God worshipped by the pagan Germans until the coming of Christianity) to rid
Germany of the deadly Jewish poison that they believed to be polluting German art
and culture, and even the nation itself. Yet when the SS began its assault on the Jews,
these perceived enemies offered no threat whatsoever to either the Führer or the
Nazi state. In their generosity to their fellow Aryans, the SS were even prepared to
extend the eradication of the Jews to neighbouring countries. The atrocities
committed by Hitler's SS in occupied Poland, Russia and the Ukraine are familiar
to anyone who has read accounts of the Second World War.

But the responsibility of the whole German nation, rather than just the SS and members of the Nazi party, has been proven in recent years. Historians such as Daniel Jonah Goldhagen have examined the records of the part-time police battalions that followed in the wake of the regular German army, which make shocking reading; letters home show how enthusiastically these supposedly ordinary men and auxiliary soldiers carried out the most appalling crimes in emulation of the SS. One member of Police Battalion 105, while taking part in the genocidal killings of Jews in Belarus, wrote to his wife telling her not to lose sleep over his actions. He added that he was taking photographs as he went along that would be 'extremely interesting for our children to see'. As Goldhagen has pointed out, there is strong evidence that the Germans involved often volunteered to take part, even when there was no compulsion for them to do so. Nor could these atrocities have been carried out on such a vast scale without the highly professional logistics needed to implement and sustain them. Shamefully, there was little or no attempt to even slow the process of human destruction by ordinary Germans, let alone to frustrate it with individual acts of sabotage. The numbers of people involved in this national programme of cruelty is staggering. Over 100,000 Germans were part of the killing process; 2 million were involved in running and policing the slave labour system that supported the German economy. In all, there were over 10,000 camps and ghettos scattered across Germany and the occupied territories. Some were purely for extermination, others for forced labour or for holding captured soldiers. Auschwitz alone had over 7,000 guards to maintain control over its inhabitants, as well as 50 satellite camps.

Later, when in custody, members of the SS and the Gestapo claimed, predictably, that they were only obeying orders. These assertions appeared beyond both credulity and decency, but to test them the American psychologist Stanley Milgram set up a revealing experiment at Yale University in 1963. The results provide a fascinating insight into the ordinary man's capacity to obey orders and inflict torture in certain conditions. Milgram selected a group of people who were told by the experimenters to deliver a series of fake electric shocks to other participants, in what was described as a therapy to improve the recipients' learning ability. Whenever the learners made a mistake they were to receive a shock of increasing strength. Those inflicting the shock knew what it felt like, having received a test shock themselves. There were eight settings on the dial of the shock machine, the last three of which were labelled 'intense' (setting 5), 'danger' (setting 7) and 'XXX' (setting 8). What astonished Milgram and his researchers was the discovery that 87 per cent of the participants continued to apply the shock as directed, even when the learner appeared to kick loudly in pain on the wall.

What was equally surprising was that two-thirds of the group happily delivered the 'XXX' 450 volts maximum, even though the display in front of them clearly showed the voltage. The subjects could not be seen by those administering the shocks; for all they knew, the learner's failure to respond to the questions was because they were already unconscious. With this experiment Milgram categorically demonstrated that normal, decent people could be persuaded to seriously harm others, purely on the orders of someone in authority. Subsequent studies have confirmed Milgram's results, and have indicated that in certain circumstances, particularly in groups, the capacity to inflict harm on others is even greater. The excuse that 'I was only doing my duty' may, after all, have relevance when deciding the guilt of those involved in carrying out the atrocities of future despots.

In despotic regimes, organizations such as the SS and NKVD are used to keep the people in a state of constant fear. This is all the more effective if those who are arrested and tortured are clearly innocent of any crime. Witnessing such injustices and unable to trust his neighbours and even members of his own family, the ordinary citizen abandons all hope and submits to the tyranny, making it extremely difficult for the despot to be overthrown. Such a tyrant emerged on the Caribbean island of Haiti in 1957, when 'Papa Doc' Duvalier was elected president. Having closely studied the careers of Hitler and Stalin, Duvalier set out to establish his own support group of secret police, the Tonton Macoutes. The name derived from old Creole language for 'bogeyman', and was traditionally used to scare disobedient children.

Duvalier found his Macoutes amongst the misfits and criminals of Haitian society. Each recruit was given a gun and some money before being let loose on his unfortunate fellow citizens. One of their first tasks was to punish the inhabitants of the poorest section of Port au Prince, who had dared to vote against Duvalier in the presidential election. A large hole was dug at a religious shrine near the city, and at nightfall trucks arrived full of opposition voters, gagged and bound hand and foot. They were thrown into the hole and covered in tons of wet cement, which was smoothed over and left to dry. The other presidential candidates immediately fled the country, leaving only the opposition leader Clement Jumelle, who was hunted like a dog through the streets but eventually managed to escape into the jungle.

Dressed in a ragbag uniform that had its origin in Italian fascism, the Macoutes, wearing sinister dark glasses, now terrorized the country. Duvalier had essentially given them free rein to rob, harass and even murder anyone in the country outside of the political elite, which they proceeded to do with gusto. Meanwhile, Duvalier surrounded himself in a mystical aura of voodoo. Images were discretely issued by the Macoutes showing Duvalier dressed in a white top hat and tuxedo, and wearing sunglasses. This was the costume traditionally worn by the voodoo god Baron Samedi who, in Haitian culture, traditionally stands at the crossroads on the pathway to death.

The great majority of Macoutes were negroes who bitterly resented the lighter-skinned mulattos (a person of mixed black and white ancestry), who formed the old elite of Haiti. Some were *bougans* or voodoo priests, particularly loyal to Duvalier, who encouraged them to inform him of any dissent they witnessed during their religious ceremonies. Astutely, Papa Doc did not ignore women: thousands of poor black females were recruited as members of the armed Fillettes Laleau. This evolved to be a force of formidable, ruthless and dedicated female thugs; some soon commanded male Macoute units of their own. As supreme commander of the Tonton Macoutes, Duvalier chose Clément Barbot, a ruthless and vindictive ex-policeman. Under Barbot, the Macoutes were given even greater licence to extort and murder in return for their protection of the president. Some members even had private cells built in their own homes, literally turning law enforcement into a cottage industry.

By 1963 the United States, now under the presidency of John F. Kennedy (1917–1963; President of the USA 1961–1963), had decided that the Duvalier regime was an embarrassment to the whole continent and that a regime change must happen. The CIA moved swiftly. Arms were sent to the United States Embassy in Port au Prince and offered clandestinely to any group of army officers prepared to stage a coup. To no one's surprise, the first to accept was the disgruntled Clément Barbot, who used the guns and explosives to attempt the assassination of Duvalier's son and heir Jean-Claude 'Baby Doc' and his daughter Simone. The plot failed: Barbot was hunted down and murdered by his fellow Macoutes. Papa Doc died peacefully in his bed in 1971, leaving control of Haiti to his son Jean-Claude who continued the corrupt family rule until the Duvalier regime eventually fell in 1986. The Haitian people turned on their oppressors, burning their houses and attacking and killing them in the street. As for Baby Doc and his wife Michelle, they were spirited away with American help and taken to live in a luxurious villa in the South of France.

CHAPTER 6

Finding a Scapegoat

It would appear difficult to stir up racial hatred in the ethnically mixed but easy-going societies of the Caribbean, but that is exactly what General Rafael Trujillo (1891–1961; dictator of the Dominican Republic 1930–1961) achieved in 1937. His domain was the greater part of the island of Hispaniola while the smaller, western section was occupied by the French-speaking Republic of Haiti. Haiti, 200 years earlier, then the French colony of Saint-Domingue, was the jewel of the French colonial empire, supplying 40 per cent of France's foreign trade and providing enough cotton for the whole French textile industry. Remarkably, the small colony was Europe's principle source of sugar in the 18th century, and had a greater volume of foreign trade than the whole of the United States. Subsequent slave revolts, and misgovernment once it became independent of France, had ruined the economy; but its once-fabulous prosperity was still resented by the citizens of the Dominican Republic. In 1937, faced with a gathering challenge to his despotic rule, Trujillo decided to divert attention from his failures by launching a pogrom against the thousands of poor black Haitians who had crossed the border and were living illegally in his country. The appeal to Dominican nationalism was underpinned by Trujillo's covert support for a policy of racial discrimination against the blacks known as *Antihaitianismo*. This involved the attempt to 'whiten' the population of the Dominican Republic by encouraging Caucasian refugees from Europe to settle there. Units of the Dominican army were sent to the border areas with orders to massacre the Haitians they found there; to give the appearance that the violence was a spontaneous reaction by Dominican peasants, the soldiers were ordered to use machetes instead of bullets. Over 12,000 Haitians were decapitated and their bodies thrown into ravines. Other Haitians were either drowned or strangled, and their small children murdered by being thrown against rocks and tree trunks. Trujillo remained in the capital, confidently awaiting the thanks of his people for ridding the country of the despised intruders. Instead, when news of the slaughter was leaked to the world, President Trujillo had to endure the wrath of a United States government that immediately set about undermining his regime. His offer of $750,000 to the families of the dead Haitians was rejected with scorn. In a further attempt to placate international opinion, he then offered to establish a refugee colony in the Dominican Republic for the French Jews currently being persecuted by the Nazis. Although his offer mollified American public opinion, the 'colony', when it materialised, housed a mere 235 Jewish immigrants.

In his purge of the Haitians, Trujillo had followed one of the cardinal tenets of despotism – when in trouble, find a scapegoat group (preferably vulnerable, badly organised and incapable of significant resistance)and then encourage your people to persecute it. According to René Girard, the political scapegoat has been with us since civilization began, for its real purpose is to shift blame and responsibility away from the majority and towards a target person or group. It also allows feelings of unresolved anger and hostility in the community to be transferred to others, whether they are guilty of the accusations against them or not. So, rather than attack each other in a dispute over policy or possessions, the majority target the weak, such as those with physical abnormalities, members of ethnic or racial minorities, or the poor. Sometimes even those with positive natural endowments such as beauty, intelligence, charm or wealth may be scapegoated. With almost the entire community in agreement, the destruction of the group or individual becomes easy. Such victims have existed throughout history, an obvious example being the medieval witches who were demonized and blamed for the community's ills before being tortured and often executed. To qualify as a witch, all an old woman had to do was lead an isolated lifestyle; their persecutors considered that they were doing nothing wrong, and often, the victims unwittingly condoned the process by coming to believe that the charges against them were true. The verdict reached, scapegoats are driven out of the community or simply killed. Once they are gone the violence ends, and those who are left are convinced that because peace has returned, the scapegoats were the cause of their problems after all.

This appears to have been the stratagem used by the Emperor Nero after the Great Fire of Rome, the largest recorded conflagration in antiquity. Although the city suffered daily fires, the one that began on the night of 18 July AD 64 was altogether different. It started in the merchant area near the Circus Maximus and spread rapidly to destroy a large part of the city. Returning from Antium, Nero took charge of the fire-fighting that was carried out by 7,000 freedmen; as well as distributing food, he provided shelter for the thousands of homeless in the city's numerous temples and public buildings. The emperor was said to have been everywhere that day, working harder than he had ever worked in his life, encouraging the exhausted fire-fighters to new efforts and without the protection of his usual cohort of guards. In spite of his obvious sincere distress at the disaster and his undoubted sympathy with the people, the suspicion soon arose that this devastating fire had been deliberately started on Nero's orders to clear the way for the Golden House. It was common knowledge that Nero was planning to build himself a vast, 300-acre palace complex that would include a 37-metre-high (121 feet) statue of himself. Then another rumour spread – that the emperor had actually been seen on the Tower of Maecenas at the height of the blaze dressed in stage costume, playing the cithara and singing the well-known song 'The Sack of Ilium'. The historian Tacitus (c.AD 55–120) insists, however, that Nero was nowhere near Rome that night but remained at Antium, over 30 miles (48 km) away. As ever in such circumstances, the mob preferred to believe otherwise. Faced with growing anger, Nero sought to divert attention from himself by providing the people with a readymade scapegoat — the mysterious new religious sect, Christianity. In choosing the Christians, he ignored the fact that although many orthodox Jews lived close to where the fire had started, none of their houses appeared damaged. Perhaps there were too many to deal with, or he had taken a personal dislike to the Christians; moreover, the Christians were already deeply unpopular in Rome, so they made an ideal minority for persecution. The dislike stemmed from their practice of openly condemning the decadence of Roman life, and their habit of describing the city as a second 'Babylon' awaiting destruction at Christ's second coming. Predictably, eyewitnesses claimed to have seen Christians dancing for joy at the flames, and Tacitus reported that some confessed their guilt under interrogation. Yet there was another reason for choosing the Christians. Not only did they criticize the Roman lifestyle; they were potentially dangerous rebels too. Their leader, the dead Christ, was seen as a man who had encouraged uprising against Roman rule, and claims that he had returned from the dead were deeply disturbing to a people wary of magic. Casting spells or attempting to communicate with the dead carried a death sentence under Roman law. Then there were the reports of bizarre rituals – for example the Eucharist, in which they claimed to consume the body and blood of Christ, magically transformed from bread and wine. What happened next is described in great detail by Tacitus:

> Nero falsely accused and executed with the most exquisite punishments
> those people called Christians, who were infamous for their abominations…
> first those were seized who admitted their faith, and then, using the
> information they provided, a vast multitude were convicted, not so much
> for the crime of burning the city, but for hatred of the human race. And
> perishing they were additionally made into sports: they were killed by dogs

by having the hides of beasts attached to them, or they were nailed to
crosses or set aflame, and, when the daylight passed away, they were used
as night-time lamps. Nero gave his own gardens for this spectacle and
performed a Circus game, in the habit of a charioteer mixing with the
plebs or driving about the racecourse. Even though they were clearly
guilty and merited being made the most recent example of the
consequences of crime, people began to pity these sufferers, because
they were consumed not for the public good but on account of the
fierceness of one man.

These brutal methods of execution were not uncommon in the Roman world
at the time; burning to death was the customary punishment for arson, as crucifixion
was for lower-class criminals. Being covered with the skins of beasts then torn to pieces
by dogs is far more theatrical, suggesting that Nero had choreographed and dramatized
the event. It bears a suspicious similarity to a mythological *tableau vivant* described by
Tacitus in his work, the *Annals*, that depicts the death of Actaeon, a legendary hunter
devoured by his own dogs. The barbarities culminated in the death of St Peter, who
was crucified upside down in mockery of the death of the Christian leader.

Until Nero, the Christians, although disliked, had never been actively persecut-
ed. This now changed, and they became the despised 'whipping boys' of Roman
society. Harassment continued for decades under Nero's successors, the Emperors
Domitian, Valerian and Diocletian. Perversely, Nero's persecution ensured that the
Christian faith flourished, and converted the entire Roman world under the
Emperor Constantine 300 years later.

Nero had been able to scapegoat the Christians by presenting them as 'outsiders',
alien to the true nature and culture of Rome. As such they were seen as naturally
inferior to the majority, and looked down upon. For the favoured group, this feeling of being superior can flourish no matter how miserable, impoverished or brutal
their lives may be. Even a nominally democratic society such as Northern Ireland 30
years ago illustrated this. To be a poor Protestant was still better than being a
Catholic, even a relatively prosperous one. Often, an obvious minority, whether in
dress or behaviour, such as Orthodox Jews, makes the ideal target for persecution.
It is also significant that every modern despot has attacked homosexuals. Even the
terminology used in the propaganda is revealing, with references to human disease
in such words as 'plague', 'cancer' and 'eradication'.

A similarly scapegoated social group were the Ugandan Asians expelled from the
country by Idi Amin in September 1972. The fact that the Ugandan economy

depended on this minority group was ignored by Amin, as he ordered 50,000 of the country's most able businessmen and their families into exile, confiscating their possessions. Many were beaten, many killed. Amin's decision was self-defeating – comparable to Hitler's insistence that all Jewish scientists leave Germany in the 1930s, even though some of them later worked on the Manhattan Project in atomic bomb research. In Uganda's case, without the entrepreneurial Asians the economy was soon near collapse. In recent times, Robert Mugabe (b.1924; executive president from 1987) has arguably helped ruin the Zimbabwean economy over the past decade by scapegoating white farmers and seizing their land without compensation. Compounding the crime, Mugabe gave the stolen land not to poor farmers but to his own favourites in government – just as Amin gave the Asians' assets not to the poor, but to members of his army.

While the majority of Ugandan Asians and white farmers of Zimbabwe generally escaped with their lives, the intellectuals in Pol Pot's Cambodia did not. During just four years of his murderous regime, an estimated 2 million people perished, mainly in the rural Killing Fields. Pol Pot seized power in April 1975 and began his rule with a simple statement of intent. He would evacuate people from the towns, abolish markets and the currency, defrock Buddhist monks, execute all members of the previous regime and establish co-operatives and communal eating for all. As his scapegoats, Pol Pot selected the entire educated elite of Cambodia. As Plato had warned long ago, 'A tyrant must keep a sharp eye out for men of courage, vision or intelligence… By ridding the city of other potential leaders, the tyrant promotes a type of mediocrity amongst the citizens.' So, Cambodian professionals such as doctors, teachers and engineers were arrested and shot in droves, while the ordinary people were driven out into the country to eke out a precarious existence, fully dependent on the state for survival. As the writer Elizabeth Becker described it in her book, *When the War Was Over*, 'Cambodia became one great labour camp where workplace and home were fused together in a piece of land from which there was no exit.' Groups of people were moved about the countryside at the whim of local commanders, and anyone even marginally connected with the previous regime could expect no mercy. Then, in emulation of his great hero Mao, Pol Pot announced a Cambodian version of the economic 'Great Leap Forward' – or the leap into even greater misery, as it became. The people were now ordered to labour in the fields for 20 hours a day, and the list of scapegoats was widened to include more recognizable minorities, such the Chinese or the distinctively dressed and strongly Muslim Cham. As in every other despotism, the Khmer regime had an infamous prison, in this case Tuol Sleng jail, where prisoners were tortured and killed after being forced to write their own 'confessions'. Tens of thousands of victims' photographs were taken when they were admitted to the prisons; these sad faces are even more moving than the famous piles of faceless skulls scattered throughout the Killing Fields. Such an appalling situation could not be allowed to continue and the Vietnamese army finally invaded the country in 1978, driving Pol Pot from power. When pictures of the destruction that had been wreaked on the Cambodian people reached the outside world, they appeared almost as shocking as those taken in the German death camps in 1945.

Even before he was elected to power in 1933, Hitler was unambiguous about the fate he intended for the Jews – the greatest scapegoats in history. Hitler viewed them as the cause of Germany's economic problems, the defilers of true German art and culture and a poisonous threat to the pure blood of the German nation. The whole race was to blame; all Jews should be driven out of the country and, if possible, off the face of the earth. It was a simple but powerful message, ideologically consistent and easily comprehended. It was further compounded by rumours, widely believed in Germany, that there existed an international Jewish conspiracy to take over the world. The evidence for this was the discovery of *The Protocols of the Elders of Zion*, a document that had originated in Russia in the mid 19th century. It was purported to be a detailed plan by the Jews to subvert national economies and set the nations of Europe at each others' throats. Although ludicrously unconvincing, it was a godsend to anti-Semites throughout the world – from entrepreneur Henry Ford in America to Hitler in Germany. Its publication in the Nazi journal the *Volkischer Beobachter* gave added weight to Hitler's warnings in his treatise *Mein Kampf* that Jews were seeking to contaminate German blood by seducing pure Aryan girls. Hitler's words paint a sinister picture of their demonic intent:

> With satanic joy in his face the black-haired Jewish youth lurks in wait for
> the unsuspecting girl whom he defiles with his blood, thus stealing her
> from her people… and it is Jews who bring the Negroes in the Rhineland
> always with the same secret thought and clear aim of ruining the hated
> white race by the necessary resulting bastardization.

Perhaps it is a measure of how the world has changed that if Hitler had written this in any western democracy today, and found a publisher, he would certainly have been prosecuted and probably imprisoned. Yet the majority of the German people at the time believed in this dark fairytale wholeheartedly, and elected Hitler to power in the full knowledge that he would make the Jews the nation's scapegoats and rigorously persecute them. As Alice Miller has stated, to eradicate Jewish badness and evil was to purge the self of its own historical experience of self-loathing. The man the nation chose to accomplish this mission on their behalf was Hitler.

There is no need to reiterate the terrible fate that Hitler imposed upon Europe's Jews, other than to remember the vast numbers that were processed through the Nazi killing machine. Whereas Vlad the Impaler had only the limited technology of his time, Himmler and his associates had the full resources of modern German industry. Documents, such as the German railways' agreement to transport Jews to the death camps – a one-way fare – or the IG Farben Company's tender for the supply of Zyclon B gas for extermination, are among the most shameful records of this period. The dispassionate manner in which all this was arranged is almost incomprehensible to later generations. As John Toland, has written in his book *Adolf Hitler: The Definitive Biography*, 'The exterminations proceeded with cool calculation. It was a tidy, businesslike operation: and the reports were couched in the arid language of bureaucracy as if the executioners were dealing with cabbages, not human beings.'

Germany's victimization of its Jews was in complete contrast to events in Italy in the early years of Benito Mussolini's fascist regime. Rather than being opponents of fascism, Italian Jews played a prominent role in its success; by the 1930s, over a quarter of all Italian Jews, well above the national average of 10 per cent, supported the Fascist PNF party. One of Mussolini's most high-profile mistresses was a Jew. Many of the 40,000 Italian Jews were nationalist rather than Zionist and one of the most prominent, Ettore Ovazza, set up an anti-Zionist journal to promote the message that Italy's Jews were wholly Italian and inseparable from the majority of their fellow citizens. But problems began during the Italian invasion of Ethiopia when the new Italian settlers in Africa were forbidden to marry blacks, and the concept of racial inferiority became topical. Subsequently, Italy saw the introduction of legislation with anti-semitic undertones, but in 1937 the majority of Italian Jews remained unconcerned. Their confidence appeared justified when the fascist government even allowed some of Germany's persecuted Jews to seek asylum in Italy, provoking the anger of the Nazi theorist Alfred Rosenberg (1893–1946), who ranted against '...this Judeo-Fascist regime entrenched in world-polluting Rome'. Although Mussolini frequently attacked minorities, the Jews were simply in the same bracket as other groups he looked down on – Neapolitans, Calabrians and southern Italians in general. Moreover, when news of the Nazi *Kristallnacht* pogrom reached Italy, almost the entire population of Milan reacted in horror, condemning the Germans as modern-day barbarians. Yet, in November 1938 Mussolini, in a craven attempt to please Hitler, followed the German lead. Against the wishes of the Italian people, he began to scapegoat Italian Jews. As in Germany, they were banned from all teaching positions, forbidden to serve in the armed forces and prevented from marrying Christian Aryans. Oddly, this discrimination was not based on racial hatred as it was in Germany, but on a need to bolster national solidarity against all perceived outsiders be they blacks, Arabs, Slavs or Jews. When the war began, such legislation increased and Jews were forced to participate in government public work schemes; but the Italian fascists still resisted the draconian measures in place in Germany.

The situation changed dramatically in 1943 when Mussolini was overthrown and imprisoned by the partisans. General Badoglio (1871–1956) became prime minister and immediately began negotiating a ceasefire with the Allies. Enraged by what he saw as a national betrayal, Hitler attempted to force Italy into a wholehearted commitment to the war, and, though he could hardly spare them, ordered a large contingent of battle-hardened German troops to be withdrawn from the Eastern Front and sent to occupy northern and central Italy. Unfortunately for Italian Jews, this was the very region where the majority of them lived. German troops together with some of Mussolini's more ardent supporters then began rounding up Jews in Rome, Milan, Genoa, Florence, Trieste and other northern cities. In total about 8,000 Jews were deported to the Nazi death camps during the occupation and about 95 per cent of them perished there. Ominously, there had been plans for a series of concentration camps in Italy itself, but they were abandoned as soon as Mussolini fell from power. Whatever the faults of Mussolini's despotism, it never demonized its Jewish citizens in the same way as Hitler's regime; the great majority of the people were opposed to deportation and many gave active support to their Jewish neighbours, 80 per cent of whom survived both the Nazi occupation and the war.

While the memory of Hitler's despotic persecution of the Jews remains vivid, his persecution of another group of scapegoats is often forgotten. The gypsies were also his victims, and unlike many of Germany's Jews, had neither the resources nor the education to contemplate escape. The Roma were ideal scapegoats, seen as wandering anti-social criminals and culturally inferior. When Hitler came to power in 1933, his administration inherited anti-gypsy laws that had been in force since the Middle Ages. But the Roma presented a problem for Hitler. The racist policies he directed against the Jews were based on their non-Aryan status, yet the Roma were one of the oldest Aryan groups in Europe. At first, Hitler tried to force German scholars to deny the truth, and to reclassify the Roma as non-Aryans; many refused, and suffered imprisonment as a result. So the Nazis abandoned the non-Aryan argument, and sought to find others. A new policy statement decreed that the Roma were not Nordic but vaguely asocial, sub-human beings and members of an inferior race. In 1937, the Roma were listed along with the Jews in the Nuremberg Law for the Protection of Blood and Honour. Marriage with non-Roma was forbidden, as was sexual intercourse between Aryan and non-Aryan peoples. The Nazi criteria for classification as a Roma were twice as strict as those applied to Jews – namely, if two of a person's eight great-grandparents were even part-Roma, then that person was a gypsy and subject to classification with the Jews, at the bottom of the racial scale. The criteria for classification as a member of the Jewish race, was anyone who had three or four Jewish grandparents – although ultimately anyone with a single Jewish grandparent was at risk of persecution.

By 1937 the Roma were being forced into concentration camps at Dachau, Dieselstrasse, Mahrzan and Vennhausen, and were joined soon afterwards by those of the German occupied countries, whose governments were ordered to co-operate with the Nazi authorities in deporting their gypsies. New arrivals at the camps were sterilized to prevent them from reproducing and the Roma were then worked to death in the camp quarry or in outlying factories. At this stage, there were no gas chambers, but thousands were shot, hanged or tortured to death. In July 1938, plans for the Final Solution were finalized and the Roma and Jews singled out for annihilation on racial grounds. Within weeks, the Roma were being transported to the death camps in Poland. In February 1943, over 10,000 Roma had arrived at Sachsenhausen for extermination following Heinrich Himmler's decision to close the Roma camps in Germany. The Roma were beaten and clubbed to death, or herded into the gas chambers. If not killed immediately, they were used for inhuman scientific experiments. Auschwitz alone held over 16,000 Roma at one point, but by August 1944 only 4,000 remained. After a visit by Himmler, the last of the imprisoned Roma were led to the gas chambers. Altogether an estimated 1.5 million Roma were murdered by the Nazis between 1935 and the end of the war in 1945.

Unfortunately, scapegoating did not die with Hitler and the Nazis. It should not be forgotten that Saddam Hussein sought to suppress the Kurds of Northern Iraq by identifying them as enemies of the state. The Kurds are considered the world's largest ethnic group although they do not have a recognised state of their own. There are approximately 25 million Kurdish people, of whom just over 4 million live in Iraq, constituting about 23 per cent of the population. For over a century these proud, independent people have posed a problem to the world community. Aware of the Kurdish dream of an independent state, the United States President, Woodrow Wilson (1856–1924; President 1913–1921), called for Kurdish self-determination at the end of the First World War in 1918, and promoted the idea of a homeland, a genuine Kurdistan. This appeared to be a probability until the Western allies reneged on the promise in an attempt to placate and please the new Turkish regime of Kemal Atatürk. There was also the perception that the Allies needed to avoid destabilizing the fragile new states of Iraq and Syria, that had been granted to Britain and France, respectively, as mandated territories. So, in the 1923 Treaty of Lausanne, the Kurdish dream of a homeland was denied and the people were divided between Turkey, Iraq, and Syria. Their first oppressors were the Turks, under Atatürk, who banned Kurdish political groups and their cultural activities. At the end of the Second World War, however, the Kurds of Iran, with Soviet support, finally established the first small independent Kurdish state, the so-called Kurdish Republic of Mahabad. But the Iranian government saw this as a dangerous example to other minorities and the Iranian army swiftly crushed this embryonic state.

In contrast to the long established Iranian oppression, the arrival of Saddam Hussein as the Iraqi leader in 1968 seemed, at first, to augur well for the Kurds. Two years after he became President, Hussein's Ba'ath Party actually reached a comprehensive agreement with the Kurdish nationalist leaders, which granted them the right to use and broadcast their own language and also allowed them a significant degree of political autonomy. But Kurdish hopes were short-lived, as the agreement was soon abandoned when the ruling Ba'ath Party decided on a new policy of 'Arabising' the oil-producing areas of Kurdistan. Kurdish farmers were deported to other areas and replaced by poor ethnic Arabs from the south, guarded by government troops. This was intolerable to the Kurds who, in March 1974, rose in a rebellion against Hussein that escalated into a full-scale war in the following year. In the ensuing chaos some 130,000 Kurds fled to Iran. Tens of thousands of villagers from the Barzani tribes were forcibly removed from their homes by the Iraqi government and relocated to barren sites in the desert south of Iraq, without any form of assistance or support. Yet Kurdish resistance continued in the north of the country, with local groups waging a persistent guerrilla war against the Iraqi military that eventually provoked Hussein into taking draconian reprisals against the whole Kurdish community. He claimed the right to use any means possible to eliminate Kurdish resistance; when his army invaded the area, all males between the ages of 15 and 70 were seized. Mass executions were carried out in villages and the surrounding countryside, while Kurds were ordered to abandon certain designated areas; any people or animals found there were killed. Human Rights Watch (HRW) estimates that Hussein's 1987–1988 campaign of terror killed at least 50,000 and possibly as many as 100,000 Kurds. His most notorious action of all, which became the centrepiece of his trial in 2006, was the attack on the town of Halabja which, with the use of mustard gas and nerve gas agents, resulted in the death of over 5,000 Kurds.

An account of what happened in central Africa just over a decade ago also shows that hatred of minorities is still very much alive. Between April and June 1994, an estimated 800,000 Rwandans were killed in the space of 100 days. Most of the victims were of the Tutsi tribe and most of the murderers were Hutus. This was slaughter on a scale comparable with anything in history. The event was sparked by the death of the Rwandan president Juvenal Habyarimana, a Hutu, whose plane was shot down above the capital Kigali. Within hours of the attack, violence spread from the capital throughout the country, and did not subside until three months later.

Ethnic tension in Rwanda was nothing new and had long existed between the majority Hutus and minority Tutsis. The Belgians who had colonized Rwanda had considered the Tutsis superior to the smaller Hutus, and had given them better jobs and educational opportunities. Resentment among the Hutus grew, culminating in a series of riots in 1959 in which more than 20,000 Tutsis were killed. When the Belgians left in 1962, the Hutus took power and blamed the Tutsis for every Rwandan crisis; the shooting down of Habyarimana's plane proved to be the final straw. In Kigali, the presidential guard immediately launched a campaign of retribution, and the killing of Tutsis began. It was led by an unofficial militia group called the *Interahamwe*, which was 30,000-strong. Soldiers and police officers encouraged ordinary citizens to take part in the murders, and in some cases, Hutu civilians were forced to murder their Tutsi neighbours by military personnel; others were offered incentives, such as money, food or the land of the Tutsis they killed. To its subsequent shame, the international community did nothing, and the UN troops withdrew after 10 of its soldiers were murdered. Finally, in July, the Tutsi-backed RPF forces invaded from Burundi and captured Kigali. The government collapsed and an estimated 2 million Hutus fled into what is now the Democratic Republic of Congo. These refugees include many who have since been implicated in the massacres. Long after the genocide, the search for justice continues with over 500 people under sentence of death and a further 100,000 still in prison. The tragedy of Rwanda revealed that the age of massacres is far from over.

CHAPTER 7

Seducing the Masses

In 1895 the French psychologist Gustave Le Bon published his seminal work, *The Psychology of the Crowd*. It is a virtual textbook for the ambitious despot. It describes how the masses can be manipulated and how to exclude them from the political process. Le Bon suggested that thousands of individuals assembled in a group could, under certain circumstances (such as at a great national event), become what he termed a 'psychological crowd'. Out of this temporary unity comes a collective mind that makes them think, feel and act very differently from how they would as individuals. Le Bon claimed that such a group had limited intelligence, and could never accomplish acts that require a high degree of insight and skill. He says, 'It is stupidity and not mother-wit that is accumulated in a crowd.' Anyone watching the ritual chanting and choreographed gestures of a soccer crowd, the beautifully shot and staged films of Leni Riefenstahl depicting a God-like Führer, let alone the mobs that greeted Saddam Hussein when he appeared in public, would surely agree. Although Hussein was almost certainly unaware of it, he used Le Bon's principles to build himself a highly effective personality cult in Iraq. Giant portraits and statues filled every public square, portraying him as a soldier, statesman and scholar. On one of his birthdays in the 1980s, Baghdad residents even woke to see giant helium-filled balloons, painted with images of Hussein's moustachioed face, grinning down from skies over the capital.

More dangerously, according to Le Bon, the individual gains a sense of his own invincibility from the association of numbers, and becomes hypnotized into group actions that may conflict with his personal moral code. Such crowd actions are not necessarily evil, as witnessed by the thousands of Burmese monks who appeared on the streets of Rangoon to oppose the military despotism, or the Chinese students who faced the tanks in Tiananmen Square. But more often than not, these actions are destructive and vindictive; the crowd hunts down their victims and attacks property. As the masses are motivated by emotion rather than rationality what they need most, Le Bon argued, is an inspirational leader – someone to excite and channel their feelings. As the crowd is only capable of thinking in images, the only way to impress it is also with images. The art of good government, therefore, is to provide the people with the right kind of image. The leaders that crowds have most admired behave like the Caesars, with symbols and emblems, an authority to overawe the people and a sword to enforce his will. While a crowd will always revolt against a weak or feeble leader, it will bow down before a strong one; so, any would-be ruler should be theatrical when addressing the people, and endow his words and language with powerful imagery. Old newsreels of Mussolini and Hitler show how closely these 20th-century dictators followed Le Bon's advice. He also added propheticaly that 'words whose sense is the most ill-defined are sometimes those that possess the most influence'. This was a lesson that would be taken on board by not only the despots of the 20th century, but by later democratic presidents and politicians too – the vagaries of George W. Bush's pronouncements on Iraq and the 'war on terror' being but a recent example.

Le Bon's essential point was that the successful leader should 'mystify' his approach to the crowd, and always appeal to sentiment rather than reason. This advice was intended for the use of democratic politicians, it was adopted by liberal and despot alike. Significantly, his most avid disciple was the political showman, Mussolini, who was so taken with Le Bon's ideas that he invited him to Rome and used him as an adviser when planning his speeches. Having then witnessed the malleability of the crowd, Mussolini wrote a revealing account of what it felt like to hold such despotic power:

> When I feel the masses in my hands knowing that they believe in me or
> when I mingle with them and they almost crush me, then I feel like one
> with them. However at the same time I feel a slight aversion, much as the
> poet feels towards the material he works with. Doesn't the sculptor
> sometimes break the marble in rage because it does not take shape
> precisely under his hands according to his vision...? Everything depends
> on that sense of control, that ability of the artists to dominate the masses.

Mussolini's concept of himself as the creative genius, using his unique talent to shape the people to his will, has been common among despots. But however creative his performance may have been, the language that he used distorted the truth and disguised evil as virtue. For example, the word 'pacification' meant mass murder; 'relocation' meant transport to a death camp.

Although, according to Le Bon, the crowd should be held spellbound by the leader it must also, at times, be placated and diverted with spectacle and entertainment. If this is done effectively, violence decreases and the population is depoliticized. Tacitus claimed that this was the way that Rome conquered Britain. After a short burst of initial violence, it was the sight of warm baths and sumptuous banquets that seduced the people into accepting Roman rule. The need for diversions had also been recognized by Plato, who noted that a tyrant often distracts the people by involving them in war, thereby diverting criticism from his domestic failures while uniting the nation in a common purpose. At times of war, the people have less time to plan the tyrant's overthrow; they are too concerned with saving their lives in battle and feeding their families to worry about their lost rights. But whatever the distraction, it makes the people less inclined to take up arms against their oppressor, as expressed in the phrase 'bread and circuses'. These words were coined by the Roman poet and satirist Juvenal (c. AD 55–130) to describe the entertainments provided for the public by the Roman emperors. Augustus, who once matched over 600 gladiators against each other in pairs, was the first to recognize the propaganda potential in these imperial spectacles. The tradition was continued by his successors. Juvenal, having lived through the reign of Nero, certainly knew what he was talking about.

One of the greatest impresarios of the ancient world was the Emperor Caligula, with his all-consuming passion for horse- and chariot-racing. During his four-year reign he spent vast sums of public money on horses and a large racetrack on his estate near Rome. Traditionally, there were four competing chariot-racing teams in Rome – the reds, whites, greens and blues. Each attracted a huge following, both patrician and plebeian alike, in the manner of modern Italian football teams. Caligula adopted the greens and would often dine at their stables, inspecting the horses and showering the drivers with generous gifts. His obvious enthusiasm and generous sponsorship of the sport earned him great popularity with the crowd. It also led Suetonius to claim that Caligula, perhaps in a gesture of contempt for the rest of the Senate, had once suggested making his favourite horse Incitatus a consul.

Caligula's frequent public appearances and promotion of 'bread and circuses' was in complete contrast to the behaviour of his reclusive predecessor, Tiberius, who preferred to remain out of the public eye and concentrate on his dubious sexual practices on the Isle of Capri. Of all the Roman emperors, Caligula was certainly the most popular, particularly at the start of his reign in AD 37. This made his steady fall from grace with the ruling class all the more perplexing. Even in his last despotic months he remained the favourite of the ordinary people, while feared and hated by the patricians. No matter how crazy his behaviour, he knew that the people still loved him; when returning from campaigning on Rome's northern borders in AD 40, he issued a proclamation saying that he would only come back if the ordinary people and equestrians still wanted him, as he wished to have no further truck with the senators. Throughout his reign, Caligula used his popularity to transform himself into a semi-divine figure, claiming that he received divine inspiration from Jupiter. His inevitable fall, when it came, was greeted with none of the rejoicing on the streets that usually followed the murder of a despotic emperor.

Caligula's intuitive appreciation of the need to entertain was shared by the Emperor Nero. But Nero was also obsessed with performing personally, in the Greek tradition, and as emperor he was always allowed to win – whatever the contest. Anyone who has watched Idi Amin battering his fellow contestants aside in a swimming gala in Kampala will appreciate why. Nero even 'won' the chariot race in the Olympic Games one year, in spite of falling ignominiously out of his chariot. His recorded victories number 1,808, making him the ultimate *victor ludorum* of history. Yet, Nero took great pains to portray himself as just another humble competitor and appeared genuinely surprised at each inevitable victory. This false humility led him to conspicuously dedicate the victor's laurel wreath to the people of Rome after each success, and the crowd would be generously showered with a form of gift token that could be redeemed for jewels, horses, slaves or even houses. Long after his death, he was remembered as the second greatest impresario of the age, and admired for his talent at making a brilliant success out of any public event. One memorable example was the coronation of Tiridates as King of Armenia, then under Roman patronage. Once Tiridates had made obeisance to Nero in the forum, in the presence of the entire senate and a cheering crowd, the Praetorian Guard led the way to Pompey's theatre, which had been specially gilded for the occasion. Here, Nero delivered a lengthy performance on the Greek lyre before changing into a charioteer's costume and charging round the arena in his favourite chariot.

Such histrionic behaviour would have been acceptable in Ancient Greece, but in more conservative Rome it was viewed by the patricians and military with suspicion and deep distaste. As Suetonius sourly commented, 'He was obsessed with a desire for popularity and was the rival of anyone who in any way stirred the feeling of the mob.' There was also a suspicion among the older patricians that Nero's encouragement of young men to perform athletics in the nude, in the Greek manner, encouraged homosexuality and undermined the virility of Roman youth. Nero paid little attention to such criticisms and in AD 57 ordered the building of a new amphitheatre on the Campus Martius, composed of stone, faced with marble and decorated with gold and ivory. No expense was spared; even the safety nets were trimmed with rare amber beads from the Baltic coast. It proved a fitting venue for the new exotic spectacles that Nero provided, which eclipsed all that had gone before. As one elderly citizen remarked admiringly, 'All the shows we saw in former years now seem shabby to us.' Once the amphitheatre was completed, Nero embarked on the construction of numerous other buildings, baths and gymnasiums, all principally for the entertainment of the people and all executed to as high a standard as possible. Perhaps the ultimate expression of his fascination with architecture and design was the Golden House. It was begun after the great fire of Rome, which had cleared a vast area of land where Nero's first home, the Domus Transitora, had stood. Work continued on the Golden House until the emperor's death in AD 68. It certainly impressed the Roman people and was described in great detail by Suetonius in his *De Vita Caesarum* (*The Lives of the Caesars*):

> A huge statue of Nero, 120 feet high, stood in the entrance hall; and the
> pillared arcade ran for a whole mile. An enormous pool, more like a small
> sea, was surrounded by buildings made to resemble cities and by a
> landscape garden consisting of ploughed fields, vineyards, pastures and
> woodlands. Here every variety of domestic and wild animals roamed
> about. Parts of the house were overlaid with gold and studded with
> precious stones and mother of pearl. All the dining rooms had ceilings of
> fretted ivory, the panels of which could slide back and let a rain of flowers,
> or of perfume from hidden sprinklers, fall on his guests. The main dining
> room was circular, and its roof revolved slowly, day and night, in time with
> the sky. Seawater, or sulphur water, was always on tap in the baths.

Nero was equally obsessed with the arts. He made frequent visits to Greece, his spiritual home, where he toured and performed in the local festivals much like a modern rock star, complete with a backing group of long-haired boy dancers. Dressed in floral tunics and with his own hair worn long and curled in the Greek manner, he would sing to the assembled crowd in seemingly interminable performances – provoking, it was said, the occasional member of the audience to feign death, just to escape the tedium. Caution was needed in these circumstances; Tacitus claimed that Nero had every audience watched by spies who were ordered to report any displays of mockery or criticism.

Under Nero, the spectacles at the Circus Maximus became ever more flamboyant, with traditional chariot races giving way to gladiatorial contests and battles against wild beasts. To retain the public's attention, the events became increasingly bizarre; Christians were burnt alive, and the fights between men and animals became ever more grotesque. At one such event, Nero himself descended into the arena to fight a lion (what the crowd did not realise was that its claws and teeth had been carefully removed beforehand). Yet all this increasingly desperate entertainment failed to halt Nero's waning popularity following the Great Fire of Rome in AD 64 and the suspicions that it had been deliberately started by the imperial impresario himself.

Not until the French Revolution would such politically motivated spectacle be seen again, when the new rulers of France used mass rallies to seduce the people. Although the Revolution soon descended into a bloody tyranny that would cost the lives of almost 400,000 citizens, it claimed at all times to be in the great tradition of the Roman Republic. One member of the Committee of Public Safety, which ruled the country with draconian violence, was the great painter and chronicler of his times, Jacques-Louis David (1748–1825). It was David who orchestrated the great festival of the people to celebrate the first anniversary of the Fall of the Bastille on 14 July 1790. From then on, David designed entire spectacles including the uniforms, banners, triumphal arches and inspirational props that became the new government's visual propaganda. These events included the Planting of the Tree of Liberty, the Festival of the Supreme Being and the vast state funeral that took place when the Jacobin polemicist Jean-Paul Marat (1743–1793) was assassinated. In many ways, David was the first great genius of modern political spectacle and the forerunner of the Nazi architect Albert Speer (1905–1981), who would choreograph the 1930s Nuremberg Rallies as a promotional machine for Hitler. But unlike Speer, David was himself fully involved in enforcing the worst excesses of the regime, including the Terror of 1793. As a deputy for the city of Paris, he participated fully in the National Convention and voted for the conviction and execution of King Louis XVI. His signature has also been found on over 30 other execution warrants. But it was as the painter of some of the greatest works of propaganda art in history that David remains supreme. Whereas Picasso (1881–1973) produced one great political work, *Guernica*, David produced almost a dozen. In paintings such as the *Oath of the Horatii* and the *Oath of the Tennis Court* he managed to capture the historic virtues of stoicism, masculinity and patriotism and apply them as an allusion to contemporary France. But it was in *The Death of Marat* that he perfected his art, elevating a bloodthirsty and vindictive journalist into a national hero martyred for his dedication to the Republic. The scene of Marat lying dead in his bath after being stabbed by Charlotte Corday recalls traditional religious works that depict the dead Christ being taken down from the cross.

As a close supporter of the tyrant Robespierre, David narrowly escaped death himself when the Jacobins were overthrown. Surviving the political turmoil, he found a new role under the absolutist rule of Napoleon – his Republicanism conveniently forgotten. *Napoleon at St. Bernard*, the portrayal of his new master mounted on a rearing horse, gesturing prophetically towards the future, is undoubtedly one of the greatest of all works of artistic propaganda. David had served and survived two masters, bloody despotism posing as liberation, and a dictatorial emperor whose methods presaged the totalitarian dictatorships of the 20th century. In his later years he served a third, the restored Bourbon monarchy. Had David lived a century later he might well have found another sympathetic patron in Mussolini, who harnessed spectacle and propaganda for the creation of his own personality cult in a manner never before seen in Europe.

Fascism and the French Revolution had much in common. Both aspired to the role of inheritor of the Roman tradition, which included providing spectacle for the people and the use of high art as political propaganda. This concept had great appeal for Mussolini. Once in power as Duce, he became obsessed with the idea of restoring Italy's lost military glory that had last existed in Roman times. Convinced that the Italian nation had been cheated of its colonial empire by the greed of others, he spotted Abyssinia, an African country so lacking in resources that it had been virtually ignored by the other colonial powers – and decided to invade. To persuade the Italian people to join him in this venture, he began using the state media to demonize its inhabitants, describing them as 'slavers', 'barbarians' and 'cut-throats'. At the same time, the imminent invasion of this inoffensive country was portrayed as an act of Italian self-sacrifice, to be carried out in the cause of civilization. Mussolini claimed it would bring relief from oppression to all the inhabitants; put simply, the invasion would be a triumph of good over evil – a brazen reversal of the actual truth. Ignoring the mild protests of the Western democracies, Italian troops duly entered the country, and, after overcoming the opposition of ill-armed tribesmen, occupied the capital Addis Ababa on 15 May 1936. The Duce then issued a bombastic and risible statement, describing the unprovoked conquest as 'one of the most just wars in history'. When the League of Nations inevitably imposed economic sanctions on Italy, Mussolini gave an almost comic tirade of speeches in which he described Italy as the victim of the piece, and declared that the sanctions were a blatant example of international bullying.

What mattered most to him, however, was that the Italian people had been woken from their sleep. They now found themselves involved in martial action that presaged a national rebirth. From now on, every public speech of the Duce's was an exercise in hyperbole involving carefully rehearsed, exaggerated gestures, the whole performance designed to arouse the maximum excitement in his audience. This was politics as grand opera in the Italian tradition, capable of involving even the poorest and most ill-educated citizen. In the case of Abyssinia, petty aggression had been transformed into a moral tale of the triumph of virtue in an exotic African setting. It was an uplifting story full of noble passion, self-sacrifice and sentimentality. Above all, it was drama elevated to melodrama, with a cast of thousands performing together to realize the Italian dream of restoring the lost Roman Empire.

In retrospect, Mussolini's claims looked ridiculous, and to the outside world he lost any credibility he had earned as a result of the early efficiency of his regime. But the Duce took little notice of international concern, being convinced that the Italian people were now united behind him. Throughout the period of the Abyssinian invasion his speeches were highly effective pieces of communication, because they drew on an Italian dramatic tradition. Italy was unique in Europe in having a popular culture based on the many small theatres and opera companies that toured the country. Presented like the plot of an opera, the Abyssinian campaign found resonance with the ordinary people, who were enthralled by this story of good and evil; it was performed by brave men for the sake of their country and it was to avenge a massacre of Italian soldiers that had occurred at Dogali, near Addis Ababa, in 1897. On the day the invasion was announced, the aptly named Ministry of Popular Culture ordered that sirens be sounded and church bells rung throughout the land. Everything was stage managed by the Fascist regime; people were ordered to assemble at a certain time at specific locations to hear the Duce broadcast the news to the nation. Presenting Italian actions as virtues made it easier for Mussolini to portray the League of Nations sanctions as petty and unjust. As a riposte, he ordered a Day of Faith celebration, at which women all over the country were asked to donate their wedding rings as a gesture of solidarity to the Duce.

In spite of Mussolini's sanctimonious bluster, it soon became clear he had used the Abyssinian venture, in the best despotic tradition, to distract the people from the growing economic and social failures of his own regime. The greatest victim of this self-deceiving propaganda was the Duce himself, for it tempted him to embark on far more dangerous military ventures. Ignoring Italy's fundamental weakness in industrial production and its lack of raw materials, he drove the nation to arm itself in search of further military glory. The opportunity arose in 1936, when he ordered his Italian Blackshirt volunteers into Spain to support General Franco in the Civil War. Three years later, he tried again by embarking on another ill-judged invasion – this time of a neighbouring country, Albania. Finally, in June 1940, Mussolini made his last and most fatal mistake by taking Italy into the Second World War on the side of Hitler's Germany. Yet in spite of all Mussolini's bellicose statements, it is doubtful that the Italian people ever convinced themselves that they were a martial and violent nation. They demonstrated their innate humanism by frustrating German attempts to deport and murder large numbers of Italian Jews later in the War. Old newsreels show the joy of the Italian armies surrendering to much smaller Allied units in North Africa, suggesting that it was the Duce, not the Italian people who was obsessed with restoring the martial legacy of Rome.

Despite Mussolini's ignominious end in Milan in 1945, later tyrants learned a great deal from his early success in seducing the Italian people – especially his use of the press, national radio and public spectacle to create an effective personality cult. One who took the lesson to heart was Nicolae Ceausescu, who became President of Romania in 1967. Mass rallies and bombastic speeches were a constant feature of his regime, but with attendance assured by the Securitate, his secret police. For the purpose of these rallies, the city of Bucharest was divided into six districts, each with a mayor and a party chief. Whenever a rally was planned at the Presidential Palace, these officials had to produce a minimum of 30,000 local people on the day, or face awkward questions. Each attendee was required to sign an undertaking to be at the rallying point at a specified time; before setting off, they were handed a flag or banner to wave and carefully searched to ensure they were not carrying alcohol. At 10am precisely, Ceausescu would appear on the balcony and the cheering would begin. It came not from the vast majority of the sullen crowd, but from the front ranks that were packed with Securitate men dressed in workers' clothes. As the Romanian journalist Petru Clej recalled, 'These men were acting as a barrier between him and the rest of us. The ordinary people did not cheer or shout much, but the volume was made up by a battery of loudspeakers that played tape-record-ed cheers.' On other occasions, up to 10,000 children would be shepherded into the square to dance and sing in unison to a rigidly choreographed formula. Then the president's wife, Elena, addressed them to the accompaniment of more tape-record-ed and over-amplified cheers. This stage-managed technique, using young children, was exactly what the Ceausescus had witnessed in Kim Il Sung's (1912–1994; in power 1948–1994) North Korea, when they visited in 1971. Nothing was left to chance in these rallies; it was evident even to the regime that the Romanian people hated Ceausescu and were capable of turning on him at any time.

A revealing insight into the ineffectiveness of this staged propaganda is given by the academic Gabriel Costache, who describes what happened when he was out walking in Bucharest one day. As he rounded a corner near the National Assembly, he was astonished to find Nicolae Ceausescu completely alone and without his usual bodyguard, addressing a group of about 100 people in the street. Although the crowd dutifully applauded his impromptu speech, they noticed as he walked away that his usual retinue of Securitate agents was missing. As it began to dawn that they had the tyrant at their mercy, they began slowly to mock and jeer at him and approach menacingly. Suddenly, the Securitate men appeared, and the crowd broke and ran away. As Costache says, 'This incident revealed for me a sort of duplicity. Ceausescu was a kind of monster but in a way we were his accomplices.'

No such doubts about their leader troubled the vast majority of the German people when, in March 1933, they democratically elected Adolf Hitler as Chancellor, fully endorsing his undisguised programme of rearmament and the persecution of Jews. Hitler was not slow to act. Within a few months, every Jew employed by the State or working in education was dismissed from their post. With the notable exception of a small number of university academics, there was virtually no protest by the German people; right from the start, the nation was happy to endorse the myth of his messianic status as saviour of Germany. There are also few examples of anyone daring to mock the Führer publicly, or to show open dissent at any of the political rallies that were staged by the Nazi party throughout the 1930s.

Hitler's success with the people owed much to the ideas and techniques that he had witnessed in Italy. It was apparent to all that Mussolini's Blackshirts were the model for Hitler's Brownshirts, and that Hitler took the title of Führer in the same way that Mussolini called himself Duce. Hitler was to use all the techniques of modern communication pioneered in Italy to continue shackling the German people to the myth of his own invincibility. One of his first moves was to appoint the architect Albert Speer to reinvigorate the annual Nuremberg Rally, the most important and ostentatious event of the Nazi year. The rallies had begun modestly enough in 1922, but under the direction of Speer their importance became supreme. Speer, with the strategic imagination of Jacques-Louis David (but without the Frenchman's artistic ability), transformed the Nuremberg arena into a vast open-air temple decked with Nazi flags and regalia, all branded with the swastika logo. The theatrical use of sound and light was masterful, creating an atmosphere of excitement and anticipation before the dramatic arrival of the Führer himself. The whole extravaganza – the marching feet, thundering drums and the portrayal of the German people united as one behind the single, visionary figure of Adolf Hitler – was captured in German film director Leni Riefenstahl's extraordinary production *The Triumph of the Will*. This film, one of the most dramatic examples of film propaganda ever made, was widely distributed nationally and internationally, carrying the message of the rallies far beyond Nuremberg to the far corners of Germany and German-speaking Europe. The success of the campaign was almost total, for it produced one of the most unusual social revolutions in history in which an entire nation subscribed without reservation to the will and ideas of a single man. Hitler's Minister of Propaganda, Joseph Göbbels (1897–1945), proclaimed his firm belief: 'Propaganda has only one object: to conquer the masses. Every means that furthers this aim is good; every means that hinders it is bad.' The result of the willing endorsement of Nazi policy by the Germans, and the almost total lack of either political or militant opposition, meant that the regime had no need to use massive violence or coercion to govern the country. The Germans behaved as though they were returning to the care of an omnipotent father who must be obeyed and never questioned; the very idea of raising a hand against him was unthinkable.

The success of the Nuremburg Rallies proved the power of politically slanted spectacle. The same techniques also enabled the Nazis to dominate the 1936 Berlin Olympics, where the sporting events were intended to come a poor second to the real hero of the occasion, Hitler. To non-believers all over the world, the Nazi extravaganza was ludicrous, and the adulation showered on this shabby little man aroused more ridicule than respect. So it was a form of poetic justice that when the war against Germany finally began, one of the weapons used by Britain was mockery: the image of Hitler was roundly lampooned by the BBC and by British newspaper cartoonists. This black propaganda undoubtedly diminished the standing of Hitler and his regime in American eyes, and helped to sway public opinion in the United States against Nazi tyranny. The BBC propaganda service was set up under the direction of a bilingual journalist, Sefton Delmer, who frequently ignored Foreign Office guidelines in creating his highly effective programmes. His boss was Hugh Carleton Greene, who later became one of the most influential and successful of all BBC Governor Generals. Presiding over a team of talented German exiles, Delmer produced material that skilfully undermined enemy morale. He created a right-wing short wave station presided over by a character called *Der Chef*, a die-hard Prussian officer of the old school, who pretended to be all for Hitler and his war. Delmer thought this would appeal to the 'pig dog' inside every German while, at the same time, injecting some doubt about Germany's conduct of the war. *Der Chef* was a huge success with his salacious stories and soon gained large audiences. The writers understood the German character intimately and so they were able to satirise and mock with impunity. One series of programmes, for instance, concentrated on the supposedly bizarre personal habits of the Nazi leaders. Much of the content was highly pornographic but after the war Delmer resolutely defended his actions. 'Do I regret this pornography which I perpetrated during my few years as a temporary government servant? I certainly do not on morale grounds. As far as I was concerned, anything was in order which helped to defeat Hitler.'

The novelist Ian Fleming also became involved by approaching Delmer with regard to setting up a radio station backed by naval Intelligence, in the war against U-boats in the Atlantic. It was to be a significant weapon against the German navy and received Delmer's full backing. The Navy managed to gain use of the BBC's 'Aspidistra' transmitter, the most powerful in the world at the time. Again, using the expertise of German exiles, Delmer created a live news station called *Atlantiksender* that broadcast non-stop popular music, including jazz and swing, interrupted by frequent news bulletins for the U-boat crews. This was not so much black propaganda as 'grey' and in essence was all the more dangerous to the German morale. Knowing that this was an enemy-controlled station, portraying events from the other side, made the U-boat crew very uneasy because they realised just how much the enemy knew about their movements. What could be more horrific than being deep below the surface and feeling that the enemy knew exactly who and where you were?

To counterbalance British complacency at home, another series of programmes by the BBC made it plain, in chilling detail, just what would be the fate of the British if the Germans ever managed to invade. Yet another series, written by Karl Otten, a confirmed pacifist, unmasked those who had betrayed the German people and had brought Hitler to power. Even by Göbbels's high standards it was impressive propaganda and all the more effective as the Reichsminister's own efforts became increasingly strident and unbelievable as the war progressed. The BBC broadcasts had the edge, with a combination of traditional British humour and the biting, satirical wit of Berlin cabaret that the exiles brought with them. So famous did the broadcasts become that even Germany's most distinguished novelist, Thomas Mann, contributed a weekly newsletter that was recorded in California and then flown to London for transmission. Curious to find out how well they had done, the BBC conducted a survey after the war and was amazed to discover that 10 million Germans had been regular listeners, in spite of persistent jamming by the Nazis, and the dire penalties that awaited anyone caught listening.

In the aftermath of the most devastating war in history, it was hard to imagine that within a few decades of 1945 another despot would appear who would develop an even greater personality cult than either Mussolini or Hitler. Using the methods of remorseless propaganda and mass spectacle, Kim Il Sung sought to stamp his image as a near god-like being on North Korea. He began by eliminating much of his country's written cultural history, replacing it with a programme of supposed modernization and the elevation of himself as the arbiter of all wisdom. What was noticeably different about Kim's regime was his concentration on brainwashing children, knowing that they would grow up to become his most faithful disciples. From the age of six, each North Korean child was subjected to a programme of relentless indoctrination that told them that the 'Great Leader' was the fount of all knowledge, the redeemer of his nation and, above all, infallible. They also learnt that Kim Il Sung had repelled the American invaders who wished to turn the Koreans into slaves, that North Korea was a paradise on earth, and that all other nations were full of beggars where vicious capitalists battened on the starving poor. In the manner of Big Brother in George Orwell's seminal novel *1984*, Kim's picture was displayed everywhere; on public buildings, on living room walls and even on the buses that carried the people to work. The obligatory giant statue, in this case 70-feet high (21 m) and made of bronze, was erected as giant totem in the centre of Pyongyang to which the passing crowd bowed in obeisance. Martial music accompanied the children to school and their parents to the factories. This was the all-embracing quality of the audio and visual propaganda that had so impressed the Ceausescus on their formative visit to North Korea.

Little changed when Kim Il Sung died in 1994. His son, the small, fat bespectacled Kim Jong-Il, simply took his place and was given the title of 'Dear Leader'. As Kim Il Sung was taken to his burial place, he was accompanied by a carefully choreographed funeral procession of several hundred-thousand screaming and crying mourners. In the manner of Lenin in Red Square, his body became a public spectacle in its own right, permanently on display in a glass case in the centre of Pyongyang. Parties of schoolchildren and workers were carried in buses from all over the country to weep as they filed past the carefully embalmed corpse. An object of continuing veneration, the older Kim was awarded the posthumous title of 'Eternal President'. Those visiting his mausoleum are subjected to a well-rehearsed paean of praise by the guides, often accompanied by tears.

Under his son, the crowd-bonding spectacles are less frequent but political control remains as rigid as ever. No contact with the outside world is allowed; there are very few land telephone lines and being found with a mobile phone is a punishable offence. Anyone bold enough to speak out against the regime is arrested and never seen again, or occasionally publicly executed as a warning to others. These days, there are few state-sponsored spectacles to divert the crowd. The economic decline of North Korea continues, and Kim Jong-Il seems increasingly vulnerable to regime change.

CHAPTER 8

Building a Personality Cult

It would have been difficult for the people of Turkmenistan to ignore their despotic ruler even if they wanted to, for the smiling face of President Saparmurat Niyazov (1940–2006; President 1990–2006) was everywhere. There was scarcely a square or open space that did not display a statue of Turkmenbashi, as he was known, or bear his portrait, beaming down from the walls of workshops and school classrooms, resplendent in hotel foyers, adorning bank notes and even vodka bottle labels. Many of the statues were as golden as the promises that he made to his people, and he was always shown symbolically facing the rising sun. The tallest statue of all stood in the centre of the capital city Ashgabat on an ingeniously designed pedestal that rotated to follow the sun. Niyazov was proud of what he had done for his country, and thought himself worthy of gratitude and respect. 'If I was a worker and my president gave me all the things they have here in Turkmenistan, I would not only paint his picture, I would have his picture on my shoulder, or on my clothing,' Niyazov is reported to have said.

Niyazov was an opportunist who was lucky enough to be in the right place at the right time when Soviet rule collapsed in Turkmenistan in 1991. As head of the local Communist party, he seized power with the help of the army and proceeded to build himself a ruthless and all-embracing personality cult. He was impressed by Kim Il Sung's regime in North Korea, particularly with the way in which Kim had asserted his intellectual and moral superiority over the people. Niyazov set out to do the same, but added his own bizarre twist by taking on the Koran. Untroubled by modesty or any awareness of his own limitations, Niyazov set himself up as a new spiritual leader whose teachings would rival those of the Prophet himself. In 2004 he ordered that sections from his own philosophical treatise, the *Rukhnama*, or Book of the Soul, be inscribed alongside verses from the Koran on a new $100-million mosque being constructed in his home village just outside Ashgabat. To make the contest more equal, Niyazov banned the construction of any new mosques in Turkmenistan; all existing mosques or churches were required to display a copy of Niyazov's new work alongside the Bible or the Koran. It became apparent to the citizens of Turkmenistan that all they needed to get ahead in this society was a thorough grounding in the great man's thoughts. Teachers and university students were selected solely on the basis of their knowledge of the *Rukhnama*; soon the English literature course at Ashgabat University consisted of the study of only one book – the *Rukhnama* translated into English. To make sure that the nation fully appreciated its good fortune, phrases such as 'the guarantor of the nation's progress and independence' and 'visionary architect of the nation's future' appeared constantly in the national media.

Elsewhere, in the Central African Republic, an even more baroque version of the traditional personality cult emerged under Jean Bédel Bokassa (1921–1996; President 1966–1977, Emperor 1977–1979), an ex-sergeant of the French colonial army. In 1966, as the new president, he began a sincere attempt to govern his poverty-stricken country efficiently. It didn't last; he soon succumbed to the temptation of self-glorification, referring to himself as the 'Saviour of the Republic', 'Man of Steel', and 'Artist and Guide of Central Africa'. What made Bokassa different from contemporary despots was his obsession with France and its culture, and his desire to imitate past European monarchs. Even his French patrons were surprised when in 1977 he decided to make the Central African Republic a monarchy, and himself an emperor. Now describing himself as 'His Imperial Majesty the Emperor of Central Africa', Bokassa consulted the history books and devised for himself a lavish coronation ceremony based on that of Napoleon Bonaparte. The justification for the expenditure was that by creating a monarchy, he would help Central Africa stand out from the rest of the continent, and so earn the world's respect. His French backers were unimpressed, but allowed the $20-million ceremony to go ahead. Guests were flown in from all over the world at the new emperor's expense; food, uniforms and even ceremonial horses were imported from France. This extravaganza eventually consumed one-third of the nation's annual budget, equivalent to the entire sum of France's aid to the country for a year. Ominously, no world leaders of any significance attended the ceremony, many considering Bokassa insane, and wary of his increasing resemblance to the Ugandan despot Idi Amin. Rumours that he enjoyed eating human flesh did not help his image in the outside world. The new 'empire' proved to be little more than another traditional tyranny, with dissenters suppressed, opposition opponents thrown into jail, tortured and murdered. Eventually his French paymasters tired of his embarrassing behaviour. When he ordered the arrest and brutal murder of protesting schoolchildren in January 1979, they finally struck. French paratroopers landed in the capital, and within hours had overthrown the emperor and carried him off into exile, so ending a personality cult that was unique in the 20th century.

If Bokassa's personality cult was unique, however, that of the Ceausescus in Romania was almost as strange. It was the first despotic double act, featuring not only Nicolae but his wife Elena too. This formidable woman exercised a role in Romanian political life far in excess of mere consort, for she also became closely involved in the politics of the regime and all but shared power with her husband. She often appeared when foreign delegations were visiting Romania and, far from confining herself to a social role, frequently became involved in negotiations. She was obsessed with becoming accepted as a scientist of international repute and with control of Romanian communism, becoming the official party boss with a central role its reorganization. By the mid 1980s she had become such an important figure in the regime that her birthday was celebrated as a national holiday. Few other woman, with the possible exception of Eva Peron, better known as Evita, in Argentina, had come so close to exercising dictatorial power in the 20th century; there is little doubt that she would have succeeded her husband as president of Romania after his death, had she not been executed with him. Her one undoubted virtue was unshakeable loyalty to this man, whom she had met when both were students. Unfortunately, she had even less capacity for human warmth, making her more despised and resented than he was. Bitter and resentful, she appeared to have affection for no one other than her husband and their two pet dogs. She constantly nagged Nicolae and all those around her, from their servants in the hideous Spring Palace in Bucharest to the most senior government ministers. As one former health minister stated: 'She was totally negative. She was mean, she always had to have her own way. She was Ceausescu's devil. As with a mentally unstable character, you tried to avoid her. He was someone you could talk to, he had a human touch, but she was unadulterated evil.' For someone so concerned with her image, Elena seemed unaware of her infamous reputation, constantly carrying out spot-checks in the palace kitchens to prevent pilfering while selfishly spending vast sums of government money on furs and jewellery for herself. It was a vice she shared with her husband, for in spite of the propaganda that praised their generosity to the Romanians, both Ceausescus were obsessed with material possessions. Gifts they received from foreign dignitaries were shown on television, to stress the supposed importance of Ceausescu and Romania in international affairs, before being hoarded away in the palace.

Although a scholar of modest achievements, Elena used the state propaganda machine to suggest that she was a highly qualified and gifted scientist whose opinion was sought on a variety of issues. It was easy to have herself appointed head of both the National Council on Science and the Council on Technology; but what concerned Elena most was the acquisition of honorary science degrees from foreign universities to give credence to her claim. These she collected like other women collect china, and Romanian diplomats were ordered to identify sympathetic institutions throughout the world. Eventually this obsession became a mania, and the bestowing of such honours the prerequisite for any state visit abroad. The more prestigious the university, the more she lusted after a doctorate. Before the infamous state visit to Britain in 1978, she had lobbied desperately for an award from either Oxford or Cambridge universities, but had to settle for a far more modest honour from the Central London Polytechnic.

The inspiration for the Ceausescus' personality cult and their vision of themselves as leaders of a new and progressive Romania had come from their visit to North Korea in 1971. Coming from the chaotic and ramshackle Romania of the early 1970s, they were pleasantly surprised by the ordered and disciplined society they discovered in Pyongyang. Neither Stalinist nor Western capitalist in character, the region retained its own resolute nationalism combined with a common determination to improve the national economy with hard work, even if this was at the expense of individual freedom. They were also impressed by the manner in which Kim Il Sung had nurtured a highly successful personality cult, and on returning to Bucharest set about establishing one of their own. Soon pictures of the Ceausescus appeared throughout the country, and the state media began devoting hours of radio and television time to accounts of their doings. They were a strangely competitive couple; just as Elena craved scientific awards, so Nicolae sought international recognition as a statesman, using Romanian ambassadors abroad to promote his image as a man of peace and understanding with a role to play on the world stage. One of the mechanisms they used was to try and persuade foreign journals and publications to publish articles praising the great man and his regime. Sadly for Nicolae, the results were constantly disappointing. A typical example was a news item from Sicily, which described Nicolae Ceausescu as one of the world's greatest leaders and thinkers. This purported to come from the 'Syracuse Academy', an institution that eventually turned out to be a small language school in a Naples apartment run by an old lady. After the fall of the Ceausescus, she revealed to a TV reporter that she had been approached by a Romanian diplomat and given a fee to publish the eulogy, which he had written himself. Praise for the Romanian despot eventually came from a far more credible source, however: the British Prime Minister Margaret Thatcher declared fulsomely (if somewhat ambiguously) that she was impressed by the personality of President Ceausescu and 'left with particular impressions about him as the leader of Romania'. Not to be outdone, the former Labour Foreign Minister, David Owen, unctuously described him as 'a statesman of world-wide repute, experience and influence'.

The inevitable consequence of any personality cult is that the subject comes to believe implicitly in his or her own myth. In Ceausescu's case, it overwhelmed his native common sense, resulting in delusions of grandeur that earned him international ridicule. Once, he stormed out of a dinner in America because a Roman Catholic Cardinal had dared to say a Christian grace before the meal; a few days later he did the same again, when the Mayor of New York dared to suggest that the Romanian people were being denied freedom of worship. This petulant behaviour was a mistake, for it demonstrated to the international community that the President of Romania was losing his judgement. In Romania, the Ceausescus' increasing arrogance was also annoying members of the government, while the poverty-stricken public were shocked to see the President's enormous Spring Palace under construction in the centre of Bucharest. The building was so grotesquely over-ornate that it was mockingly compared to a bad-taste version of the Palace of Versailles. As discontented as they had become, the Romanians kept their anger to themselves. For five centuries they had endured the rule of the Ottoman Turks, and had learnt from bitter experience to stay silent or risk death from their Islamic masters. There is little doubt that Ceausescu was fully aware that it was the Christian religion with its powerful imagery that had sustained the people during this long period of Turkish oppression. Ever the opportunist, he now used it to enhance his own personality cult. What he offered Romania was a new Communist Holy Trinity, with himself at the head and Elena and the people making up the triumvirate. In government propaganda, phrases such as 'the saviour', 'the sacred word', and the 'unifying nimbus' were increasingly used to indicate divine approval for Ceausescu's actions. One poem composed in his honour even paraphrased the Nicene Creed with the words, 'Man will return to Eden and the Ceausescu Era will have no end'. Slavishly promulgated by the media, such catchphrases were designed to stay in the memory and be repeated in the manner of traditional religious responses. It became common practice to refer to the leader (without irony) as 'The builder of the outstanding stage in the millennia-old existence of the Romanian people'. This extended to every section of Romanian society, including the intelligentsia, who vied with each other in praising the great man in the hope of gaining favour with him or his wife. The Romanian historian Dan Berindel later confessed that he had been one of them, and had been fully prepared to debase himself in return for having his work published and a decent flat in Bucharest. As he recalled, 'I too was placed in a position where I had to quote from Ceausescu's works in order to get my own published… one could quote something unexceptional like "whoever ignores history is like a child that grows up without knowing its parents".'

The bureaucracy involved in maintaining state censorship was mind-numbing. Officials in the Central Committee of the Communist Party spent months, sometimes years, laboriously checking the contents of every book submitted for publication. There was one simple criterion for publication; each work must refer sympathetically to the President and quote from his writings and speeches as often as possible. The more quotations used, the more likely the chance of success. To disguise their humiliation every writer, academic or journalist subscribed to the myth that there was no official censorship in Romania. Nor did there need to be, for everyone understood the unspoken rules. The same subservience was shown by Romanian television executives, who vied with each other to gain favour with the Ceausescus by constantly extending coverage of their daily activities. Eventually the President and his First Lady were on Romanian screens for over two hours every day. All other programmes, particularly foreign imports, were heavily censored by the Securitate, whose agents examined them thoroughly for anything that might blemish the image of the leader or his wife. News coverage was particularly difficult; whenever the Ceausescus were filmed speaking (a daily and interminable occurrence), every hesitation or mispronunciation had to be carefully erased from the scene before broadcast. There was one other problem to be dealt with, too, and that was the diminutive stature of the president. Whenever Ceausescu appeared with other people, for example when greeting foreign dignitaries, he had to be shown in a way that disguised his relatively short stature – the same problem faced by North Korean film crews shooting Kim Jong-Il today. Nicolae Ceausescu was just five feet six inches (1.7 metres) tall. Visiting French dignitaries such as the lofty General de Gaulle (1890–1970) and President Giscard d'Estaing (b.1926) were a particular problem, as they could never be shown standing next to their host. Even the Romanian cameramen filming the events were required to be no taller than Ceausescu himself; failure to comply with this unspoken rule resulted in instant dismissal, and the certainty of no future work in the Romanian media. Anyone who protested publicly was thrown into jail, went into voluntary exile – or simply vanished.

The cultivation of the Ceausescu personality cult did not depend on appearance alone. In the manner of Kim Il Sung, the president sought to portray himself as a man of great practical abilities with a keen understanding of economics. Just as Kim Il Sung had encouraged his people to refer to him as 'The Great Leader', so Nicolae Ceausescu promoted himself as 'The Genius of the Carpathians'. Unfortunately, he also modelled the Romanian economy on that of North Korea. Rigid state control stifled initiative and led to falling production, recalling discredited Stalinism. The result was economic collapse. Food rationing had to be reinstated, and the country was brought to a near standstill by a chronic energy shortage. The blame for the ensuing hardship was fully, if silently, attributed to Nicolae Ceausescu. To the Romanians, it was now abundantly clear that 'The Genius of the Carpathians' was just another inept despot, living a life of luxury while the country was on the brink of starvation. The end, when it came, was swift and dramatic; on 21 December 1989, the crowd started to barrack the president in Revolution Square. The look of total incomprehension on Nicolae's face has become one of the defining moments of the end of Communism. Escaping from their palace by helicopter, the Ceausescus made for the border, but were betrayed, arrested and summarily executed on Christmas Day. Since his removal, Romania has begun to prosper under free enterprise. It has been suggested that when North Korea eventually rids itself of Kim Jong-Il, it could do worse that model itself on the resurgent economy of the new and liberal Romania.

Of all the 20th-century despots, none built a personality cult with more dedication and panache than Mussolini in the 1920s. As a professional journalist, he had acquired some of the skills necessary to persuade the public of his ideas, and in many ways he became the role model for all subsequent dictators of the 20th century. His careful self-promotion certainly showed the way to Hitler and Chairman Mao. Mussolini started with the significant advantage of being Italian, and therefore heir to the great Roman imperial tradition. The historic stiff-armed Roman salute became the most recognizable gesture of his new fascist regime, and the symbol of the *fasces* an important visual icon in the creation of a new Italy. Mussolini's intention was to elevate his image from that of an ambitious bourgeois journalist to a latter-day emperor, with all the qualities of a secular messiah. It was this fusion of Roman history with Roman Catholicism that gave his personality cult its undoubted appeal at a time of both economic and spiritual depression.

His first task on coming to power on 29 October 1922 was to establish himself as the most dominant and talked-about political figure in Italy. Even his bid for power, the famous March on Rome a few days earlier, had assumed messianic proportions; fascist disciples from all over Italy had flocked to his cause, making it inevitable that he assume the role of prime minister. At this time the fascist threat was minimal and the ironic truth of Mussolini's March on Rome was that he and most of his black-shirted followers travelled to Rome from Milan by train, first class. The 'crisis' had begun on 24 October, 1922 when Mussolini had declared before 60,000 people at the Fascist Congress in Naples that 'We want to become the state!' In spite of these bold words he then retired to Milan. Meanwhile, the Blackshirts, who had occupied the Po plain, gathered at strategic points of the country. On 26 October, former

Prime Minister, Antonio Salandra, warned the current incumbent, Luigi Facta, that Mussolini was demanding his resignation and preparing to march on Rome. King Vittorio Emanuele III then added to the crisis by claiming that there were more than 100,000 fascists ready to converge on Rome and unleash a bloody civil war. The King claimed that as a result of this imminent danger, he had no alternative but to call on Mussolini to form a government. In reality, there were between just 10,000 and 25,000 Blackshirts ready to march, mostly unarmed, positioned and located at least 50 miles (80 km) from Rome and without any communications with the so-called fascist military command in Perugia. The military threat was so insignificant that it could easily have been crushed by the Italian army, but the monarch threw his clandestine support behind Mussolini. He choose to use the powers granted to him under the constitution and refused to countersign a decree from Facta, calling for the suppression of the Blackshirts by the army. The latter, whose loyalty to the king was unquestioned, now had the excuse to condone the army's intention to stand aside and allow Mussolini to come to power. Although Facta decided, as an insurance policy, to order a state of siege for Rome, on 28 October, the King refused to authorise this, thereby all but handing power to Mussolini. These facts were ignored by the new regime and, to satisfy his inordinate vanity, Mussolini created the heroic myth of the March on Rome. The numbers involved – a mere 300 or so Blackshirts – were grossly inflated into a mythical army of 300,000 dedicated heroes, led by Il Duce on horseback. Four years later, he felt confident enough of his sway over the Italian people to abandon the democratic constitution altogether, and seize power as the world's first fascist dictator. In the process he suppressed free speech and introduced a comprehensive system of centralized government that he described as 'totalitarianism'. Under this new system, all political debate was replaced with state conformity that could be neither opposed nor questioned. Citizens had to obey orders, much as Mussolini and Hitler had been required to do as soldiers in the First World War.

As a journalist, Mussolini had developed a genius for self-promotion, making himself the subject of the articles that he wrote while he was editor of the Milan newspaper *Il Popolo d'Italia*. He had also studied books on psychology and was particularly influenced, as we have seen, by Gustave Le Bon's book on the behaviour of crowds. This research was now put to good use; it soon became obvious that the Duce was a master of oratory and crowd manipulation. Determined to drag Italy out of its perceived lethargy, Mussolini began to change many aspects of Italian life, commencing with the national calendar. Just as the French Revolutionaries had introduced a new calendar to symbolize the creation of a new era, so in Italy the year 1922 became Year One of the Italian rebirth. This innovation, at least, caught the imagination of the Italian public. In Milan, a school of mystical fascism was established to celebrate the event and to promote the cult of 'Il Duce'. As the dictator himself claimed, 'Fascism is a religious conception of life... which transcends any individual and raises him to the status of an initiated member of a spiritual society.'

Italian fascism relied heavily on the image of the Duce. His portraits were everywhere, supplemented by the sound and vision of fascism on the move. The new party slogans, *Credere, Obbedire, Combattere* (Believe, Obey, Fight) and *Mussolini ha sempre ragione* (Mussolini is Always Right), were drummed relentlessly into Italian ears by state radio. The Italian press was also involved; the weekly illustrated magazine *Illustrazione Italiana* in particular ensured that the Duce was portrayed in a positive light, with every issue dominated by stories about him or a member of his family. Aware of the devotion traditionally given by the people to the birthplace of saints such as St Francis of Assisi, the Duce's own birthplace at Predappio became a shrine, revered by the faithful as a kind of modern Bethlehem.

Securely in power and with the socialist opposition behind bars, the Italian Fascist Party had little to do but concentrate on the deification of its leader, while the press was banned from revealing details such as the state of his health or his age. Thousands of images show the Duce posing in a theatrical manner, whether it be stripped to the waist helping to drain the Pontine Marshes, or in military uniform addressing the crowd from the balcony of some provincial town hall. Appearance was everything; the Duce's office in the Palazzo Venezia in Rome had to be located in one of the largest rooms in the entire city, where he sat at one end like a character in a Verdi opera.

The success of the publicity campaign was obvious from the start and appeared to confirm Mussolini's belief that Italy had been waiting for such a heroic figure to arrive. The words 'Viva Il Duce' appeared everywhere, and was soon shortened to a visual shorthand – the word 'Dux' or the single letter 'M' carried the message on public buildings, street corners, classroom walls and even, in a typically Italian sartorial touch, on brooches and embroideries on women's clothing. No one could leave their house without being stared at by the Duce, which for some provoked a curious sense of guilt and unease. As one writer observed, 'Mussolini's head fixed me with severe eyes. My God! What did I do wrong? ... It is impossible to find a hidden place, a discreet corner where the severe face of the dictator is not observing you.' Intentional or unintentional, the staring eyes of the despot, even the avuncular gaze of Comrade Stalin, soon became synonymous with the oppression of modern despotic regimes.

Although dictator and regime may have appeared as one, much of Mussolini's early success came from his ability to separate himself from the limitations of his fascist government. Mired in corruption and incompetence, it was the fascist politicians who were held responsible for the failings of the system, not the dictator himself. As one parliamentary deputy admitted, 'The Fascist leaders who surround him express the most bourgeois mediocrity and nothing more... Mussolini emerges above them in a conspicuous, absolute way not so much for his intellect, culture or ability but for the sheer insolence of his *personality*.'

Admiration for this new colossus of politics was not confined to Italy alone. Mussolini was increasingly eulogized in the foreign press, both in Europe and the United States. One of his most enthusiastic admirers, the *New York Herald*, praised him in November 1923 as a man who deserved his place in history, and a worthy successor to Garibaldi. Similar comparisons were made in the British press, the London *Daily Telegraph* applauding the British government's strange decision to invest him with the Order of the Bath for his services to politics. It helped that the new Italian fascist regime could be seen, particularly in the United States, as a bastion against the menace of Communism; the Duce himself, in spite of his bluster, was viewed as far more benign than either of the hatred ogres of Soviet Russia, Lenin and Stalin. As the famous American columnist Will Rogers wrote in 1926, to his later embarrassment, 'Dictator form of government is the greatest form of government: that is if you have the right Dictator.' The historian Simonetta Falasca-Zamponi reveals in her book *Fascist Spectacle* that between 1925 and 1928 more than 100 articles about Mussolini were published in the US press, while only 15 appeared on Stalin. He even met with the approval of that most formidable opponent of European dictators, Winston Churchill. On a visit to Rome in January 1927, Churchill stated that Mussolini was the greatest living legislator, telling the beaming dictator that:

> 'If I had been an Italian I am sure that I should have been wholeheartedly
> with you from the start to finish in your triumphant struggle against the
> bestial appetites and passions of Leninism. I will, however, say a word on an
> international aspect of fascism. Externally, your movement has rendered
> service to the whole world.'

It was not politicians alone who were taken in by Mussolini. The eminent psychologist Sigmund Freud sent him a signed book dedicated to 'a Hero of Culture'. With friends like these, it was difficult for Mussolini to provoke enemies. Internationally respected and lauded at home, his success led to his near-deification; daily, schoolchildren all over Italy were required to recite an almost blasphemous verse that included the words:

1. Nero playing while Rome burns. A 19th-century impression of the despot as artist. The rumour that he ordered part of the city to be burnt in AD 64 to make way for his Golden House led to his unpopularity and eventual overthrow and murder.

2. Ivan the Terrible accepting the submission of the Tatars at the fall of the city of Kazan. His despotic cruelty was driven by a religious mania and the conviction of his divine right to rule Russia. His rampant paranoia eventually deteriorated into near insanity.

3. Napoleon crowns himself Emperor of France. The Enlightened Despot at the height of his triumph. Although Napoleon brought stability and reform to France he suppressed individual freedoms. His military adventures finally brought disaster to his country and led to his own exile on St Helena.

4. Joseph Stalin, the smiling, avuncular despot whose paranoia led to the deaths of millions of Russians by execution, imprisonment and starvation. Stalin took the credit for the triumphant Red Army in the Second World War but was posthumously denounced as an incompetent tyrant by Nikita Khrushchev in 1956.

5. Hitler Triumphant. The Führer entering the Sudetenland without a fight in 1938. One of the greatest mass murderers in history, Hitler made no secret of his intentions to exterminate the Jews yet was elected democratically as Chancellor of Germany in 1933.

6. Hitler and Mussolini arrive with their aides Hermann Göring and Count Ciano at the Munich Conference in September 1938. Hitler's assurances to Britain and France that he would not invade Poland soon proved to be worthless and a year later Europe was plunged into bloody war.

7. Il Duce Speaks. Mussolini used his gift for oratory and mastery of propaganda to persuade the
Italian people that totalitarianism was the way ahead. His alliance with Hitler and decision to declare
war on the Allies when Hitler appeared victorious was a monumental blunder that sealed his fate.

8. Nicolae Ceausescu with his grim-faced wife, Elena. The fall of their despotic regime in Romania began with the one of the bravest displays of public dissent in modern history and ended with their flight and summary execution on Christmas Day 1989.

9. The young Muammar Gaddafi soon after seizing power in Libya. His vision of an Arab people united under his own brand of Islamic Socialism soon proved a failure. He abandoned his support for international terrorism when seriously threatened by the United States.

10. Saparmurat Niyazov the self-proclaimed visionary of Turkmenistan. Personality cults do not
come any greater, with thousands of his statues and images adorning every town and village in
his country. He remained virtually unchallenged as leader throughout his 21-year dictatorial rule.

11. Saddam Hussein found hiding in a cellar in 2003. The brutal despot of Iraq ruled his country with an iron fist. What turned out to be a bluff over the development of weapons of mass destruction led to an invasion of Iraq by United States and British troops and ensuing bloody chaos.

12. Kim Il Sung, founder of the modern despotic state of North Korea, was much admired by the Ceausescus of Romania. In 1950 he invaded the democratic South so provoking the Korean War. His establishment of a nuclear arms industry was one of his most dangerous legacies to the world.

13. Mao Tse-tung, the supreme ruler. Mao's radical policies of 'The Great Leap Forward' and the 'Cultural Revolution' proved a disaster for China but the eradication of illiteracy and the dramatic improvement in life were significant achievements. His ruthless elimination of political rivals has been compared to that of Joseph Stalin.

14. Pol Pot. The Cambodian despot drove his people into the country in an attempt to impose his own rigid, communist orthodoxy. In Pol Pot's 'Killing Field' an estimated 1.5 million people were executed or worked to death. He escaped retribution by dying while awaiting trial in Cambodia.

15. Kim Jong-Il on a film set. Known to his people as 'Our Dear Leader', Kim inherited both his father's police state and his personality cult. In the dangerous game of 'cat and mouse' with the United States over nuclear weapons he has proved remarkably successful, however.

16. General Trujillo inspects the US Navy. Trujillo used the army to seize power in the Dominican Republic. Under his regime the country became a family fiefdom with all opposition brutally eliminated. Tiring of his brutalities the United States conspired in his assassination in May 1961.

17. 'Papa Doc' Duvalier. Mild in appearance but despotic by nature, François Duvalier ruled Haiti
from 1957 until his death in 1971. He controlled the people by way of Voodoo curses and his
Tontons Macoute thugs. His son, 'Baby Doc', continued this tyranny until deposed in 1986.

18. Idi Amin Dada deposed Milton Obote as President of Uganda in January 1971. His superficial
amiability and clownish behaviour disguised a ruthless despot capable of such barbarities as the
murder of many of Uganda's educated elite. When deposed by an invading Tanzanian army in
April 1979 Amin retired to luxurious exile in Saudi Arabia.

19. Bokassa the Emperor. A Francophile with delusions of grandeur, Jean-Bédel Bokassa admired Napoleon and in emulation, crowned himself Emperor of the Central African Republic in 1977. Like Idi Amin, Bokassa was an African tyrant who personally participated in murder. He was deposed and forced into exile by French paratroops in 1979.

20. Robert Mugabe, the survivor. His near destruction of Zimbabwe's once prosperous economy has been accompanied by increasing brutality towards anyone opposing him. The only beneficiaries of his despotic rule have been his allies in ZANU–PF who have maintained him in power.

'He descended to Rome, on the third day he restored the Italian state. He ascended into high office and is seated on the right hand of our Sovereign. From there he came to judge Bolshevism. I believe in the wise. The Communion of Citizens. The forgiveness of sins. The resurrection of Italy. The eternal force. Amen.'

That the Vatican should have endorsed such sacrilege is staggering, even though Pope Pius XI (1857–1939; in office 1922–1939) had earlier described Mussolini as a 'man of Providence'. The support of the Pope gave the Italian people every reason to believe that this stocky, pugnacious man had become a kind of god. Stories of him instantly taming wild horses or restoring the sick to health began to appear in the Italian press. Once, he was shown driving through Rome with a lion cub on his lap to demonstrate his astonishing mastery of the animal kingdom. Anyone walking through Rome at night was encouraged to look up at his office window in the Palazzo Venezia, where they would see the light in his window still burning – a symbol of his commitment to working long hours to serve the Italian people. It seemed there was no end to his powers; when he visited Sicily in June 1923, the potentially disastrous lava flow from Mount Etna suddenly and mysteriously ceased. Small wonder, then, that the long drought in Libya immediately ended in March 1937 with the arrival of the Duce's plane in Tripoli. When he survived four assassination attempts in one year, merely suffering a wounded nose, his status as a near spiritual being was assured.

Mussolini's propaganda extended, however, to more worldly associations, designed to portray him as a man of his time. He was frequently shown in and around aeroplanes – the ultimate symbol of modernity in the 1920s – or driving fast cars. Images of Mussolini the intrepid aviator filled the press, accompanied by dramatic stories of his daring. One report claimed he had refused anaesthetic when operated on for a wound during the last war. In 1926, the Fascist propaganda machine issued a decree requiring a newsreel featuring the Duce in action to be screened before every feature film that was shown in Italian cinemas. Unlike the later dreary coverage of the Ceasesecus' meetings with foreign visitors and speeches to sullen workers, Mussolini constantly appeared in dramatic situations all over Italy. His speeches were exciting; he brought a message of hope and progress to the Italian people, delivered in plain, no-nonsense language. One of Mussolini's greatest strengths was his mastery of popular oratory; sentences were deliberately short, his words simple and direct, but they were delivered with force and passion using every cadence of the Italian language. The content frequently had far less substance than the packaging. As he said himself, after a particularly rousing address to the people of Mantua in

October 1925, 'Mine are not speeches in the traditional sense. They are elocutions, a contact between my soul and yours, my heart and your heart.'

Throughout his years of triumph, Mussolini never once forgot his role as triumphant saviour of his people; but after the fiasco of the botched conquest of Abyssinia, and the even greater disaster of Italy's alliance with Hitler, everything changed. Ignoring the lesson of the First World War – that the industrial power of the United States would decide all future world conflicts – he ordered his ill-equipped nation into battle as the lackeys of Nazi Germany. At home, the economy was unable to sustain the large army he had committed to battle. Hunger and deprivation returned to the country, and the façade of the great dictator crumbled with surprising speed. Italy was defeated by 1942. Mussolini was overthrown by his own fascist government and then captured by Italian partisans. Photographs of him after his rescue by German paratroops show a pathetic figure, whose face reveals the knowledge that the end is near. They bear an uncanny resemblance to those of Hitler decorating members of the Hitler Youth for bravery as the Russians close in on his Berlin bunker. Shabbily dressed and with his coat collar turned up, Hitler appears an almost furtive figure as he limps along the line of boy soldiers, patting cheeks and gripping arms in an unconvincing manner. The fate of Mussolini was even more ignominious, shot with his mistress, Clara Petacci, then hung upside down in front of a Milan petrol station, to be spat at and kicked by a vengeful Italian mob.

Hitler's squalid end was in complete contrast to his meteoric rise to power as the saviour of Germany. Like Mussolini, he established a highly successful personality cult that in the early years of his rule made him as popular abroad as he was in Germany; he also had the good fortune to arrive on the political scene at a time when the mass media offered new opportunities for communicating with the people. Not only had the German press become more sophisticated; nationwide radio and provincial cinemas could bring the Führer's propaganda to every small town in Germany. With the Mussolini experience as their guide, Hitler's Nazi propagandists were able to establish an even more effective personality cult. However, the raw material that Joseph Göbbels, Minister of Public Enlightenment and Propaganda, and Hans Fritzsche (1899–1953), Head of the Wireless News Department, had to work with was not exactly promising. Hitler was far less prepossessing than the squat but impressive Mussolini. At first sight, he was almost totally lacking in physical charisma, being below average height with wide hips and narrow shoulders. His legs were noticeably short for his height, and he was so hollow-chested that his uniforms had to be specially padded to compensate. Physically, he would not even have met the requirements for joining his own elite guard of the SS.

Furthermore, his dress sense in the early days of his rise to power was woefully inad-equate for a man with such huge political ambition, and was hardly helped by his brown, rotting teeth and long, dirty fingernails. His provincialism showed in his Bavarian national costume with its childish lederhosen, white embroidered shirt and feathered hat, although when delivering an important speech, he would abandon the Bavarian costume in favour of a common-looking blue lounge suit that robbed him of all distinction. Even his gait was comical. According to one observer, 'It was a very ladylike walk with dainty little steps. Every few steps he would twitch his right shoulder nervously while his left leg jerked up as he did so.' At the trial following the unsuccessful Munich Beer Hall Putsch, when Hitler had attempted to provoke a national uprising, the journalist Edgar Mowrer was astonished to see the little man who had caused so much trouble. From Hitler's appearance alone, Mowrer doubt-ed if this could really be the messiah who was about to save Germany. 'Was this provincial dandy, with his slick dark hair, his cutaway coat, his awkward gestures and glib tongue, the terrible rebel? He seemed for all the world more like a travelling salesman for a clothing firm,' he wrote.

Yet Hitler's one redeeming feature, mentioned by every witness, was his mesmer-ic eyes – bright blue, bordering on violet, they seemed to transfix every member of the audience when he spoke. A policeman who had previously disliked him intensely grudgingly attended a Nazi rally, and found himself gazing at the future Führer as he entered the hall. Hitler looked straight at him with his hypnotizing and irresistible stare, and the man was lost. 'From that moment,' he told his friends the following day, 'I became a National Socialist. Heil Hitler!'

He may have lacked the physique or bearing of a Wagnerian god, but Hitler certainly had the right message, at the right time, to captivate the German people. The entire nation was still suffering from the humiliation of losing the Great War, combined with economic misery brought about by the financial collapse of the Weimar Republic. To a desperate people, Hitler seemed no ordinary politician, but a god-like figure from the German past who had come to save the nation and lead the people back to prosperity, self-respect and power. For this reason alone he was greet-ed with almost universal approval and admiration. As the historian Eberhard Jackel wrote, 'What they felt for him was an almost childlike devotion to a beloved father, a devotion that could easily dissolve into compassion.' Given this climate, it was simple for his underlings to create a powerful personality cult around the Führer. As if to complement his incarnation as the father figure of a reborn Germany, his birth-days at once became one of the most important events in the Nazi calendar. A new national 'Father's Day' was created, which commenced with modest celebrations of

1934, progressed to the interminable military parades of 1939, and ended with a final macabre celebration in the Berlin bunker as the city was falling to the Russians. The myth of Hitler as untainted redeemer of his people was so successful that his mistakes were blamed, like Mussolini's, not on the man himself but on the fallible timeservers in his party. For this reason there was precious little opposition, with a few notable exceptions, at any stage of his despotic rule, from 1933 until 1945. Even when it was apparent that the war was irretrievably lost, the people remained faithful, and were shocked and outraged by the Officer's Bomb Plot led by Count von Stauffenberg. Acting quickly, Hitler went on German radio within a few hours of staggering wounded – but still alive – from the Wolf's Lair; he explained what had happened and demanded the nation retain its loyalty to their Führer. His appeal was a complete success, and at a stroke he regained not only control of the nation but also the renewed love of the German people. To have felt nothing but sympathy for a man who had wasted the lives of millions of young men, and had brought the country to the very edge of disaster, was an extraordinary phenomenon. It possibly justifies the claim that Hitler's was the most successful personality cult in history.

Although less dramatic than Hitler's, the cult of Stalin was destined to survive his death and continue for several years, until it was memorably denounced by Nikita Khrushchev (1894–1971; premier of USSR 1958–1964) in February 1956. Addressing the Supreme Soviet, he began with the words, 'Comrades, the cult of the individual acquired such monstrous size chiefly because Stalin himself, using all conceivable methods, supported the glorification of his own person.' The national recognition that Khrushchev was correct contrasted dramatically with the unprecedented mourning that had swept through the Soviet Union three years before, when the news broke that the great Stalin was dead. Huge crowds of weeping mourners had flocked into Red Square to see his body lying in state in the Kremlin; several hundred of them were crushed to death in the melée. Even those who had suffered under his cruel and despotic rule, and there were millions of them, seemed suddenly bereft. It was as if a member of their own family had died. Some lamented the passing of the charismatic leader who had led them triumphantly through the Great Patriotic War; others were shocked to realize that they now faced a bleak and uncertain future, bereft of the firm hand that had controlled their lives for decades. 'What shall we do now that Comrade Stalin is dead? What shall we do?' lamented one young Russian found kneeling on a Moscow street.

Some commentators believe that Stalin's personality cult had been successful partly as a result of the Russian peasants' traditional need to worship God through a single human being. In the past, this had been enshrined in the person of the Tsar, the little father of his people, a good and honest ruler who would protect them from dishonest officials and tyrannical landlords. Certainly Stalin looked the part, with his comforting moustache, smiling face and gentle gestures. The image was further enhanced by his ubiquitous pipe, which proved to be little more than a stage prop to reassure the people, for he hardly ever lit it. The character presented to the Russian people was that of kindly 'Uncle Joe', dedicating his life to providing a better future for his people. The Russians' need for a constant and protecting presence, even in death, was astutely provided by the Central Committee of the Communist Party when Lenin died in 1923. His embalmed body was put on display in a mausoleum in Red Square, and soon became a site of pilgrimage for the Communist faithful from all over Russia. In 1953 Stalin joined him, but his embalmed corpse was summarily removed on the orders of Khrushchev eight years later – still some five years after his address to the Supreme Soviet – and banished to an obscure burial site near the Kremlin wall. He justified this by saying, 'The further retention in the mausoleum of the sarcophagus with the bier of J.V. Stalin shall be recognized as inappropriate since the serious violations by Stalin of Lenin's precepts, abuse of power, mass repressions against honourable Soviet people, and other activities in the period of the personality cult make it impossible to leave the bier with his body in the mausoleum of V. I. Lenin.'

The only flaw in Stalin's otherwise successful personality cult was that he genuinely hated the limelight and preferred to manipulate events from behind the scenes. Only appearing in public when absolutely necessary, he would sit at the edge of every discussion group at the Kremlin, saying little but observing all. Much of his slow and measured style of public speaking derived from the discrete lessons he had received at the Moscow State Theatre in the early 1930s, where he also learned to use his pipe to enhance his image. He was instructed to smile frequently, to introduce telling pauses in his speeches, and to gaze deeply at his audience at frequent intervals. As his confidence grew he introduced little touches of his own, such as returning the applause when he finished a speech in the manner of a modern footballer clapping back at the crowd. Stalin avoided flamboyant uniforms on public occasions; like Hitler, he wore only one simple decoration – Hitler's was the Iron Cross First Class, and Stalin's the badge of Hero of the Revolution. The message of both was unequivocal – we possess the noble virtues of simplicity and accessibility. The obvious similarities between the personality cults of these two has been well documented. One of their many biographers, Richard Overy, suggests that they needed and utilized ritual adoration, and to be constantly in the public eye – if not in person, then in image. Above all they presented themselves as messianic figures sacrificing themselves for the sake of their people, and therefore free from all normal moral constraints.

The progress of Stalin's personality cult was in direct proportion to the elevation of his visual image, as seen on posters and display material of the time. Throughout the 1920s and 1930s his face grew in size as he tightened his grip on the Soviet Union. When he first took over from Lenin in 1924, images of his face were always smaller than that of the dead leader's and he was always shown standing behind him. Over the years, it grew insidiously larger until they were given equal visual weight. By the late 1930s Lenin had disappeared altogether and Stalin was the single dominant figure in all government display material. The turning point was the May Day Parade of 1932 at which, for the first time, the colossal statues of Lenin and Stalin were of equal size. When a film biography of the departed leader, *Lenin in October*, appeared in 1937, historical fact was ignored; Stalin was present in almost every scene as the wise adviser, encouraging Lenin's every move. Likewise, in all Communist Party literature Stalin steadily replaced Lenin as the fount of Communist wisdom. In 1934 every schoolchild in the Soviet Union was given a copy of the great leader's philosophy, much as Chinese children would one day be given a copy of *The Thoughts of Chairman Mao*. This document heaped fawning praise on the great leader, describing him as 'the inspired guide of the proletariat' and 'the wisest man of our times'. All artistic representations of Stalin, or anything written about him, were governed by an official rulebook – *What to Write about the Life and Activities of Comrade Stalin* – that artists or writers ignored at their peril. In essence the myth of the portrait became the reality, shackling Stalin to his own contrived image and making it impossible for him ever to abandon either his pipe or his trademark moustache. (The German people would probably have been aghast if Hitler had shaved off his moustache, too.). Nor was his cult confined to visual imagery; by the 1940s, the very name of the leader had been imposed like a brand on towns and cities throughout the Soviet Union. Apart from Stalingrad, there were Stalinsk, Stalinogorsk, Stalinbad and dozens more. One communist party member even summoned up the courage to write to the head of Soviet cultural affairs, complaining that the Stalin name cult had gone too far. 'In the end, this sacred and beloved name may make so much noise in people's heads that it will have the opposite effect.'

Although this advice was ignored in the Soviet Union, it might well have found favour with one of Europe's quieter despots. Dr António Salazar (1889–1970) of Portugal, who became dictator of Portugal in 1933, had witnessed the excesses of the personality cults in Italy, Russia and Germany. He maintained his low profile rule until he was incapacitated by a stroke in 1968, carefully avoiding the trademark rallies and gaudy military uniforms favoured by Mussolini and, to a lesser extent, his close neighbour, General Franco in Spain. A sombre figure, determined to promote traditional values in his country, Salazar maintained an iron grip on Portuguese society. Like Stalin, he had as a young man contemplated becoming a priest before studying law at Coimbra University. His political ideas derived from a passionate commitment to Roman Catholicism that led him to take to the streets to oppose the socialist views of the Portuguese First Republic. When he came to power, Salazar introduced a new constitution similar to the fascist system that already existed in Germany and Italy. With the inevitable support of the army and the security police, Salazar brought authoritarian rule to Portugal. However, it was not as bloody as other dictatorships, and a personality cult of the leader – or even any glorification of the ruling party – was totally absent. Rather than pursuing a grandiose idea of foreign conquest (as Mussolini had done), Portugal maintained its significant colonial empire in Africa; and rather than make dramatic changes in social policy, Salazar introduced his own concept of the 'Estado Novo' or New State, by which Portugal would be guaranteed stability but would enjoy only modest economic growth. Although his economic system was corporative in nature, it was based on the Papal encyclicals *Rerum Novarum* and *Quadragesimo Anno*, that were supposed to prevent class struggle or the triumph of materialism.

For the next 35 years, Portugal was run as a low-key bourgeois dictatorship with the grey-suited Salazar at its head and the Roman Catholic Church its ethical driving force. To keep his fiefdom in order and free of subversive left-wing contamination, Salazar relied heavily on the PIDE secret police, an organization that was consciously modelled on the German Gestapo. Dissidents were vigorously pursued; the state's principal enemy was the international communist movement based in the USSR. However, Salazar's regime was moderate compared to other European dictatorships, such as Franco's. Aware of 20th century philosopher Karl Popper's dictum that a society can be threatened from the right as well as the left, Salazar eventually banned the National Syndicalists, Portugal's main fascist party, for being 'too pagan and too totalitarian'. As befitted the little world that Portugal had been reduced to, his own party, the National Union, existed merely to support the regime and promoted little else, ignoring the outside world and its dangerous political theories. Although careful to keep his distance politically, there is no doubt that Salazar had great sympathy for fascist Italy and admired what Mussolini was doing there. He was equally sympathetic to General Franco and gave him his full support during the Spanish Civil War. In many ways, Franco and Salazar complemented each other – even to the extent of keeping their countries neutral in the Second World War, in spite of the obvious temptation to join Hitler's side in the early years.

As a result of Salazar's highly conservative economic policies, the wealth of the ruling oligarchy increased significantly while the Portuguese people became amongst the poorest in Europe. The much-vaunted stability that he had delivered led only to stagnation in the long term, and was compounded by Salazar's own distrust of materialism. He remained convinced that any significant rise in living standards would inevitably 'leave in darkness all that is spiritual' in the human being. In other words, it was important to keep the people poor to keep them pious. He was wary of providing an open education that would allow the Portuguese to develop subversive ideas, so spending on higher education was carefully controlled and all literature and publications heavily censored. Obedience and acceptance of one's lot were the order of the day. Suspicious by nature, Salazar made the administration of Portugal peculiarly his own, delegating little and taking a keen interest in every aspect of government. The result was national apathy; the people gave up even attempting to have a say in the running of their country. The nation's isolationism was compounded by Salazar's own reluctance to travel abroad after the Second World War, or to allow Portugal's overseas possessions their independence. Small wonder that his colourless obscurantism appeared increasingly irrelevant in the late 20th century.

While dictatorships and their associated personality cults were a relatively new experience for modern Europe, they were an established fact of life in Latin America. None was more flamboyant in the years following the Second World War than that of Rafael Trujillo of the Dominican Republic. Trujillo had little interest in political theory, other than instinctive admiration of the ornate fascism that had characterized the rule of Mussolini. In reality, Trujillo was little more than a typical Dominican *caudillo* or warlord, who exercised absolute control of his country. As a declared anti-communist, he was treated with sympathy by the United States, which encouraged him to outlaw the PCD, (Dominican Communist Party) at the start of the Cold War. In return, Washington was happy to turn a blind eye to Trujillo's venal and despotic rule, and only too pleased to have a loyal ally at the centre of the Caribbean. He proceeded to rule the country like a feudal lord for 31 years, holding the office of president from 1930–1938 and 1942–1952. In between, he still retained absolute power while leaving the ceremonial affairs to puppet presidents such as his brother. Safe from outside political interference, after 1947 Trujillo set about building himself a monstrous personality cult that contrasted markedly with both his physical stature and the strategic importance of his country. Always meticulously dressed in military uniform, decked out in gold braid and garish decorations, Trujillo presented himself to the people at interminable military parades. His overweening conceit required that the highest mountain in the country become Pico

Trujillo; the capital city, Santo Domingo, was renamed Ciudad Trujillo and embellished with dozens of new civic buildings of doubtful architectural merit. The obligatory statues of Trujillo, an estimated 100,000 of them, appeared everywhere. In a practical touch, the board of public works provided drinking fountains in his honour for every town. These bore the simple legend 'Trujillo provides water'. Even the Nigua Insane Asylum had a poster on its wall proclaiming 'We owe everything to Trujillo'. Like dictators in Christian countries, he ordered that his portrait appear alongside or instead of that of Christ in every house in the Dominican Republic. This new role as a semi-religious figure must have appealed to him, for he then declared himself 'Godfather of the Nation' and offered to personally baptise any child born during his presidency. To almost universal surprise, he went on to keep his word, and actually performed the ceremony for the thousands of babies that were brought to his palace. An astute populist, he also ensured the loyalty of poor workers by ordering that their traditional Creole dance music, the *merengue*, become the national music of the Dominican Republic; he frequently pleased the crowd by dancing to it himself in public.

But there was a far more sinister side to Trujillo's rule. His enemies were ruthlessly dealt with, killed and often dismembered, their remains thrown into his shark grotto or fed to a ferocious pack of dogs. His legendary nepotism reached absurd proportions, as when he made his 7-year-old son a colonel in the army and a general at the age of 10. Equally fatuous, but in the established despotic tradition, were the titles he assumed, such as 'First Journalist of the Republic', 'Genius of Peace', 'Protector of All Workers', 'Saviour of the Homeland' and 'Undefeated Generalissimo of the Dominican Armies'. He organized a campaign to lobby for the Nobel Peace Prize for himself, and the Literature Prize for his wife. The corrupting nature of power had divorced him completely from the real world.

CHAPTER 9

The Pursuit of a Big Idea

Throughout history the aspiring despot has sought to justify the seizure of power by claiming that it is in a good cause – that he is either obeying God's will, or following the principles of an all-embracing political system. In the case of both Hitler and Stalin it was the pursuit of a totalitarian system, Nazism and Communism respectively. In pursuit of the 'big idea', the end justifies the means and the promise of some form of golden future is all that is needed to explain the imposition of present misery. But long before modern political ideologies were conceived, it was still a single big idea that motivated ancient tyrants. In the case of Qin Shi Huang, the first emperor of China, the concept was of a unified country free of foreign interference, governed by a single ruler. Until Qin appeared in the 3rd century BC, China was divided into six separate kingdoms, each constantly at war with the others. The future despot endured a typically miserable and humiliating childhood as a hostage at the court of the King of Zhao. Returning to his own state of Qin as its child king in 247 BC, he eventually seized full power at the age of 21 and then began an aggressive campaign against the neighbouring Chinese kingdoms. One by one he attacked, defeated and annexed them, having armed his troops much better than his rivals. Advances in military technology now allowed the casting of individual weapons for foot soldiers, so making them the deciding element in battle; in the past, wars had been decided by a small number of aristocrats mounted on chariots.

When a kingdom was conquered, it became part of the Qin nation and enjoyed the same rights and responsibilities. It also shared a written system of justice that was unique in Asia at the time. Other measures were equally enlightened, such as the abolition of feudalism and the appointment of a civilian governor to administer each of the 36 regions of the unified China. To minimize the endemic corruption of Chinese society and to discourage rebellion, these governors were regularly moved to different regions to prevent them establishing a local power base. To further avoid the risk of an armed uprising, Qin ordered that every weapon in civilian hands be handed in to the authorities and then melted down – literally turning swords into ploughshares. All members of defeated royal houses and their families and attendants, an estimated 120,000 people, were then ordered to leave their defeated kingdoms and move to the Qin capital at Xianyang where the Emperor could keep them under close observation – much as Louis XIV would later do with his potentially rebellious nobles at the Palace of Versailles.

These far-sighted reforms were merely the start of a long unification process that continued throughout Qin's reign. Perhaps the single most important measure was the development of a single script for the different Chinese languages. For the first time in Chinese history, written communications could be sent from the capital Xianyang right across China, so making both commerce and government far more efficient. Even today, the different spoken languages of Mandarin and Cantonese share the script that was devised under Emperor Qin.

Yet this man remains condemned by many historians for his attack on Chinese literature, which showed he was more afraid of ideas than he was of people. In a move that made the Nazi book burnings of Göbbels look mild, Qin ordered that all the books in China, with a few exceptions, be burnt. Those excluded were books that mentioned himself or were of practical use, such as medical treatises or building manuals. Every work of poetry and philosophy, particularly Confucianism, was to be destroyed. Anyone who did not complete the task within 30 days was branded on the face before being sent to labour on building the Great Wall; on one occasion, Qin ordered that 469 scholars who continued to disobey him be buried alive. Anyone daring to talk about the lost books, or to quote from them, was summarily executed. In what was an early form of police state, those who knew of any transgressions and did not report them suffered the same punishment. All other laws introduced by Qin were enforced equally ruthlessly, with such penalties as cutting off the left foot or branding on the face for stealing, or being torn apart by chariots for treason. Perhaps the cruellest edict was that if just one person was found guilty of a crime, he was to be killed along with his family, his extended family, his fellow classmates, villagers, teachers, friends and acquaintances. Yet this barbaric assault on Chinese culture contrasted strongly with Qin's continued fascination with practical reforms, such as the unification of the currency into just two kinds of coinage, gold and copper. Measurements and axle length were made uniform, so that cartwheels anywhere in the country would fit the ruts in the roads; public works projects were initiated, including a system of canals for better irrigation and transport. New roads were constructed to link the towns and cities throughout China, making trade far easier. These innovative roads were indeed one of the great achievements of his reign, built to exact specifications – 300 feet (91 m) wide and lined with pine trees planted at 30-foot (9.1 m) intervals – they have survived in part to this day. There were three major highways, totalling over 4,200 miles (6,759 km) in length – even longer than the Roman roads that led from Scotland to Rome itself.

By 215 BC, Qin Shi Huang was the ruler of a completely unified country. In that year he sent 300,000 troops with his most successful general, Meng Tian, to China's northern border, where he defeated the barbarian Huns threatening invasion and then went on to recover China's lost territories in the region. After this, Qin ordered the building of what would become his most lasting physical monument: the Great Wall of China. It could at least be said of Qin's despotic reign that it was for a purpose that can still be appreciated in the context of modern China. Grandiose works that satisfied his vanity but drained the economy became an obsession in his later years, driven by his second and far more personal idea – the pursuit of immortality.

Qin Shi Huang had already started taking practical steps to prolong his life when his doctors prescribed a therapy long believed to increase longevity – group sex with multiple partners. To this regime his new court physician, Xu Fu, suggested adding a substance to his diet that was supposed to prolong life indefinitely. So it was that the emperor began taking the deadly liquid metal that would soon kill him – mercury. There was also a Chinese legend that spoke of the Peng Lai islands, where immortals were said to reside forever thanks to a mysterious elixir. Qin Shi Huang now commanded Xu Fu to mount an expedition to find them; thousands of soldiers were conscripted to carry out the search.

Meanwhile and for many years previously, a vast new imperial palace and emperor's tomb had been under construction, involving 700,000 workers. It was ready just in time for Qin's death in 210 BC. Accompanying him to the afterlife were his terracotta warriors – a testament to the incredible skills and organization of Chinese craftsmen at the time. In a last act of tyranny, however, the emperor ordered that the workmen who had laboured to make his tomb should be entombed alive with him, so that they could not divulge the secrets of what it contained. It was an appropriate gesture for a man whose brilliance as a ruler was only matched by his capacity for callous and ruthless cruelty. An epitaph for him was written by one of his own officials, Heou, who declared, 'Though he has suppressed the feudal lords and reunited the empire he is a man who received from heaven a violent, cruel and despotic nature… only his judges and executioners can approach him and gain his favour while his 75 scholars of vast learning must content themselves with empty titles, for they are not employed in any work worthy of them.'

Judging by the performance of the Roman emperors two centuries later, Qin's reign was a model of efficiency, and of sustained – if brutal – progress. But while he was driven by the quest to modernize a disorganised and archaic society, the Roman emperors were content to live in the reflected glory of past achievements. The great road system that linked the empire to Rome was largely completed by the time that Augustus became emperor in 27 BC, and the barbarian tribes, although a constant threat, were kept at bay by the power of the legions. Technical innovations were few, and the principles on which the empire was administered had long since been established. Consequently, there was little need for reform within Rome itself that could be used by an aspiring emperor to justify a coup. There was also little need for overseas expansion, for Rome had conquered all that it wanted of the known world. Not until the reign of Constantine in the 3rd century AD would a single ethical idea – the conversion of the Roman Empire to Christianity – be used as a justification for the seizure of power.

Consequently, the earlier Roman emperors had only their personalities or their promises of rewards to supporters to support any claim to the throne. There could be no appeal to nationalist sympathies, for the only nationalists known to the Romans were barbarian tribes such as the Gauls and Goths. Inward looking and selfish, these regimes were both politically and sexually incestuous, as power became concentrated in the hands of a few scheming patrician families. The rules of both Caligula and Nero are just extreme examples of this increasingly degenerate Rome; their fall was more the product of their own flawed characters than of administrative weakness.

Nationalism was absent from the medieval as well as the ancient world. Both the Mongolian warlords, Genghis Khan and Tamerlane, ruled at a time when their peoples were driven by a common urge to conquer – not out of a sense of Mongol nationalism, but purely for plunder and out of the sheer exuberance of conquest. They were not concerned with building settlements, but only with transportable booty that they could eventually carry back to their homeland. It was not until the arrival of Vlad Tepes that territorial nationalism would be invoked as justification for a ruthless regime. With the fall of Constantinople on 29 May 1453, the Turkish Sultan Mehmet II appeared to have the whole of eastern Europe at his mercy, and he proceeded to mop up the remaining Byzantine possessions in the Morea unopposed. While the rest of Christendom wondered what to do about the Turkish threat, Vlad Tepes of Walachia moved swiftly, securing his throne by uniting his people in a nationalistic and Christian-inspired struggle to throw off Turkish rule.

The first modern invocation of the 'big idea' was the demand for social equality and justice that underpinned the French Revolution of 1789. It became the justification for the state tyranny that followed, its protagonists determined that it must be defended at all costs. Later historians saw the significance of the French Revolution in a very different light. Arnold Toynbee in his monumental work, *A Study Of History*, identified it as the moment at which our civilization ceased growing and began to disintegrate. By comparing the Revolution to events in numerous past civilizations, Toynbee was able to identify the eruption of class war as the single common factor in the start of social disintegration. This began, he claimed, with an explosion of civil violence caused by the tyranny of the ruling class. Toynbee's words echoed those of Edmund Burke who thought that the democracy demanded by the French Revolution, and later adopted in principle throughout Europe and America, was a dangerous call for 'fearless' rule that would crush the individual. Most dangerous of all was the adoption of universal suffrage, which would mean that the majority of citizens no longer considered themselves as loyal subjects of the state, but as individuals who recognised no authority but their own wishes, which was the rule of selfishness. In the end, the French Revolution was not a protest against a particular tyranny, but against authority in general. It marked the time when authority stopped being the master and started being the servant of its charges. The ideas that drove the Revolution were an immediate danger to all other European nations. Since late 1791 the other monarchies had followed events in France with growing alarm, as they witnessed the marginalization and humiliation of King Louis XVI. Should these ideas spread throughout Europe, then long-established dynasties would soon be under a similar threat. Consequently, an anti-revolutionary alliance led by Prussia and Saxony began to emerge, causing the Assembly in Paris to introduce ever more draconian measures to discourage any attempt at a counter-revolution.

On 20 April 1792 Austria declared war on France and the new Minister for War, Charles Dumouriez, was faced with having to challenge a powerful enemy with a force that had lost the greater part of its officer corps. Suspicion of all foreigners now induced a national paranoia that led the Assembly to declare the fatherland in danger. Although the King had opposed the recruitment of the new militia, thousands converged on Paris to join up. In a desperate move to maintain law and order, the Assembly appealed, unsuccessfully, to the King to abdicate in favour of his son. Rather than face the consequences of a humiliating treaty with the enemy, the Assembly eventually united in a determination to fight on, knowing that any agreement would inevitably involve the restoration of the monarchy and imprisonment or worse for themselves. Robespierre expressed their anger and frustration in a speech that accused the King of being in traitorous contact with the Austrian invaders. New decrees were issued ordering the deportation of recalcitrant priests, the abolition of the royal bodyguard and rapid recruitment of a 20,000 strong militia to protect Paris against any attempt at a royalist coup. As the armies of Austria and

Prussia gathered on the borders to threaten the new French Republic, the Jacobins under Maximilian Robespierre induced the Convention to ratify despotic measures, thus weeding out the supposed traitors in their midst. Their argument was that this 'fifth column' would join the invading armies to overthrow the hard-won freedoms that French citizens now enjoyed. As a result of this national paranoia, over a thousand aristocrats and supporters of the old regime were dragged out of the Temple prison in Paris and butchered in the streets, while the deputies in the Convention began denouncing each other in the manner that became familiar in Stalin's Russia of the late 1930s. A climate of fear and insecurity descended on France; no one involved in public life appeared safe.

The situation was striking: this was not the despotism of a single individual, but of a group. In many ways it demonstrated Gustave Le Bon's theory that in unusual circumstances, the members of a group abandon their individual ethical principles and join together in an emotional action that can often be tyrannical. The almost hysterical banding together of a group of nominally democratic politicians had never occurred before. Nor could the situation last; the protagonists, terrified of mutual denunciation, began to turn on each other like rats in a trap. Only with the overthrow of Robespierre and his Jacobins, followed by the advent of Napoleon and the return of a single authority, did any sense of individual safety return to the French people. The simple basis on which The Terror had briefly succeeded was that the end justified the means; the rights of the individual had to be sublimated to the security and preservation of the new state. This was something new in history. It would show the way ahead for future despots, who would use the same excuse to justify the most fundamental oppression of the individual.

The effect of the French Revolution was devastating, and not just because it demonstrated how people could be motivated by the ideal of freedom; it also showed how chaos can occur in a revolutionary situation, and how law and order can be restored by a strong single individual unconcerned by political issues. One keen student of the Revolution was José Gaspar Rodríguez de Francia in faraway Paraguay. A devotee of the Enlightenment and a keen reader of Voltaire, Jean-Jacques Rousseau and the French Encyclopaedists, Francia was destined to be the first of many Paraguayan despots who modelled themselves on Napoleon. His childhood was predictably traumatic, spent in the company of an eccentric father and lunatic brothers and sisters. When Francia was born in 1757, Paraguay was a relatively small, landlocked South American country ruled by Spain; by the time he became president in 1814, it had become independent of both its colonial master and neighbouring Argentina. The only man with the necessary diplomatic, financial, and administrative skills to run the country, Francia immediately proclaimed himself dictator for three years, and then for life. Once in power, his character appeared to change from reclusive intellectual – he possessed the largest library in Asunción – to man of action. With remarkable energy he proceeded to impose on Paraguay what Scottish historian Thomas Carlyle has described as 'the boldest and most extraordinary system of despotism that was ever the work of a single individual'. The whole power of the state, both legislative and executive, became vested in his single person. All that was required of the people was to obey his commands; these were enforced by the army, which consisted of 5,000 regular troops and 20,000 militia, who were naturally given many privileges that were denied the ordinary people. However, the national finances were accurately and frugally administered, and disputes were settled objectively in the courts of law. Unusually for such a regime, no government sinecures were allowed, and every official was compelled to work honestly; even monks were sent out to work in the fields (not slaughtered, as they would later be in Pol Pot's Cambodia). In an act of revenge against the elite of Spanish descent, who he thought had discriminated against him because of his supposed impure blood, Francia forbade them from marrying each other – so forcing them to choose spouses from among the native population.

Francia's big and very strange idea, emulated to a lesser degree by later despots such as Enver Hoxha of Albania (1908–1985; ruled 1944–1985) and Kim Il Sung of North Korea, was that of total exclusivity: to cut his country off completely from the outside world, and let it develop in isolation. Communication with any other nation was forbidden by law, and nearly all forms of foreign commerce were banned. Paraguay's trading vessels were left to rot on the riverbanks; no one could engage in trade without a licence from the dictator. Virtually the only imports allowed were guns and ammunition for the army, used to enforce the ban. All Paraguayans were forbidden to travel abroad, and this already landlocked country now became almost hermetically sealed from the rest of an immense and thinly peopled continent. Those foreigners who found their way in by accident or design were arrested, for Paraguay had become a mouse-trap – easy enough to enter, but very difficult to leave. Three European explorers, colleagues of the great botanist Alexander von Humbolt, who wandered in by mistake were detained there for years. Sometimes, by special permission of the president, an individual might be allowed to leave; but such occasions were rare. Guards were placed along the borders to prevent anyone passing in or out, and were ordered to seize contraband materials, such as books that might contain subversive ideas. Anyone bold enough to attempt escape faced not only the border guards but the formidable natural barriers of wide rivers and virtually impenetrable jungle. The only practical means of escape was by boat down the river Paraguay, a journey attempted by a French visitor who set out to escape in 1823 with five negro servants. The bid for freedom ended in disaster, one man dying of fatigue and another of snakebite. Near death himself, the Frenchman and his remaining companions finally surrendered to the rural militia.

Although commerce with the outside world was lost, Francia carefully fostered Paraguay's internal industries, such as farming. But the dangers of isolation became apparent in 1820, when devastation by locusts produced a nationwide famine. Unable to import food from outside Paraguay, the country faced disaster until Francia ordered, under the threat of dire punishment, that the farmers immediately re-sow their land with a second crop. The resulting harvest was so successful that the system was adopted permanently, so doubling the national agricultural yield each year. Soon rice and cotton were also being cultivated, and new industries such as textiles introduced. Written accounts of Francia's regime emphasize both its far-sighted wisdom and its flagrant violation of the simplest principles of justice. Internal espionage destroyed free speech; people were arrested without charge and disappeared without trial. Interrogation and torture took place in the so-called Chamber of Truth, and each year, over 400 political prisoners were sent to a detention camp where they were shackled in dungeons and denied medical care. Yet at Francia's death in 1844, Paraguay had developed a strong, prosperous economy, and its independence had been secured at a time when its continued existence as a distinct country seemed unlikely. In spite of his strange theories, Francia left a country at peace, with full government coffers and with many new industries flourishing. Throughout his reign, he remained tremendously popular with the lower classes despite having trampled on their human rights, and having imposed an authoritarian police state based on espionage and coercion.

While Francia had pursued his idea of Paraguay as an isolationist state with marked success, his successor but one, Francisco Solano López (1827-1870; dictator of Paraguay 1862–1870), did exactly the opposite. López had the bright idea of involving his small country in unprovoked aggression; his attempt to make Paraguay the dominant power in the region was a total disaster, and resulted in the near-disappearance of the small country as an independent state. A pampered child, López was groomed from early childhood to inherit the presidency from his father Don Carlos López (1790–1862), Francia's successor. Made a brigadier general at 18, López went off to France to buy arms on behalf of the government. In Paris he acquired an admiration for Emperor Napoleon III (1808–1873; Emperor of France 1852–1870) and an infatuation for an Irish-born adventuress, Elisa Alicia Lynch. Returning to Paraguay with the arms and Elisa, he became obsessed by the grandeur he had seen at the French imperial court, and conceived the fatuous idea that little Paraguay could challenge the military hegemony that Brazil and Argentina exercised over the smaller Latin American countries. He began by sending the Brazilian government a letter, demanding that it stop interfering in the revolutionary struggle that was taking place in neighbouring Uruguay. When Brazil predictably ignored his request, López ordered Paraguayan troops to seize a Brazilian-owned merchant ship docked in the river at Asunción. All those on board, including the Brazilian governor of Mato Grosso province, were thrown into jail. Then, before Brazil could respond, López struck again, ordering an expeditionary force to invade diamond-rich Mato Grosso and burn down the capital, Cuiabá.

Not content with provoking the most powerful nation on the continent, López next picked a quarrel with the second. He sent the rest of his small army to support the Uruguayan president Atanasio Aguirre against Brazilian-backed rebels; but to reach Uruguay, the Paraguayan troops had to cross Argentinian territory. When the Argentine president, Bartolomé Mitre (1821–1906), refused to allow them to pass through the province of Corrientes, López declared war on Argentina too. On 13 April 1865, Marshal López (as he now styled himself) seized two Argentine warships moored in the Bay of Corrientes, and announced that Paraguay had annexed the two adjoining Argentine provinces of Corrientes and Entre Ríos. Unfortunately, the revolutionaries had seized power in Uruguay, and joined with Brazil and Argentina in declaring war on Paraguay. After a few initial successes, López was driven back by the combined armies surrounding his country. This inevitable defeat seemed to provoke a severe mental collapse; now he convinced himself, in true despot fashion, that he was surrounded by treachery. Ignoring the desperate military situation, he ordered his soldiers to arrest thousands of supposed traitors who he claimed were plotting his downfall. Many of Paraguay's most prominent citizens were dragged off to execution, among them his own mother, his brothers and brothers-in-law, together with cabinet ministers, judges, prefects, military officers, bishops and priests. Thousands of others, including Paraguay's long-suffering soldiers and generals, went to their deaths before firing squads or were hacked to pieces. In all, over nine-tenths of the civil service were executed, together with more than 200 foreigners, some of them members of the diplomatic legations in Asunción. López might well have been insane at this point, for he attempted to have himself canonized by the local bishops before escaping with a few followers. He headed to Paraguay's northern frontier, where he was eventually hunted down and killed by the invading troops. López's ludicrous attempt to make himself the 'Napoleon of South America' had resulted in the death of half the Paraguayan population, and had come close to wiping his country off the map.

The most significant motivating idea of 20th-century despotism was that of total-itarianism, based on either left- or right-wing political ideology. In return for the promise of a better and well-ordered life, the individual was expected to sublimate his personal interests and freedoms to total control by the state. The dictatorial regimes that resulted from it were as conservative and anti-democratic as any in history. In practise, totalitarian government meant the rule of a single individual under whom social or political change was impossible. These new leaders were the familiar despots of the past, but rebranded by their supporters as men driven by ideas that could benefit the whole community. Their arrival was only made possible by the disillusion and despair that followed the end of the First World War in 1918. There was a perception, particularly in central and eastern European countries, that the government and the ruling classes had failed the people, and that young men had been slaughtered in vain. These nations generally lacked a tradition of strong democratic government, but retained a history of internal ethnic conflict made more acute by the steady growth in nationalism. When the new totalitarian dictators appeared in Russia, Italy and Germany they had the great advantage of being able to use the new sophisticated communication techniques of cinema and radio to promote themselves and their ideologies. The result was a society in which the regime governed and controlled every aspect of an individual's life. Everything became subject to state control under the modern dictator – the economy, politics, religion, culture, philosophy, science, history, entertainment and even thought itself. In many ways this was the completion of a process that had begun during the First World War, when both the national economy and individual rights were subordinat-ed to the task of winning, whatever the human cost.

The word totalitarian was first used to describe the all-embracing society of fascist Italy under Mussolini, where every aspect of life, from industrial production to sport, was rigidly controlled by the state. As the dictator said in October 1925, 'All is for the state; nothing and no one are outside the state.' This was the most compre-hensive definition of fascism ever given, and it appeared to many international observers that it could be equally well applied to Stalin's communist Russia. What gave Mussolini's regime its distinct character was its leader's cheerful commitment to violence as a state objective. Even before the disasters of the First World War, Mussolini had in 1909 declared himself a disciple of the revolutionary syndicalist George Sorel, and his theory of a permanent struggle between the proletariat and the bourgeoisie. Sorel believed that this conflict could re-energise society and produce a whole new system of moral values, but only if the state kept up a constant stream of rapid and profound social reforms imposed from above. This would be a never-ending process, with fulfilment always just out of reach. In this way, individual members of society would remain constantly galvanized for future effort. This theory of the need for constant action was shared by the Italian Futurist art movement, whose leader Filippo Marinetti (1876–1944) had proclaimed a decade before Mussolini came to power that 'There is no beauty if not in struggle... War is our only hope, our reason for living, our only will.' Or as Prezzolini, another of the Futurists, wrote, 'So-called gentility, silence and politeness are often the synonyms for cowardice, lack of argument, weakness of mind... The violence we employ has nothing to do with hatred for others but with love of ourselves.'

Mussolini's achievement was to incorporate these artistically derived concepts into his own big political idea for regenerating Italy, using the Italian Fasces of Combat organization that he founded in 1919 to bring it about. A party so committed to violence naturally provoked profound hostility from the more traditional and democratic Italians. The Fascists responded vigorously by attacking their opponents with cudgels and forcing them to drink massive doses of castor oil. Fascism and violence were inseparable; in 1921 alone, between 500 and 600 socialists died on the streets of Italian cities, and hundreds of left-wing libraries, bookshops and cultural centres were destroyed. Mussolini ensured that Fascist thugs were lionized by the party; when occasionally killed, they were beatified, just as the Nazis created martyrs such as Horst Wessel.

The regimes of Fascist Italy, Nazi Germany and Soviet Russia used the forces of the state to repress both discussion and dissent among the people. Put simply, state terror would be visited on anyone who disputed the ruling party or challenged its ideology. In the Soviet Union the task was easier, for Stalin inherited an established totalitarian system that had been forged by Lenin. Hitler, however, had to create one from the disjointed elements that formed the Weimar Republic. His genius was to realise that a charismatic individual delivering the simple but magnetic ideas of National Socialism held great appeal for a mass audience. Moreover, when combined with a mystical nationalism that sought to unite German-speaking peoples throughout Europe, it presented a formidable challenge to the existing discredited political parties. The emotional message of a resurgent Germany attracted the young, too, who flocked to the Nazi flag in their thousands. In 1931 a survey showed that 40 per cent of all Nazis were under 30 years of age, and 70 per cent were under 40.

Elected chancellor by a democratic majority, Hitler was soon able to delegate the daily administration of his regime to able and efficient subordinates. Leading Nazis were given considerable freedom to develop the detail of any broad strokes of policy suggested by Hitler, without the constant interference that plagued Russia in the

1930s. The most obvious example was the complicated logistics of implementing the Final Solution of the Jewish problem. Once Hitler had agreed to wholesale extermination in principle, the details were left to the likes of Reinhard Heydrich, Artur Sess Inqart and Adolf Eichmann to develop and carry out. Although this may seem simple and efficient delegation, it should be remembered that Hitler was notoriously lazy. Stalin, by contrast, viewed the input of his subordinates with increasing suspicion, and any individual success as a potential challenge to his own supremacy. Lacking Hitler's almost insouciant disregard for detail, he involved himself in all the minutiae of communist policy, particularly security and the purges generated by his rabid paranoia. Whereas Hitler avoided personal involvement with the concentration camps, Stalin poured over death lists on an almost daily basis.

Both the great 20th-century despots were able, in the early years of their rule, to present their respective ideologies as being of material as well as abstract benefit to the people. The early years of Nazism produced a booming economy in Germany, and the consequent surge in employment led to a significant rise in the standard of living for the average German. Visitors to the country in the mid to late 1930s were impressed by the economic progress they witnessed, and tended to minimize the dangerous rhetoric that Hitler and his leading supporters were spouting. The National Socialist system appeared to be working well; there were new autobahns to drive on and new houses for the workers to live in. Few outsiders attributed the booming economy to the ominous build-up in the armaments industry. The British politician David Lloyd George, who visited Berlin in 1936, reported approvingly:

> I have seen the famous German leader and also the great changes he has
> made. Whatever one may think of his methods – and they certainly aren't
> those of a parliamentary country – there can be no doubt that he has
> achieved a marvellous change in the spirit of the people, and in their
> economic and social outlook.

Despite Hitler's increasing demands for the restitution of supposed German territory, international opinion was agreed that the Führer appeared to have worked a near-miracle on the economy and had restored the self-respect of the German people. As John Toland, a later biographer of Hitler, succinctly wrote, 'If Hitler had died in 1937 he would undoubtedly have gone down as one of the greatest figures in German history.' It was after the Austrian Anschluss the following year, when Germany virtually annexed Austria, that the brutal oppression that was an integral part of National Socialism was revealed. Only then did observers begin to realize the full threat of the Nazi regime. But the insouciance of the Western democracies in the 1930s has no better testimony than *Time* magazine's choice of Hitler as its 'Man of the Year' in 1938, and of Stalin the following year.

One great advantage that Hitler had over his fellow despot was that he was able to develop his Nazi philosophy virtually without historical precedent. Stalin had far less room for manoeuvre having inherited Communism; as a materialist creed, it allowed little escape into the heady metaphysics of Volk and bloodline that Hitler enjoyed. Nor was Communism bound to nationalism in the same way as Nazism. Without these abstracts, Stalin had to establish a personality cult that depended more on an image of efficiency, combined with that of a father figure: more the stuff of production figures than of torch-lit processions to the altar of nationalism. Only with the Second World War could Stalin invoke the historic crusade of the courageous Russian people to drive out the foreign invader. This brought him a popularity that he had never previously enjoyed, and Soviet propagandists capitalized upon it by comparing him with the great (if controversial) figures of the past, such as Ivan the Terrible and Catherine the Great.

For all his supposed economic achievements in the 1930s, Hitler ended the Second World War dead and with his reputation in tatters. Not only was he now the most reviled despot in history, but his plan to restore the German nation had led it to unparalleled disaster. One of the most culturally respected societies in Western Europe had become the most reviled, and its people were left to carry the burden of guilt for Hitler's generation for decades. Perhaps the only positive outcome was that no other advanced nation would again support a totalitarian regime; Nazi Germany demonstrated that all-embracing dictatorship leads inevitably to disaster. Unfortunately it took several more decades before the Soviet Union learned a similar lesson. Success in the Great Patriotic War (1941–1945) enabled Stalin to sustain Soviet tyranny, cloak himself in nationalism and continue his paranoid rule over the Russian people and the newly acquired satellite nations of Eastern Europe. But Stalin, always far more cunning than Hitler, realized that he must change his ways; although the persecution of dissident individuals continued, it was far less rigorous than it had been in the late 1930s. With the Western democracies weakened by the cost of the war, Stalin now enjoyed a golden period in which he was able to offer the Soviet economy and social system as a viable alternative. Not until his death, when full details of his long tyranny were released, did the world realize that the monster of Soviet Communism was responsible for even more deaths than Hitler.

Despots with a big idea have never, so far, reappeared in Europe. They continued to arise in Latin America and Africa, but because of their irrelevance to world politics, they were largely ignored. One such tyrant operating in a political backwater was François 'Papa Doc' Duvalier of Haiti, the close neighbour of another petty despot, Rafael Trujillo of the Dominican Republic. Duvalier's big idea was the concept of negritude. This was a movement begun in the 1930s by a group of black Haitian and American intellectuals who believed that their common black identity should lead them to reassert their racial pride and reject white dominance. The movement had taken root in Haiti as a reaction against the materialism and crude racism demonstrated during the American occupation of the country in the 1920s. A decade later, the young Duvalier joined the movement, believing that blacks like himself should concentrate on their blackness and their roots in Africa rather than model their society on America. Their journal *Les Griots* championed this *noirisme*, and called for the black people to assert their innate superiority over the mulattoes who had traditionally ruled Haiti. Part of this belief involved the rejection of the white man's Christianity and the promotion of African-derived Voodooism as the true religion of the people. Duvalier's writings at this time give a clear indication of how he would implement negritude should he come to power – they are as firmly described as Hitler's resolve to destroy the Jews in *Mein Kampf*. Once elected president, Duvalier moved swiftly to implement his policy by dismissing those of mixed race from positions of power and putting his black supporters in their place.

As Duvalier was inspired by the concept of a brotherhood of blacks, so Saddam Hussein was motivated in his early years by the cause of Pan-Arabism. When the Iraqi monarchy was overthrown in 1958, it was replaced by the military dictatorship of General Kassem, which relied heavily on communist support. Five years later Kassem himself was gone, murdered by a group of Sunni Ba'th army officers that included Saddam Hussein. Following a spectacular and ignominious defeat by Israel in the 1967 war, when Egypt, Syria and Jordan were devastated by Israel's preemptive strike, the cause of Pan-Arabism seemed lost; but then both Iraq and Syria came under the control of a Ba'thist party committed to restoring Arab self-respect by destroying Israel and ending American meddling in Arab affairs. These ambitions were highly popular throughout the Arab world, promising as they did the restoration of the Arab community as a powerful world force. When Saddam Hussein became president of Iraq in 1979, he set about implementing this strategy with the help of the Sunni minority, which inevitably marginalized the Kurdish and Shi'ite majority. Aware of his fragile position, Hussein began concentrating power in the hands of his closest Sunni supporters, who came mainly from his home town of Tikrit. Although militarily competent, the new Iraq that emerged under Hussein was a social and economic disappointment, and any prospect of his regime restoring past

Arab glory was soon lost. In reality, Hussein's Iraq was little more than a primitive despotism, in which he and his allies took whatever they wanted but where most still lived in poverty. The influence of the much-vaunted Ba'thist party was equally illusory. It became a vehicle for corruption and, as the only political party allowed, the recruiting ground for the brutal secret police, the Mukhabarat. This organisation worked hand-in-glove with the Ba'thist party militia, which placed its spies and informers throughout the army to make sure that loyalty to Hussein was maintained.

Hussein's subsequent misjudgements and blunders included a disastrous war with Iran, a failed attempt to annex oil-rich Kuwait and, worst of all, an ill-judged game of bluff with the United States that resulted in the invasion of his country and the total destruction of his regime. Ironically for Hussein, if he had maintained good relationships with his neighbours and with the United States, he might well have proved an able ruler. Artificially created countries like Iraq, its borders decided by international agreements after the First World War, only hang together under firm rule. Yet Hussein's dangerous games were to bring about his downfall, and with it the end of an Iraq-led Pan-Arab state in the Middle East.

Having seen the collapse of Nazism and the disgrace of Stalin, Nicolae Ceausescu was content to avoid fundamental totalitarianism. No great theoretical ideas underpinned his inward-looking regime. He concentrated on promoting his own brand of pragmatic communism, combined with an unusually thorough personality cult. Yet he had one obsession that would earn him the hostility of almost all Romanians: what he grandly described as systematisation. In reality, it was little more than a crude scheme to raze half of all Romania's historic villages to the ground – villages that had remained unaltered since the Middle Ages. In their place he proposed building a series of new 'agro-industrial' mini-towns. The main beneficiary would be Ceausescu himself – the new towns would be easier to police, and the vacated land would be freed for increased agricultural production. Although the original plans for this nationwide vandalism had been drawn up in 1972, the actual demolition did not begin until the late 1980s. Uniquely, Ceausescu managed to unite both sides of the Iron Curtain in opposition to it: as well as protests from cultural and environmental groups all over Western Europe, other communist countries and members of the Warsaw Pact protested, too. What appalled the protestors was not only the loss of thousands of historic buildings, but that systematization was a cover for Ceausescu's real motive – an assault on the ethic minorities of Romania who lived in the old villages. As these minorities had no voice outside the country and as their plight was being ignored by their own government, a Belgian organization, Operation Villages Roumains, was set up with the aim of twinning every village in

Romania with one in the West. It was hoped that this would offer them a voice, and perhaps some form of protection. The move proved to be remarkably successful; although there were gloomy reports of bulldozers flattening historic Saxon and Hungarian villages, only two were actually demolished. These also turned out not to be the homes of ethnic minorities, but Romanian villages close to Bucharest. Their destruction showed what could have been – the inhabitants were given just 24 hours to vacate their houses before they were flattened and the land ploughed up; they were then rehoused in badly built apartment blocks nearby. That Ceausescu rapidly abandoned systematization showed that by the 1970s, even a communist despot could no longer afford to ignore international opinion. Nevertheless, a more low-key form of the scheme continued. In many small towns the old houses were demolished, and the inhabitants relocated in grim new apartment blocks; and although the country towns and villages were largely saved, the capital city of Bucharest came under assault from Ceausescu's bulldozers. Still obsessed with his pet theory, he ordered one quarter of the old city to be demolished to make way for a massive modern development. The entire Uranus district, comprising 10 churches (some with exquisite wall paintings), three historic synagogues and a maze of old streets embellished by villas and small houses were destroyed to make way for Ceausescu's gargantuan new palace. That an area the size of Venice had disappeared, along with over 2,000 square metres of murals on the walls of the Monastery Vacaresti, did not concern him; it was actually portrayed as a benefit to the Romanian people. Like most of his despotic decisions, it was taken unilaterally, for he was reluctant to delegate authority to subordinates and remained obsessively involved in matters of relatively minor significance. His style of policy implementation involved frequent reorganization, constant administrative reshuffling, and rotation of officials between party and state positions.

This monstrosity built in the already discredited Stalinist style was second in size only to the Pentagon in Washington, D.C. The citizens watched in horror as it rose to dominate the Bucharest skyline. What made it even more distasteful was that it was constructed without regard to cost, at a time when severe austerity measures had just been introduced. It was not in any way for the benefit of the Romanian people, but solely for the personal use of Elena and Nicolae, and furnished with the greatest opulence. Nearby was the Palace of the People, another example of monumental Stalinist architecture, standing on a new avenue lined with apartments reserved exclusively for the party faithful and the Securitate. This avenue, longer than the Champs-Élysée, in Paris, was not completed before the Ceausescus' fall; for years afterwards, the rusting cranes served as a memorial to the lost despot. Yet out of

Ceausescu's grandiose architectural schemes there appeared to come one final success. For over a century, there had been a dream of constructing a ship canal to connect the Danube with the Black Sea. Work had begun in 1949, but when criticized by the communist party chief Gheorghiu-Dej (1901–1965) five years later, it was abandoned at the reputed cost of the lives of 60,000 convicts, peasants, priests and ex-landlords who were used as slave labour. Housed in a Russian style gulag at Capul Midia, they endured a harsh climate, disease and beatings. Convinced that the project must be completed, Ceausescu ordered work on the canal to be resumed in 1973. Employing modern machinery rather than convicts armed with shovels, the canal made good progress, although it still required 30,000 workers and was the biggest investment project of its time. This, if little else in Ceausescu's regime, proved to be a remarkable success when it was completed in 1984. But three years later it was running at only a 10th of its capacity, and in the dictator's final years had been written off by the Romanian people as yet another of his white elephants.

The vandalism that the Romanian dictator had wreaked on Bucharest bore a curious similarity to the damage inflicted on the city of Asunción in Paraguay by José Gaspar Rodríguez de Francia, just over a century earlier. Asunción, too, had charming but ramshackle architecture with little uniformity of style, and streets that ran in a haphazard pattern. Francia became obsessed with altering the look of the city, much as he already controlled the lives of its inhabitants. Ignoring the natural topography and without consulting any architects or surveyors, he set out for the city centre with a small army of clerks and masons. Once there, he set down a theodolite and took a straight line sighting to the horizon, then ordered everything in its path – including houses, trees and hills – to be removed, and a new 40-foot-wide (12 m) street to be constructed in their place. Thousands of houses were demolished over the subsequent months, leaving their inhabitants in roofless misery. Anyone who protested was thrown into prison. Existing watercourses were filled in and the cityscape levelled, so that when the rains came large sections of the new works were washed away, creating chaos. It was a classic example of the despotic power of a single megalomaniac.

CHAPTER 10

A Pretension to Culture

Had Hitler been allowed to study art, as he desperately wanted to as a young man, the world might well have been spared the disaster of his political career. Rejected by the Kunstgewerbeschule, Vienna's leading art school, he sank into depression and resentment against a society that had refused to recognize his creativity. Then he channelled his obsession with art into politics. If he had been allowed to join the school, he would have studied alongside the young Oskar Kokoschka (1886–1980), soon to become the most famous Austrian painter of his generation and representative of everything that Hitler loathed about modern art. His unshakeable belief that he knew best in cultural matters was not unique; it has been a characteristic of despots since history began. Many, like Hitler, have claimed to be artistically gifted or shown a keen and interfering interest in their national culture, but none more so than the Emperor Nero. Yet Nero was merely inheriting a tradition that had been established by Caesar Augustus, a pre-eminent patron of the arts during his reign. Patronage of the arts was just one of the measures introduced by Augustus while his political reforms, although apparently benign, were to mark the beginning of the end of representative institutions in Rome. While retaining them in name, Augustus made the people subject to his personal rule as he annexed the roles of consul, tribune, chief priest of the civic religion and public censor. He also claimed to be the *princeps*, first citizen among equals and father of the country, in a primitive form of totalitarianism that would inspire Mussolini to create the office of Il Duce almost two millennia later. Augustus became the virtual dictator of Rome while retaining the resemblance of representative government. Yet he put his power to good use, encouraging and promoting the arts to a degree that no previous Roman leader had ever contemplated, and setting an excellent example to his successors. Augustus was particularly influential in promoting a new architecture that was to transform the city, fully justifying his claim that he 'found Rome a city of brick and left it a city of marble.' Much of the new building work was paid for from his own purse or by members of his household and entourage. It is easy to see where Mussolini derived his inspiration for the programme of monumental civic buildings that were erected in Rome during his period as Italian leader. Under Augustus many of Rome's greatest buildings, such as the Forum, the Ara Pacis Augustae, the Baths of Agrippa, and the Pantheon, were established. Like the Emperor himself, the style of building combined conservatism with innovation and drew inspiration from the architecture of Ancient Greece.

Literature, too, flourished under Augustus, producing what became known as the Golden Age of Roman Literature. In a subtle use of his power, Augustus only allowed poets and artists to be patronized by himself and his family. This enabled him to identify the best poets who could further the ideology of the Augustan government. Under this system some of Rome's greatest writers such as Virgil (70–19 BC), Horace (65–8 BC), Ovid (43 BC–AD 17), Propertius (c.48–15 BC), and Livy (59 BC–AD 17) flourished. Virgil, in particular, produced the *Aeneid*, a new national epic that emphasised the virtues of piety, respect for authority and fortitude in the face of adversity – the very Stoic virtues that Augustus desired for Rome and that his descendant Nero would betray.

As a young man, Nero not only received a good general education but was encouraged by his tutors to study poetry, drama, sculpture and painting in detail. Whatever his failings as emperor, he had a lively and inquiring mind, and would frequently hold dinners for the leading poets of his day. None, of course, could refuse; all were flattered to be asked to discuss their work, although, according to cynics, Nero often stole their best lines and passed them off as his own. These soirées were later extended to include the leading philosophers, such as Seneca (c.4 BC–AD 65), who were invited to debate the finer points of moral issues with the future despot of Rome. Nero's greatest passion, however, was for music. Showing his commitment to becoming an accomplished singer, he often lay down with heavy lead weights on his chest to strengthen his diaphragm. These exercises were accompanied by a special diet and the use of purgatives, in the odd belief that they would improve his performance. Pliny the Elder (AD 23–79) claims that on certain days of the month, the emperor would eat nothing but a strange dish of chives preserved in olive oil to sweeten his voice. He had also learnt to play musical instruments, his favourite being the cithara (a stringed instrument resembling a lyre), which he often played during the Juvenilia games held in Rome. Such vulgar public exhibitionism did not endear him to the members of the Praetorian Guard, who would become his eventual nemesis.

In ancient Rome, sport and the arts were considered part of the same cultural ethos; Nero's obsession with winning chariot races was therefore the perfect complement to his desire to triumph in music and drama. He also shared the universally held Roman obsession with Greek culture, and as a keen Hellenist he sought to revive the Greek games. These events combined sporting prowess with artistic performance –

young men of high social rank competed against each other in oratory, poetry, singing and instrument playing. Nero's enthusiasm for the visual arts was equally profound, as was the personal interest he took in design. The coinage produced during his reign was the finest in Rome's history; the well-executed and highly detailed portrait of Nero as the God Apollo, which appeared on the larger denomination coins, is testament to his personal involvement. Even the lesser brass coinage is of a very high standard. Curiously for a man of such personal vanity, the coinage was allowed to depict the ageing process – later editions reveal his increasingly bloated appearance.

Nero's artistic pretensions also extended to architecture. He became the leading patron of his day, encouraging Roman builders to be more adventurous in their use of vaults, domes and arcades. Always keen to back interesting projects, it could be said that he took Roman architecture literally to new heights, as the buildings completed during his reign were generally taller than those of the past. Nor was his influence confined to the city of Rome alone, for he took an equal interest in rural projects such as villas and canals. Given that he died at the relatively early age of 31, his effect on Roman architecture is remarkable. Perversely the Great Fire of AD 64, for which he was unfairly blamed, should have provided the opportunity to rebuild a large section of the city; but the suspicion and hostility of the people made this impossible. His other ambitious plan – to extend the walls of Rome as far as the port of Ostia – also had to be abandoned in the face of public hostility, along with his dream of constructing a grandiose new city to be named after himself. The one project that did proceed was his new palace, the Golden House. This was a vast structure over 120 acres in area, far larger than the present-day Vatican City and built more in the style of a country villa than a traditional Roman town house. As the huge building began to rise on the summit of the Velia Hill, there were dark comments from Nero's critics, including the poet Martial who described it as '…the hated entrance hall of the cruel king'. Decorated with the finest gold and precious stones, it would have been a splendid sight, with wall designs so innovative that the later painters of the Renaissance copied many of the themes and visual idiosyncrasies. In spite of the splendour of the architecture, Tacitus, who watched its construction with fascination, was more impressed by the way that Nero had incorporated the natural beauty of fields and lakes into the overall design.

In literature, Nero played a significant role as patron by encouraging the flowering of what became known as the age of Silver Latin. Most of his contemporary writers credit Nero with both supporting them financially and encouraging members of his entourage to do the same. Among the many poets who enjoyed his patrimony was Gaius Petronius, whose work the *Satyricon* mocks the gilded but decadent life at court. Nero was also credited with having an unusual eye for new talent, and encouraging young writers to perform at court. Although his predecessors Augustus and Tiberius had written poetry in both Latin and Greek, Nero far surpassed them. A real competitor in everything he did, he was as determined to win at poetry competitions as he was in chariot races; understandably, he always started as the favourite, for it would have been a bold judge who denied the emperor victory. One of his more memorable performances was given at Naples in AD 64, when he performed in Greek. Visiting Alexandrians applauded him with rhythmic clapping that so impressed him that he ordered Roman audiences to do the same. 'The Greeks alone know how to appreciate me and my art,' he confided to one of his attendants. Shortly before his death he embarked, like a present-day rock star, on a farewell tour of Italy and Greece, arriving back in Rome dressed in a Greek cloak and wearing the Olympic crown that he had been allowed to win. Unlike previous emperors, he entered the city through the Augustan arch – not with soldiers and the banners of military victory, but with the laurel crowns for winning drama and music competitions borne ahead of him by actors and musicians. To the very end, he remained far more committed to the arts than he was to just government. Even when he had been proclaimed a public enemy, and was waiting for the arrival of the soldiers who planned to murder him, his main concern was for his reputation as an artist and performer. With the help of a faithful servant, he eventually managed to stab himself to death as he murmured his famous last lament, 'Ah, what an artist dies with me.'

No future despot ever showed the same obsessive interest in the arts, let alone the compulsion to participate as Nero did. Yet every modern dictator has been acutely aware that control of the national culture was a prerequisite for control of the people. What is fascinating is how seriously these totalitarian regimes took the issue, and how closely involved each despot became himself. There were great similarities of cultural style between the three leading totalitarian regimes of the 20th century – Nazi Germany, Soviet Russia and Fascist Italy; all three had a common obsession with grandiose architecture, large-scale pageants and the elevation of 'folk' art as the national culture. What they despised and attempted to ban were any expressions of international Modernism and the *avant garde*, which included atonal music, jazz and abstract art. These were considered decadent, subversive and, in Germany, fatally infiltrated by the despised Jew.

Hitler's own obsessive involvement reflected his frustrated career as an artist. This he blamed on his poor education, and the fact that he was the archetypal outsider in Prussian-dominated German society. Not only was he Austrian, he was not even Viennese, having come from a small provincial town. At the Linz Realschule that he attended in 1900, he was looked down upon by the other boys as a country bumpkin and a poor academic performer who particularly resented having to learn French. His teacher complained that no boy he had ever taught was sulkier than young Hitler. Intriguingly for a man who would claw his way to controlling most of Europe, he was unusually lazy and continued to be so even when Führer of Germany. Incapable of self-criticism, he blamed his failure to pass the leaving exam entirely on his teachers and the influence of the Jews on German education. But when he was rejected by the Kunstgewerbeschule art school in Vienna, there was not a single Jew on the selection panel; his report claimed that he lacked the necessary academic qualifications and talent. It is a sad irony that the one person in Vienna who continued to buy his paintings was Samuel Morgenstern, a Jew. The grim landscape watercolours that he produced at the time appear dead and lifeless, and are in complete contrast to the dynamic and progressive work being produced by other German artists. Given his own lack of artistic imagination, it is small wonder that Hitler loathed the shining innovation in the work of his fellow Austrian Oskar Kokoschka, along with the adventurous canvases of 20th century artists Kandinsky, Klee and Grosz – all of whom were vilified by the Nazis. Hitler became so keen to rid German art of international al contamination that he fully backed the infamous exhibition of so-called 'degenerate' art, the Entarte Kunst, that opened in Munich in 1937 and toured every major German city. As Hans Hinkel, Hitler's chief cultural adviser, said at the time, 'Hand any of these paintings to an ordinary worker and he couldn't tell the top from the bottom… art for the experts is not art… a new German art must be created for the people.' Hitler shared these ultra-conservative tastes, declaring that German art must in future reflect the truths of eternal beauty, not transitory fashion; above all, it must be national in subject matter, and without the slightest taint of Jewishness. Surprisingly, only 6 of the 100 artists pilloried in the Entarte Kunst were actually Jewish. The huge attendance at the exhibition indicated that either the German people overwhelmingly shared Hitler's taste in art, or else that they were taking the last opportunity to see some of Germany's most important modern paintings. The latter may well be true, for when a complementary exhibition toured the country – this time of Nazi-approved art – it attracted less than a fifth of the audience. Hitler's favourite painter was said to be Adolf Ziegler, who became known mockingly as the 'master of the German pubic hair' for his leaden studies of monumental Nazi storm troopers and their blonde maidens. Yet Hitler's well-known hatred of 'degenerate' art is an important clue to his personality, for, as Alice Miller maintains, his rejection of Modernism implied a rejection of colour – and colour represents feelings. To an emotionally repressed misfit like Hitler, colour and feeling were dangerous and must be repressed at all costs, in the same way that his father had crushed his son's vitality to maintain control in the family. Order and certitude were prized by Alois Hitler and imposed on his son. The vague and imprecise lines used in modern drawing were almost as bad as splashes of colour for a man such as Hitler – both were a threat that could lead to loss of control.

Predictably, the Führer's taste in architecture was as ossified as his taste in painting. It had been formed through observation of the new buildings being erected in Austria and Germany during his youth. It was the period of German neo-Baroque architecture that appeared under Kaiser Wilhelm II (1859–1941; German Emperor and King of Prussia 1888–1918) and this, together with Classical Romanism, became Hitler's favourite style. Because of his obsession with 'blood and soil', Hitler was keen to create buildings and structures in places of historic significance that would bond the people together. In the ambitious architect Albert Speer, Hitler found a man who could make this vision manifest – not with the archaic neo-Baroque, but with his own soulless version of 1930s Modernism. Curiously, Speer was determined to ignore modern methods of construction using steel girders and reinforced concrete; instead, he wanted to give his buildings a sense of monumental timelessness by using stone and other traditional materials. This accorded well with Hitler's own plans for a vast new capital city in which to celebrate anticipated future victories. As Speer recalled in his memoirs, 'The Romans built arches of triumph to celebrate the big victories won by the Roman Empire, while Hitler built them to celebrate victories he had not yet won.' Although the plans were condemned by architectural critics as manifestations of Hitler's absurd megalomania, Speer's vision would have been appropriate to the new and greater German empire if Hitler had won the war.

If Albert Speer was Hitler's supreme architect, then Joseph Göbbels was his genius of communications. As the first Minister of Propaganda in history, Göbbels was largely responsible for establishing the system of biased information without which any modern government cannot function, be it democracy or despotism. Credit for establishing the Führer myth and of successfully promoting the image of Hitler as the Messiah-redeemer must be given to this man, who was content to play a supporting role to his leader. Given total control of the media, including radio, press, publishing, cinema and the arts, he ruthlessly annexed the whole of German cultural life to his own department and set about 'cleansing' it in the name of the Nazi state. Freedom of expression disappeared throughout Germany; Jews, socialists and all other political opponents were swiftly ejected from any position of influence. On 10 May 1933, Göbbels celebrated this annexation of German culture by organizing an event that came to symbolize both the nihilism and the barbarity of the Nazi regime. Outside the Berlin Opera House, over 25,000 volumes of 'un-German' books by Jewish and left-wing authors (including the works of two of German's greatest living writers, Berthold Brecht and Thomas Mann) were publicly burnt by SS storm troopers and Nazi students. As Mann said later in exile in America, 'They were burning books that they were incapable of writing.' This onslaught on the nation's established culture was as ruthless and fundamental as Mao Tse-tung's later destruction of the Chinese tradition in the Cultural Revolution. Within two years, German culture was completely under the control of the Nazi party. Every branch of the arts was subject to the Führer's interference; his attempt to destroy any taint of Jewishness in German music, to break 'the Jewish stranglehold' as he described it, was particularly malevolent – if ultimately futile. Some of the world's most eminent soloists, such as Jascha Heifetz and Artur Schnabel, were banned from performing in public; the great Berlin orchestras were nationalized, and three of the world's most important composers – Arnold Schoenberg, Paul Hindemith and Bela Bartok – were driven into exile in America.

While Hitler attempted to obliterate much of what had made German culture so vibrant and innovative in the early years of the 20th century, Stalin was putting his own peculiar stamp on that of Soviet Russia. Like Hitler, the Russian dictator considered himself the sole arbiter of good taste for the entire nation. The best-educated tyrant since Nero, Stalin was a fount of artistic wisdom. Much of his cultural self-assurance resulted from the excellent teaching he had received at a religious seminary in Georgia, where his mother had sent him in the hope that he would become an Orthodox priest. But unlike Hitler, Stalin had worked hard and passed exams; moreover, he was particularly well read, not only in politics and history but also in Georgian and Russian literature and in Classical Greek. As a student he had written poetry in Georgian, his verse containing strange, cold images that give a premonition of his later isolation. The image of Stalin as a man of letters may be surprising, but his library at the Kremlin contained over 20,000 books. He was known to read avidly whenever he could, consuming over 500 pages a day and frequently annotating the margins with comments and reflections. Some of his books revealed a keen interest in world history, particularly those of an authoritarian nature such as Machiavelli's *The Prince*, Hitler's *Mein Kampf* and Clausewitz's *On War*. His personal copy of *The Prince* had been given to him by his mentor Lev Kamenev when they shared exile and friendship together in Siberia, but this did not stop Stalin having Kamenev shot 20 years later. Given his obsession with repressing dissent throughout the Soviet Union, Stalin's reading tastes suggest a surprisingly open mind. During the General Strike of 1926, he became fascinated with British history and even began to learn English, as well as French and German. True to character, he always kept his erudition a secret from those around him, and sought to give the impression that he knew far less than he really did.

In general, Stalin continued the Leninist tradition, in which culture should reflect the importance of industrial labour, of selfless service to the state and of the need to promote healthy bodies and strong family values. For this reason he maintained a strict censorship of the arts that excluded all romantic freethinking and politically incorrect ideas. Soviet Russia under Stalin was above all a serious society, committed to economic rather than social progress. There was no time for ephemera; anything amusing or light-hearted was banned, even harmless love and detective stories and comic books. The cultural life of the Soviet Union became as conformist as the politics, the only conflicts being the constant personal spats between artists battling with each other for patronage within the state system.

What Stalin feared most was the public mockery that occurred before the fall of Trotsky in 1928, when organizations such as the Revolutionary Association of Proletarian Writers encouraged its members to criticize the regime. But what he failed to appreciate was that this rare burst of artistic freedom was beneficial to the state. It re-energized Soviet culture; it encouraged artists to believe that bourgeois Western culture was doomed, and should give way to the radical ideas that sprang from the great Russian Revolution. Driven by his own paranoia, Stalin viewed all cultural output with extreme suspicion, whether it was inspired by radical or conservative ideas. Soon after he came to power, he banned Russia's leading artists, writers and composers from revealing their work in public without his specific approval. For the composer Dimitri Shostakovich, the insecurity became a nightmare. It was impossible to predict just how Comrade Stalin would react; each premiere became a nail-biting experience. In 1936, at the premiere of Shostakovich's new opera *Lady Macbeth of Mtsensk*, Stalin was seen to slump back in his seat, a look of undisguised contempt on his face. It was clear that the opera's innovation and musical discordance was not to his taste. The following day Shostakovich was inevitably attacked in *Pravda* for having composed a 'muddle instead of music'. From that moment on, the composer went in genuine fear of his life, knowing that he could be arrested and eliminated at any time – a fear shared by anyone foolish enough to risk innovation in his or her work.

Although Stalin knew little about the technicalities of music, he considered himself an expert on the process of filmmaking. Lenin had once said, 'For us the cinema is the most important of the arts,' and his successor fully endorsed the importance of the medium. Party archives reveal that Stalin was constantly sending Soviet filmmakers his own ideas for projects, and attempting to get involved in the production process – rather like a Soviet version of a Hollywood studio boss. He loved to watch films, too, and whenever possible would order a film to be screened at the Kremlin after dinner. Many of these were Russian productions, the directors waiting nervously on hand for Stalin's reactions. Appropriately, Stalin inherited Göbbels's own film library, looted from the wreckage of Berlin at the end of the war, and was amused to discover that they had the same taste in Hollywood classics. Göbbels's particular favourites included the Charlie Chaplin films, Hollywood light comedies and *Tarzan the Ape Man*. The two men also shared a penchant for Westerns starring Spencer Tracy and Clark Gable. Stalin's favourite star was John Wayne, although he was often scathing about Wayne's well-known anti-Communism; he once told Nikita Khrushchev that Wayne ought to be assassinated to shut him up. Over the years, Stalin's interest in films and filmmaking became increasingly obsessive as he attempted to exercise a dominant control over Russian productions. Even the great film director Sergei Eisenstein, thought to be favoured by Stalin, was called to the Kremlin and ordered to drastically re-edit his great epic *Alexander Nevsky*, which told the story of Russian foot soldiers defeating mounted German knights in the 13th century. Given that Stalin was in the process of agree-ing his infamous non-aggression pact with Hitler, Eisenstein's anti-German scenes were particularly embarrassing. Eisenstein was wary of offending the dictator a second time. Before shooting his two-part film *Ivan the Terrible* in 1944, he submit-ted the entire script to Stalin. Each scene was then discussed in great detail, with the director being told revealingly, 'Yes, Ivan was very cruel. You can show that he was cruel. But you must also show the reasons for his cruelty.' Even when given permis-sion to proceed, Eisenstein remained apprehensive of Stalin's reaction. With Part One completed, he suffered a crisis of conscience and made Part Two so non-controversial that Stalin was again affronted, dismissing the work as 'some kind of nightmare'. The film was immediately banned.

In architecture as in film, Stalin dictated the cultural principles that he considered appropriate to the world's most dominant communist nation. As the leading propo-nent of Socialist Realism, he championed public rather than private space. The public spaces in every Soviet city were decorated with monumental buildings, such as the appropriately named Joseph Stalin Palace of Culture and Science. In the manner of his fellow despots Ceausescu and Francia, he swept aside historic build-ings to make way for the new civic leviathans that rose to characterize Moscow's post-war skyline. Luckily, the plans for a 1,250-foot-high (381 m) tower featuring a tall sculpture of Lenin were abandoned, although the historic Church of Christ the Saviour in central Moscow had already been demolished to make way for it. However, it was not buildings but the Moscow metro, with its spacious stations clad in marble and decorated with huge glass chandeliers, that became the most eye-catching reminder of Soviet Classicism.

Although he had closely monitored the cultural output of the Soviet Union throughout the 1930s, Stalin was careful to maintain a low profile himself. But after the spectacular, if hard-won, victory of the Soviet Union over Nazi Germany, he emerged into the limelight to associate himself personally with the general atmosphere of triumph. National heroism was celebrated in all branches of the arts, with Stalin portrayed as the vital force that had saved the nation from disaster. To the rest of the world, unaware of his terrible crimes against his own people, Stalin was the avuncular figurehead of world communism. Secure in his control of the Russian people and idolized by communist sympathisers everywhere, Comrade Stalin kept his leaden grip on Soviet culture, enforcing the cult of Socialist Realism and punishing all who deviated. Among his victims were the writers Osip Mandelstam, Isaac Babel and Boris Pilnyak, who were either imprisoned and killed or died of starvation in the gulags. Fittingly, it was exiled dissident writers like Boris Pasternak who first alerted the public in the Western world to Stalin's appalling abuses of human rights.

The grandiose projects beloved of Hitler and Stalin would have been impossible in Mao Tse-tung's China. Although large, the country had neither the resources nor the engineering tradition to undertake monumental architecture. What increasingly concerned the Chairman was the need to reform what he termed the 'culture' of China, but appears in reality to have been the totally inadequate educational system. The Western idea that the artistic and cultural life of a country was relevant to its political life did not apply in China. When he came to power in 1949, Mao was at first content to leave the artists, writers and composers to their own devices. But in 1966, he realized that comprehensive reform of education and culture could revitalize his flagging revolution and distract his critics. In many ways, the Chinese Cultural Revolution that followed was Mao's response to a challenge for power by some of his closest supporters, who were opposed to the growing influence of his wife, Jiang Qing, and other elements in his regime. Many felt that the current educational system favoured the urban young, particularly the families of party officials, at the expense of deprived children living in rural areas. Aware of growing opposition, Mao seized the initiative by ignoring party members and appealing directly to the military and the young to support his ideas for change. The Revolution began in August 1966, when a group of high school girls began demonstrating on the streets of Beijing. Their actions, clearly encouraged by the ruling hierarchy, sparked off a whole series of demonstrations and near-riots by young people all over China. As Mao had anticipated, he was seen as the spiritual leader of the movement and his *Little Red Book* became its bible. This work had been first published two years earlier, and soon became one of the most significant publications in history, selling over 900 million copies. It became essential reading for every Chinese citizen; not to carry a copy invited a beating. Not only was it a form of identity card, proving the bearer was committed to the Revolution, but it was the most important book studied in school. Chanting passages from the *Little Red Book*, students marched through the streets of all the major cities; they were legitimized with the quasi-military title of 'Red Guards', and given free railway passes to travel all over the country. Under their strident pressure, some of Mao's closest colleagues and critics were forced to resign, including Liu Shaoqi, who had recently been president of the Republic, Zhu De, and Deng Xiaoping, later to emerge as leader of a post-Mao China.

As under the first emperor of China, the works of the great philosopher Confucius were attacked as being bourgeois by committees set up to harass and often physically attack anyone suspected of disloyalty to the great Mao. The agitation culminated in the city of Wuhan in July 1967, when the rioting got out of control and regular army troops were sent in to restore order. This event proved to be the turning point in the Cultural Revolution; within a year, the more excessive behaviour of the Guards had been curbed. But the effects on government had been highly damaging. Over two-thirds of the old Central Committee members had gone, while years of steady work and progress had been thrown away. Worst of all was the effect on Chinese culture and education: virtually a whole generation had lost the chance of proper schooling and a university education. Mao's despotic attempt to hang on to power by encouraging mob tactics against some of the most important traditions in Chinese culture had proved a near disaster. As the Cultural Revolution waned, a new pragmatism appeared, and Zhou Enlai and Deng Xiaoping re-emerged to lead the country along a more appropriate and practical path.

CHAPTER 11

The Enlightened Despot

It would be easy to dismiss all despots as savage unprincipled tyrants with closed minds and totally lacking in any sense of responsibility towards their subjects. But in the early 18th century a new concept of monarchy appeared that challenged the unethical tyranny of many past rulers. These men and, for the first time, women became known as Enlightened Despots. For the first time in history European monarchs felt their traditional absolutism conditioned by a new sense of liberalism and responsibility towards their subjects. Having been exposed to the ideas of the Enlightenment it now occurred to them that they should exercise their rule for the good of the people; a simple and, to the modern mind, obvious concept which had seldom been considered worth pursuing. The accepted belief was that a king or queen ruled solely by the divine right of God and should exercise ruthless control of their subjects. Any benefit that might result for the people themselves was of little or no importance.

The ideas that brought about this fundamental revolution in monarchical thinking began to evolve in France in the writings of the Philosophes – a group of philosophers who sought to define the principles for evolving a more morally worthwhile and just society. Their suggestion was that a social contract between the king and the people should be introduced. At the same time the traditional influence of the Church should be diminished and intellectual freedom, education, science and commerce encouraged. These ideas had particular appeal to a later group of reformists, the Physiocrats – a school of French economists, founded in 1756 by François Quesnay, who were eager to show that despotism could be morally justified if the monarch followed certain economic principles of the Enlightenment. As well as advocating free trade and agricultural improvement, the Physiocrats recommended the abolition of all traditional feudal, economic and political privileges. In their place would be a simple and effective set of laws presided over by an absolute monarch who would ensure 'social freedom' for all. The appeal of the Physiocrats' theory was that it promoted change but left the now enlightened monarch, firmly and safely in place. So given a minimal framework of legal order guaranteed by the sovereign, society would find the greatest happiness without undue regulation and harassment. What made this doctrine so appealing was that in contrast to earlier social and political thought it assumed the basic goodness of human reason and the belief in a self-regulating society.

The two most important ideas that the Enlightened Despot was expected to encourage were the social contract and the preservation of individual liberty. For centuries the justification for absolute monarchy was that the king was accountable to God and to no one else. This was the same belief that Ivan the Terrible had used to justify his despotic rule over the Russian people and which the French bishop Jacques-Bénigne Bossuet (1627–1704) eloquently expressed a century later. In 1662, Bossuet preached his famous sermon 'On the Duties of Kings' to an appreciative Louis XIV, nominally the first of the Enlightened Despots, at the Palace of the Louvre. Bossuet stated that as monarchs are placed in power by God alone, any disobedience shown to a monarch is equivalent to disobeying God himself. It also follows that since monarchs rule by divine right they are answerable to no one but God. For this reason the king should centralise his government and bring his nobility under tight control. Any attempt to thwart the royal will or provoke an uprising was, Bossuet believed, blatant defiance of the Almighty. As an example of such sacrilegious behaviour he cited the case of Oliver Cromwell, in England, who had overthrown his rightful and God-given king, Charles I.

Delighted to receive such distinguished support for his own concept of monarchy, King Louis XIV followed Bossuet's advice almost to the letter by tightening his control over the governing of France. As a precaution against rebellion he also ordered his nobles to assemble together under his watchful eye at Versailles. For the 72 years that Louis ruled France (the longest reign of any major European monarch) he maintained his own brand of absolutism although he remained condemned by the philosopher Montesquieu who defined a true despot as 'a single person who directs everything by his own will and caprice. Without laws to check him, and with no need to attend to anyone who does not agree with him, a despot can do whatever he likes, however ill-advised or reprehensible'. This Louis XIV certainly did and, although the military power of France increased dramatically during his reign, his attempt at enlightenment had limited success. With much of his time taken up by the daily elaborate rituals at Versailles, Louis failed to reform his administration with the more ambitious ideas of the Enlightenment; success in government continued to depend more on an individual's social status than on his innate abilities. Above all it was Louis's failure to reform the antiquated financial system during his reign that brought about the eventual downfall of the entire French monarchy.

As much of the revenue came from the sale of state offices and privileges it only encouraged the preservation of vested interests. France may have been the wealthiest country in Europe at the time but the only taxpayers were the unfortunate peasants. The nobility and most of the bourgeois paid nothing as did the Church that owned between 5 and 10 per cent of all the land. The result was that, in spite of the theoretical national wealth, the King's government remained chronically poor – a ridiculous state of affairs for an absolute monarch. Even the King's belated attempt at financial reform in 1661, by taxing everybody alike to pay for his increasingly costly wars, was a failure due to widespread evasion. So rarefied was the social ambience that emanated from the court at Versailles that it was even thought to be degrading and a sign of one's social inferiority to pay taxes.

Louis XIV could also be found wanting as an Enlightened Despot in the matter of religious toleration, which had been one of the Philosophes' key demands. From early in his reign Louis encouraged the persecution of the Jansenist Catholics, a sect that believed in predestination, but his most controversial action was against the Huguenots. These 2 million Protestants were considered a potential threat to the security of the state in spite of being a loyal and industrious group that had contributed a great deal to the French economy. For years the Catholic Assembly of the Clergy had urged the King to take action against these 'heretics'. The arrival of the King's new mistress at Versailles, the fervently Catholic Madame de Maintenon, added to the clamour. Under the terms of the Edict of Nantes, issued a century earlier, freedom of conscience had been granted to Protestants. The Edict was carefully scrutinized and decrees issued that made it more difficult for a Huguenot to find a position in any of the professions. This was a similar, if less inhumane, policy as that adopted towards the Jews when Hitler came to power in 1933. Under Louis XIV the French Huguenots were effectively excluded from any government posts while being bribed with cash inducements to convert back to Catholicism. Further harassment included billeting troops on Huguenot households. In October 1685, Louis finally gave in to Catholic pressure and revoked the Edict of Nantes completely. The replacement Edict of Fontainebleau effectively made Protestantism illegal in France and as a result, 200,000 Huguenots fled the country – a plight echoed by that of the Asians expelled from Uganda when Idi Amin tightened his despotic rule. The loss was almost as devastating to the French economy as the departure of the Asians would prove to be to that of Uganda. Driven from France the Huguenots descended on Brandenburg, Prussia, Holland and Britain. Such a sudden influx of refugees, talented and hard working as they were, caused a great deal of resentment against France among these European nation.

With Louis XIV setting such a poor example of Enlightened Despotism the European monarchs that followed him could hardly fail to do better. One of the most successful was King Frederick II of Prussia who appears to have well-earned his reputation as Frederick the Great. Unlike Louis XIV, Frederick inherited a stable kingdom with all its finances in good order. Moreover, his father had already established a well-ordered and highly centralized state run by an efficient bureaucracy. Frederick began his reign in 1740 in the best Enlightenment manner by introducing a number of reforms that included the abolition of torture in Prussia and a bold policy of religious toleration that was even more liberal than that of Holland or England. All religions, even the Jews, enjoyed equal toleration and their members qualified for state office. As Frederick later claimed with total justification, 'I have never persecuted anyone from any sect… all religions are equal and good and as long as those practicing are an honest people and wish to populate our land, may they be Turks or Pagans, we will build them mosques and churches.' As proof of his enlightened attitude Frederick ordered the retention of Jesuits as teachers in Prussia even after their suppression by Pope Clement XIV (1705–1774; in office 1769–1774). True to his word Frederick attracted a diversity of talent to his country, not only the Jesuit teachers, but also Huguenots and Jewish merchants and bankers from Spain. Unlike Louis XIV, Frederick also took a bold approach to land reform – abolishing the serf system which tied tenant farmers to specific properties for life – and reduced the role of the nobility in his administration by employing educated civil servants from the middle classes. Above all, he set about unifying his disconnected realm by challenging the traditional power of his neighbours, the Austrians. Frederick's wars against Austria weakened the Holy Roman Empire while providing Prussia with new lands and a military prestige that would prove vital for the 19th century unification of Germany. Success at war, however, encouraged Frederick's taste for expansionism and led to what became known as the First Partition of Poland in 1772. This exercise in early *lebensraum* had an uncanny similarity to the proposed division of Poland that Hitler suggested to Stalin in 1939. By this cynical act of unprovoked aggression Frederick acquired most of West Poland and its 600,000 inhabitants. In spite of his despotic action Frederick did make a genuine attempt to improve the lot of the poverty stricken Poles by developing the infrastructure of the new territory. Both the Polish administrative and legal codes were replaced by the more efficient Prussian system and 750 new schools were built, creating a dramatic improvement in Polish education. As for the Poles themselves, Frederick looked upon them with scorn and was highly contemptuous of the szlachta nobles comparing them to the Indian Iroquois of Canada. Again his scorn for the Poles has a disturbing similarity to that of Hitler almost two centuries later. In an attempt to improve the economy of his new possession Frederick encouraged German immigrants to settle there, planting the seeds of a bitter dispute that would eventually help to spark off the Second World War. Prussia soon benefited from her new territories, the province of Silesia alone providing her new industries with much needed raw materials. Canals were built, swamps drained and new crops such as the potato and the turnip introduced.

Frequently dressed in shabby old military uniforms, Frederick the Great made little attempt to develop a personality cult of his own and preferred to refer to himself as 'the first servant of the state'. Under his Enlightened Despotism Prussia grew to become the fifth of the European great powers along with France, Austria, Britain and Russia. As a military commander he was the idol of his age introducing new standards of discipline into an army that became the most feared in Europe. Frederick began his reign knowing that he possessed a well-trained army, a full treasury and with a desire to establish a martial reputation for himself. For the next quarter of a century he confronted Europe with his army and generally emerged victorious. Victory came at a heavy cost to the Prussian people, however, for as many as 250,000 Prussian soldiers died in battle on top of enormous civilian losses. Whole provinces were devastated by warfare and their populations scattered. To pay for his campaigns Frederick debased the Prussian currency and much of the population was reduced to poverty. Although his military record remains outstanding, later historians have questioned the basis for his reputation. The Prussian army was controlled by rigid discipline that made common soldiers more fearful of their own officers than they were of the enemy. There was also an excessive insistence on performing drills, repetition that made the soldiers appear more like marionettes than warriors. This helped to discourage innovation and initiative, as did Frederick's policy of having his generals so closely monitored that none was prepared to exercise independent action without the King's approval. If a battle went badly Frederick would hold a grudge against those concerned for decades.

Although his reputation for courage was never challenged, it is known that Frederick twice left a major battlefield under dubious circumstances, that of Mollwitz in 1741 and Lobositz in 1756. Nor was his self-confidence as resolute as his reputation maintained. After the defeat at Kolin in 1757, he was seen sitting on the ground for hours, aimlessly drawing circles in the dirt with a stick, before riding away from his army claiming that he needed to rest. Again after losing at Kunersdorf in 1759, he relinquished command to a subordinate in a fit of pique, telling his officers that he might as well be dead. Nevertheless, the man who brought Prussia through three brutal wars, oversaw its reconstruction and secured its status as a great power, was far more than the sum of his negative traits. While Frederick did not necessarily seek battle for its own sake, he held nothing back once the fighting started. His enemies responded by denying him the initiative whenever possible, fighting only under favourable conditions and limiting their tactical commitments.

Determination and a degree of luck characterised Frederick's successes. At the Battle of Mollwitz, early in his reign in 1741, the fight seemed lost until Frederick urged his infantry to make one last effort that finally turned the day. When the Austrians surprised the Prussian camp in the Battle of Soor, four years later, Frederick clawed victory out of defeat by inspiring his men to great fighting power. Even when deceived by enemy tactics, as at the Battle of Hochkirch in 1758, an engagement far more serious than Frederick had at first anticipated, he managed to turn the tide and lead his troops to a significant victory. Of the 'Enlightened Despots', only Napoleon can rival the 'hands on' military leadership of Frederick the Great, and it is no surprise that their campaigns were used by the military theorist, Carl von Clausewitz, to illustrate his theories in his seminal book, *On War*. Nor should it be forgotten that Frederick was also one of the last European sovereigns to lead his men in battle and his legendary courage led to six horses being shot from under him. Napoleon Bonaparte considered him one of the greatest commanders of all time and when he visited Frederick's tomb in Potsdam in 1807 he remarked to his officers in tribute, 'Gentlemen, if this man were still alive I would not be here.' Yet Frederick the Great's military abilities were matched by his artistic talent and a commitment to culture that was unequalled by any ruler since the Emperor Nero. Almost single-handedly he transformed the insignificant city of Berlin into what his contemporaries described as 'The Athens of the North'. To his court he welcomed many of the most celebrated French writers of the age including the philosopher Baron d'Holbach and the great Voltaire himself. Under his patronage many illustrious buildings such as the Berlin State Opera, the Royal Library and St. Hedwig's Cathedral were built. His crowning achievement was his summer residence, the Palace of Sanssoucci at Potsdam, a building that was widely admired and considered by many to be the finest example of Northern German rococo architecture. As a musical performer Frederick excelled at his favourite instrument, the flute, for which he wrote 121 sonatas and 4 concertos as well as an orchestral symphony and other pieces. His creativity was all the more surprising given his constant military campaigning and yet he also found time to study Freemasonry and to perfect his knowledge of French, English, Spanish, Portuguese and Italian as well as Latin, Greek, and Hebrew.

Frederick's main rival as the most Enlightened Despot in Western Europe was a woman, the Empress Maria Theresa of Austria (1717–1780; reigned 1740–1780). Twice their countries went to war over Silesia, and twice Frederick convincingly defeated the might of Austria. Francis I, the Holy Roman Emperor, was the nominal ruler of Austria but he tended to leave the day-to-day administration to his wife. This arrangement was as unique at the time as the fact that they had both married for love. As testimony of their sincere love Maria Theresa bore her husband 16 children, one of whom would later become Marie Antoinette (1755–1793), Queen consort of Louis XVI of France. After her husband's death in 1765, Maria Theresa continued to rule Austria as joint Regent with her son, Joseph II (1741–1790; Holy Roman Emperor 1765–1790), who relied heavily on his mother's experience. In a similar manner to Frederick the Great, Maria Theresa set about implementing fundamental administrative and economic reforms that reflected the principles of the Enlightenment. She had, however, one serious disagreement with both her husband and son: whereas they fully embraced religious tolerance, she retained an almost despotic bigotry against non-Catholics. Maria Theresa thoroughly distrusted Protestants, particularly the English, and in 1741, she also expelled the Jews from Prague. Another manifestation of her strict Catholic morality was the establishment of a decency police force that was ordered to patrol everywhere, especially in notoriously easy-going Vienna, and to arrest anyone suspected of immorality. The victims of this unenlightened purge were mainly prostitutes who were transported off to remote villages and left there. Far more progressive were her law reforms that abolished witch burning, torture and, remarkably for the times, capital punishment and established its replacement with forced labour. As Frederick had done in Prussia so Maria Theresa did in Austria, centralizing the administration and strengthening the monarch's powers. Towards the end of her reign even her religious intolerance was tempered by the influence of her son and in 1781 the enlightened Edict of Tolerance was issued which granted Protestants almost equal status with Catholics throughout the Empire and lifted the restrictions on Jews, allowing them to participate fully in trade and to enjoy the educational opportunities that had previously been barred to them.

Another German-born princess who fully justified her reputation of Enlightened Despot was the Empress Catherine of Russia (1729–1796; reigned 1762–1796). Unlike her Austrian contemporary, Maria Theresa, Catherine loathed her husband Grand Duke Peter (1728–1762; Tsar of Russia 1762) and he fathered neither of her two children. She had good reason for hating her husband, for when his mother, the Empress Elizabeth, died in 1762, Peter began plotting the murder of his wife. Catherine struck first and with the help of her lover, Gregory Orlov, and the backing of the Russian Army she had Peter arrested, imprisoned and swiftly murdered. For the next 30 years Catherine ruled the country alone with a unique-ly Russian combination of enlightenment and despotism. Many of her reforms were the continuation of initiatives begun by her predecessor, Peter the Great, 50 years earlier. Less prone to military adventures than Peter had been, Catherine focussed instead on reforming Russian society. Her first problem was an empty state treasury – the result of her predecessor's extravagant life style and a costly war with Prussia. Catherine's solution to the crisis was to issue a decree secularizing the property of the clergy and seizing it for the state. This bold action brought swift returns, for the Russian Orthodox clergy owned one third of all the land and serfs in Russia. Now fascinated by economics, Catherine then created what may well have been the world's first modern think tank when she established the Free Economic Society in 1765, to discuss the modernization of agriculture and industry. Many of Europe's leading economists of her day, such as Arthur Young and Jacques Necker of France were attracted to join. It was a forum in which Catherine was able to display her own intellectual abilities and her opening speech to the forum was full of references to the ideas of the 18th century French philosopher Montesquieu, the Italian penal reformer Beccaria and the influential economist Mercier de la Rivière. Catherine eventually implemented many of the reforms suggested by this body but other aspects of her rule were decidedly less enlightened, particularly her treatment of the serfs. She began by trying to improve their miserable situation but found her propos-als hotly challenged by her own nobility. In 1773, realising that the promised reforms would not occur, the serfs rose in revolt in what became the greatest uprising in Russian history before the Communist revolution of 1917. Houses were burned and landlords murdered as the serfs rampaged through the country but when their leader Pugachev proposed marching on Moscow, Catherine acted decisively. The rebellion was brutally crushed and Pugachev publicly beheaded but the event had convinced Catherine of the urgent need for reform. Catherine was careful to protect herself against further uprisings by allying herself with the nobility. She even courted their favour by announcing that she was, herself, the 'first landlord of the realm.' To ensure no re-occurrence of the Pugachev event Catherine introduced a policy of rural decentralization by which Russia would be divided into 15 large areas and further subdivided into hundreds of administrative areas. These areas would then be admin-istered by members of the local gentry. Ultimate control, however, would continue to rest with her in Saint Petersburg. As a result of these reforms, serfdom as an insti-tution became stronger than ever and even spread to new areas, in particular to areas of the Ukraine that Russia had obtained in the partitions of Poland. Although

Catherine's government had, in essence, confirmed an already-existing system of serfdom in the Ukraine, it now confined it as a legal entity. A series of laws, fiscal in nature and issued from 1763 to 1783, forbade Ukrainian peasants from leaving their estate without the landlord's permission and directing them to remain 'in their place and calling.' Catherine the Great also extended serfdom throughout Russia by giving huge grants of state lands and peasants to her favourites at Court. By 1796 serfs comprised over 50 per cent of peasants and 49 per cent of the entire population. The power of the landlords had also increased as they could now sentence their serfs to hard labour in Siberia or, if they escaped, have them recaptured by the military. There were also ameliorating measures, however, as the new laws promised the serfs, somewhat ambiguously, the ultimate protection of the state. This attempt at compromise was in reality a failure, for Catherine's decision not to fully abolish serfdom violated one of the most important principles of the Enlightenment. Far more progressive was her encouragement of foreign investment in the economically underdeveloped areas of Russia and her requirement that the notoriously ignorant Russian nobles improve their education.

Exceptionally well-read and highly cultured, Catherine considered herself a true child of the Enlightenment so when she heard that the French government had threatened to stop the publication of the *Encyclopédie* because of its irreligious spirit, she proposed to the author Denis Diderot that he complete his great work in Russia under her protection. Catherine also enlisted the great Voltaire to her cause, and corresponded with him regularly for 15 years. In return for her patronage, Voltaire praised Catherine as 'The Star of the North' and the 'Semiramis of Russia', a reference to the legendary Queen of Babylon. Though they never met, Catherine mourned him sincerely when he died in 1778 and rapidly acquired his famous collection of books giving it pride of place in her own Imperial Library. In spite of her admiration for the French philosopher she failed, like Maria Theresa, to follow Voltaire's belief in religious tolerance. Instead she continued to affirm the primacy of the Russian Orthodox religion throughout Russia at the expense of other faiths. Yet as patron of the arts she was supreme and promoted European culture far more successfully than any Russian leader before or since. Her intention was to show the world that Russia was a truly civilized European nation capable of great artistic achievements. Part of this campaign involved the total modernization of the capital city, St. Petersburg. Italian architects were commissioned to redesign and expand the Winter Palace, making it one of the most majestic palaces in the world. French architects then arrived to construct an art gallery next door, The Hermitage, which was filled with masterpieces by Rembrandt, Raphael and Leonardo da Vinci.

Catherine's love of reading was reflected in a new library that contained over 400,000 books. Other fine buildings soon followed including an opera house, an university and an academy of art and science. Catherine's greatest achievement was to transform the backward city of St. Petersburg into one of the major cultural centres of Europe, capable of attracting some of the most eminent artists, writers, musicians, scientists and scholars of the age. Her personal talent was for writing and, as Frederick the Great proved to be an accomplished musician, so Catherine the Great became a gifted writer. She produced several books including an educational manual for young children as well as comedies, novels and memoirs.

Catherine the Great had much in common with her eccentric neighbour King Gustavus III of Sweden (1746–1792; reigned 1771–1792) who also aspired to be an enlightened monarch. But Gustavus became obsessed with restoring the golden age of Swedish power that had prevailed a century earlier. Gustavus's most formative experience was a visit to Paris in March 1771 that was a diplomatic triumph. Well known as a Francophile committed to the ideas of the Enlightenment, he was courted by all the leading French poets and the philosophers. Gustavus returned to Sweden full of enthusiasm for reform, with a secret agreement in his pocket that committed the French government to giving substantial amounts of French gold to him, in return for diplomatic support. With his new funds Gustavus now attempted to break the power of the Swedish nobility that had ruled the country in all but name for decades. But to the Swedish aristocracy Gustavus's attempt at centralizing the administration appeared to be little more than a gross act of despotism aimed specifically against its members. Although warned by his uncle, Frederick the Great, to act with care and not to violate the present Swedish constitution, Gustavus ignored the advice and informed the Parliament that he was taking sole charge of the government pledging that he would only act in the true Enlightenment manner and as 'the first citizen of a free people'. His words warned the deputies that their own political supremacy was now under threat. It was a strange reversal of the position in France where Louis XIV, an absolute King, was increasingly under pressure to cede power to others. Yet in Sweden the monarch was proposing to turn the clock back and take sole control of the country – even though he proposed to govern under the principles of the Enlightenment. Predictably the aristocracy rebelled against what they saw as new despotism and Gustavus had great difficulty in suppressing the uprising. Yet his actions had won him the support of the lower classes, glad to be free of aristocratic tyranny, and enabled him to abolish most of the hereditary privileges of the nobility even though it would cost him his life. Given the constant battles, both military and civil, that he endured it is remarkable that

Gustavus found time to write plays and to create such cultural achievements as the Royal Dramatic Theatre, the Royal Swedish Opera, the Royal Swedish Ballet and the Swedish Academy. A Freemason like his Prussian uncle, he also delighted in every branch of literature and the arts until an assassin's bullet cut short his unique experiment in government. His attempt to rid Sweden of weak government, corruption and impotence led to his own assassination by disgruntled nobles in March 1792, at a masked ball in Stockholm – an event which later became the inspiration for one of Verdi's most popular operas, *Un Ballo in Maschera*.

No account of the era of Enlightened Despotism would be complete without Napoleon Bonaparte. Not only was he its most famous exponent but also his all-embracing rule of France presaged the rise of totalitarianism a century later. Napoleon's remarkable rise from humble artillery officer to Emperor of France can be attributed to the ruthless and clear-sighted pragmatism that allowed him to combine despotic control of the French nation with a programme of enlightened reform. This unusual pragmatism can be seen, for example, in the practical way that he dealt with the tricky problem of religious belief. As a product of the Enlightenment, Napoleon was immune to devout beliefs and was able to use religion as a tool to accomplish his political ends. Like Karl Marx, he believed religion to be little more than the ethical cement that held society together. According to Napoleon, religion promoted national unity and prevented class war by keeping the people meek and passive. Quite happy to pass himself off as a Catholic in France or to lead the conquered Egyptians into believing that he had a sincere interest in Islam, Napoleon had only one belief and that was in himself and the single star of his own destiny. To Napoleon the Catholic Church was simply a tool to be used ruthlessly for his own benefit. When he first came to power in November 1799 he realized that, having been excluded from involvement in the State by the Revolutionaries, the French Church would be only too grateful to recover some of its power in return for supporting his regime. As he cynically said, '50 bishops paid by England lead the French clergy today. Their influence must be destroyed. For this we need the authority of the Pope.' The result was the Concordat signed with the Vatican in a move that would be emulated by Mussolini when he came to power in 1922. Under the Concordat the French State recognized Catholicism as the favoured religion but not as the state religion even though the clergy would now be selected and paid by the State. It was a clever move by Napoleon that won the favour of the Church while making sure that it stayed firmly under his personal control.

As with other Enlightened Despots, one of Napoleon's priorities was to create a fully centralized authority that would provide more efficient government under his personal guidance. In a country the size of France this entailed recruiting thousands of officials to run the various national and local organizations that were now created. Much of the groundwork had already been done for him during the Revolution when the old institutions linked to royal patrimony were swept away at a stroke. To finance his new bureaucratic structure Napoleon ordered that the upper classes, the richest 2 per cent of the population, be efficiently taxed providing the extra revenue needed to support his armies and administer the conquered territories. With this new funding he was also able to stimulate the economy and bring about long needed improvements to the infrastructure of France. Roads that had been deteriorating for decades were finally repaired and new bridges and canals were constructed with loans from the new Bank of France. Having seen how hunger had provoked Revolution in 1789, Napoleon made sure that the price of bread was rigidly controlled by the state and never allowed to rise more than by a modest amount. With an efficient administration in place his next step was to reform the antiquated French legal system. In 1804, he introduced his Code Napoleon that provided the first single legal system for all France. The Code made everyone equal before the law as well as guaranteeing freedom of religious conscience and secularizing the state. Some of its provisions, particularly those regulating working conditions, were immediately condemned as old fashioned, despotic and contrary to the spirit of the Enlightenment. Workers rights to collective bargaining or to determine their own wages and working conditions were made illegal. Trade unions were outlawed and a system of new labour permits controlled the free movement of workers within the country. These measures later proved to have an uncanny similarity to the draconian labour laws introduced by the Nazis when Hitler came to power in 1933. More positively, under the Code Napoleon there was no recognition of social class and the purchase and sale of military commissions were abolished. Under Napoleon's enlightened government people were expected to make their way up in society on the basis of promotion through ability. Most importantly a new state system of public education was put in place which combined a secular curriculum with schools managed by the State rather than the Church as in the past. This efficient system provided Napoleon with capable officials necessary to administer his laws and trained officers to man his army. It was managed by a national board of education that remains little altered to this day. These were undoubted achievements that improved the lives of millions as well as offering the common people the opportunity to participate in the running of the state. Yet for all his enlightened policies Napoleon remained a despot who had seized power and refused to relinquish it. His state police kept a careful eye on potential subversives and any who openly opposed him were immediately imprisoned. It was once said of Napoleon that although he could provide for the administration of justice between man and man, he could not provide it between the citizen and the ruler. Under the Napoleonic legal system political offences were heard in camera by special tribunals of quasi-military character and not by a jury in open court. Although juries might decide on other criminal matters they were certainly not permitted to interpose between the despot and any of his subjects.

Having seen the disastrous consequences of what happens when both a monarchy and a revolutionary council lose control of public opinion Napoleon resolved to control it with rigid authority. He went about this task in the manner of a modern dictator using a mixture of censorship and paid spies to control the press. Under the self-made Emperor dissent was virtually impossible as newspapers came under state control, with printers and booksellers forced to swear an oath of allegiance to Napoleon personally. By his despotic control of public opinion Napoleon reversed many of the liberal gains of the Revolution, for he believed that too much political liberty and an excess of free speech would threaten both the security and the efficiency of his new state. There was also disappointment among his female citizens because Napoleon's reforms had not done sufficient justice to women and had even deprived them of many of their social and legal gains achieved during the French Revolution. Although the Code led to an increase in women's rights in some areas it diminished them in others: under the Napoleonic system women had now to ask the approval of their husbands before making certain legal commitments such as disposing of property. A divorce became much harder for a woman to obtain and moreover, a woman's husband could imprison her for adultery while as a man he could escape all legal censure.

When he came to write his memoirs, while in captivity on St. Helena, Napoleon naturally played down the despotic aspects of his rule while congratulating himself on the enlightened ones. His most startling assertion was that his real motive in plunging the continent into a bloody war was to create a United States of Europe, a union he claimed would free Europe forever from tyranny. Napoleon's rise to power had been as meteoric as that of Hitler would be and his fall was almost as disastrous. Napoleon still remains one of the greatest enigmas of history and yet his ascent to power had changed the world by spreading France's revolutionary ideals, making it impossible for any future ruler to turn back the clock. Feudalism was dead and the new nationalistic nation was born with the bourgeoisie in ascent. The traditional despot monarch had gone but the self-made dictator was about to arise.

CHAPTER 12

The Promise of Efficiency

When Mussolini came to power in October 1922, he set about the task of renovating the Italian economy with remarkable energy. The illusion of newfound national competence was symbolized by the supposed dramatic improvements in the Italian railway system, a story of technological rebirth that was spread nationally and internationally by the Fascist propaganda machine. It claimed that the Duce was transforming one of the most decrepit railway systems in Europe into one of the best, with clean, efficient and punctual trains. In reality, the dilapidated Italian railway system had been largely renovated long before Mussolini's arrival and, as many were to later testify, time-keeping under Fascism was no better than it had been under a liberal democracy. But claiming other people's achievements for oneself was nothing new in Italian history. Machiavelli had given similar credit for supposed efficiency to the Renaissance despot Cesare Borgia, who claimed to have restored order in the Italian Romagna long after it had been achieved by others.

Mussolini's apologists continued to claim that whatever the faults of his regime, at least he got things done. There is a common misconception that despotisms are more efficient than democracies; because no time is wasted in consulting groups, committees or outside organizations, the despot can act swiftly and decisively. Decisions that would take weeks to reach in a liberal democracy can be made in a matter of seconds. The supposed efficiency that results from one man's vision can become the justification for seizing power and ending group participation in events. This was the excuse used by men such as Julius Caesar, Oliver Cromwell and Napoleon Bonaparte. But in the end, Cromwell ruled England with the same authoritarian principles for which he had previously condemned King Charles I. Reigning alone as Lord Protector, he ignored the reasoned protests of dissidents; he dissolved the same parliament that he had championed and from which he received his authority. He then imposed taxes without the consent of the people – the same offence for which Charles I had been condemned – and lived in royal state at Hampton Court Palace. Furthermore, he sought to create a dynasty by passing power on to his son. Having begun as a champion of justice and reform, Cromwell ended up as an unpopular despot. Men like Cromwell have always claimed that their seizure of power was done to save the country from chaos. Sincere or self-delusory, Cromwell joined the ranks of tyrants who have used the same justification as Ivan the Terrible – that he was acting on God's will. As a Second Adventist, Cromwell believed that Christ would shortly return to establish the reign of the saints upon the earth, and that he must prepare the way. He had no time for such frivolities as art and beauty. His troopers were encouraged to destroy stained glass and statuary in churches throughout England, just as the Taliban in Afghanstan blew up the ancient statues of the Buddha in the Bamyan Valley. Cromwell may have produced an efficient administration with the help of a large standing army, but his despotism and intolerance were not in the English tradition of open democracy. The public rejoicing that greeted the restoration of Charles II in 1660 showed that Cromwell's vision had not been shared by the people.

In times of national danger, a strong unifying character is often needed to co-ordinate the struggle for survival. Winston Churchill played that role for Britain in 1940, but he did so without seeking the special powers of a dictator that either his main protagonist or his principal allies possessed. The problem, as British philosopher and economist John Stuart Mill saw in the 19th century, is that even if a good and capable man can be found to play the role of enlightened despot, the office itself soon corrupts the individual. As Mill wrote in his great work *On Liberty* 'it has long been a common saying, that if a good despot could be ensured, despotic monarchy would be the best form of government. I look upon this as a radical and most pernicious misconception of what good government is.' Moreover, a single man with absolute control implies passivity on the part of the people. If the people are non-political people, they become non-intellectual, and vice versa: lively politics stimulate all the functions of a society. Renaissance Florence was far more creative and lively as a republic than it was under the mildly despotic rule of the Medicis. In fact, there is no example in history of despotism that did not lead to both intellectual and moral degeneration.

However, one despot stands out as having achieved efficiency, albeit at the price of ruthless action against anyone who opposed it. Qin Shi Huang's policies brought about a unified China whose basic political system would last 2,000 years. He began with the reform of the Chinese language, which had previously varied in form from area to area. To fund these improvements, Qin Shi Huang began taxing the people heavily; therefore, despite the obvious benefits of his reforms, national resentment of him grew. His ceaseless energy and constant striving for change were in contrast to the traditional passivity of Chinese society. The nobility, increasingly sidelined by

Qin's reforms, were further antagonized by the banning of all books that advocated other forms of government, together with the writings of the great philosophers of the past. Not until the 20th century would any ruler attempt the ambitious social reforms that characterized this great period of Chinese history. It could even be said that modern China has made such rapid economic progress because of the centralized system of state management that Emperor Qin put in place over 2,000 years ago.

In the smaller societies of the ancient world, there was less need for the vast bureaucracy that characterized China under Qin Shi Huang. The Greeks and Romans were content to leave their social structure and economy much as they had inherited them. But the great Mongol leaders, Tamerlane and Genghis Khan, emulated the Chinese in establishing a highly efficient communications and administrative system to govern their huge territorial empire. By the end of the 13th century, this empire stretched from the Pacific Ocean to the plains of eastern Europe, and included most of Asia. Throughout this vast region the same Yassa or legal code prevailed, bringing all the tribes with their different laws under one legal system. It was claimed by the Mongol chroniclers that this virtually eradicated theft, murder, adultery, sodomy, fornication, usury and sorcery. Genghis Khan also introduced a rapid and highly effective communication system, involving riders who constantly changed mounts as they galloped across Asia with orders and messages. Some riders could cover over 200 miles (322 km) in a single day, travelling along new post roads that also enabled merchandise to be transported over long distances.

But it was the Mongols' military efficiency, both in weaponry and tactics, that really impressed their contemporaries. As the writer Cecelia Holland has described it in her essay, *The Death That Saved Europe*:

> The Mongol army looked strikingly like a modern army, set down in a
> medieval world... a general co-ordinated the movements of tens of
> thousands of men, across mountain ranges and in unknown territory, as
> precisely as movements on a chessboard. In battle, through a signalling
> system of coloured banners, he could advance thousands of men at a time,
> send them back, turn them, and direct their charges – and when he gave
> orders, his men did instantly what they were told.

This combination of organizational self-discipline, flexibility, aggression and, above all, mobility, allowed the Mongols to defeat larger armies constantly. Their attitude towards conquered peoples was both efficient and pragmatic; as nature-worshipping animists, they had no oppressive ideological ideas to enforce other than the demand for loyalty and obedience. Nor did they concern themselves with religion, allowing complete religious freedom in every region that they controlled. As the Mongols were horsemen on the move, they did not produce crops or goods that could be sold – they were dependent on the taxes they levied. For this reason, they were keen for their conquered peoples to prosper and produce more revenue. Genghis Khan encouraged anything that would help trade prosper, including the practical sciences, paper-making and printing, and the use of the compass and gunpowder. It has even been suggested that the Mongolian development of more sophisticated musical instruments, such as the violin, laid the ground for the music of the Italian Renaissance a century later.

The Mongolian leaders' military efficiency would have been much admired by later European despots such as Vlad Tepes and Ivan the Terrible. While the Mongols moved freely across the Asian steppes, Vlad the Impaler was confined to his small corner of the Balkans by the might of the Ottoman Empire. Vastly outnumbered in his struggle against the Turks, he devised a particularly effective form of guerrilla warfare, using the rugged landscape to his advantage. Sometimes his scorched earth policy involved drawing the enemy deep into areas of Walachia where he had destroyed his own villages and poisoned the wells; then, as they retreated in despair, he would attack them again. The demoralizing effect of all this on his enemies was obvious. Even his greatest opponent, Sultan Mehmet II, the conqueror of Constantinople, was heard to lament that he could never defeat a man capable of such terrible and inhuman actions.

Ivan the Terrible faced similar difficulties in dealing with both external and internal challenges. Given the disruptive and tyrannical nature of his regime, there could have been little opportunity for social or economic improvement in 16th-century Russia, but his one tenuous claim to reform was his willingness to open his country to foreign trade. An opportunity occurred in the summer of 1553, when an English ship arrived unexpectedly off the White Sea coast in a misguided attempt to discover a northern passage to India. The captain was an Englishman, Richard Chancellor, sent on a voyage of discovery by a consortium of London merchants. He bore a letter of introduction from King Edward VI of England (1537–1553; reigned 1547–1553) to 'all kings, princes, rulers, judges and governors of the earth'. News of this approach from a land far beyond his borders, and almost beyond his comprehension, intrigued the Tsar, who summoned him to Moscow. There Chancellor, although critical of the plain and unadorned buildings, was impressed by the fine gold cloth worn by Ivan and his nobles, 'the barbarous Russes', as he called them. When the ice had cleared the following spring, Chancellor set off for home carrying a letter for the English king, in which Ivan asked him to send more ships so that mutually beneficial trade could be established between the two countries. It was another two years before Chancellor returned, this time in ships from the newly formed Merchant Adventurers Company. After unloading their cargoes at the port of St Nicholas they took on wax, tallow, furs and felt in return. The return voyage was a disaster (the ship was wrecked and Chancellor drowned), but the route had been established and trade began to flourish – although the Russians were infuriated to learn that they must pay English customs duties. A decade later, the new trading route was so busy that the newly formed English Muscovy Company was occupying five houses in Moscow, trading by land throughout the kingdom and even involved in joint missions to Persia with the Russians.

Given Ivan's paranoid nature it is surprising that he was prepared to open his country to total strangers, but developing trade with England was to prove a farsighted move. It established a window to the West that would later be used by Peter the Great to introduce Western technology to Russia; it pioneered the vital sea route for the supply of Allied armaments to the Soviet Union in the Second World War. Unlike Ivan, Stalin took little interest in trading with the West until he desperately needed strategic supplies to halt the German invaders in June 1941. Throughout the 1930s he was more concerned with the internal renovation of the ailing Soviet economy. Russia had traditionally concentrated on agriculture rather than industry, and even with Lenin's reforms, Soviet manufacturing production lagged far behind that of America, Britain and Germany. What was urgently needed was new investment in the coal, iron and steel, and power industries. Only then could the communist regime fulfil its promise to the workers to increase their standard of living and show the rest of the world that Socialist planning could really work.

The first step, Stalin decided, must be the centralization of the entire Soviet economy under a single body, the State Planning Commission, which would formulate policy and issue instructions from Moscow. These orders would then be passed on down the line to individual factories, businesses and farms throughout the Soviet Union. The overall strategy would be based on a series of Five-Year Plans that decreed the minimum performance levels required and set the national targets for industry and agriculture. The resources needed to achieve this massive improvement in efficiency would be provided by central government. Such rapid and fundamental changes would have been a near impossibility under a capitalist system, but the established structure of Stalin's totalitarian regime made it far easier – not only did the state already own all the factories, mines and farms, but it also controlled the vitally important transport system too. The greatest problem was the co-operation of the workers, a human resource that was far less predictable than the supply of raw materials. So, to ensure compliance, fundamental new labour laws were decreed. Ordinary workers were harshly disciplined if they dissented on the shop floor; poor workmanship and unjustified absence were rigorously punished. In complete contrast to Pol Pot's later policy of driving people out of the cities, Stalin was determined to drive them back in. Millions of peasants were ordered to leave the land and move into the towns and cities to work in the new factories that were being built. But right from the start, the production targets were too ambitious – a 250 per cent increase in total industrial output and a 350 per cent increase in heavy engineering simply could not be met. Furthermore, given the deteriorating international situation throughout the 1930s, the new factories had to be able to adapt quickly to the manufacture of tanks, weapons and airplanes in the event of war. The attempt to meet these unrealistic quotas led inevitably to an appalling deterioration in conditions, with workers regularly having to labour for 11 hours a day. Particularly harsh was the payment of wages in food rations, so those who did not work, did not eat. Everywhere, the government propaganda machine urged its victims to work harder and longer. As an example to others, 'Heroes of Production' were selected and then lionized by the media. One such hero was chosen because he was said to be 500 per cent more productive than the average worker.

The cost of all this on human health and happiness can only be imagined, and even the central planners realized that unless more sophisticated technology was provided, the Plan was doomed to failure. So a drive began to produce more agricultural machinery, so increasing farm productivity and releasing even more workers to join the urban workforce. To make agriculture itself more efficient, Stalin introduced a new system of collectivization that involved grouping small, scattered farms together into one big collective, or Kolkhozy. In theory, the peasant farmers could then pool their resources of animals, tools and labour for the benefit of the whole community. At harvest, they would sell their produce to the state at a set price, and reinvest any profits they made. In practice, it all proved far more difficult than Stalin had envisaged. The problem with the plan was that it ignored the small farmer's instinctive conservatism and natural desire to remain an individual, not just one of a group. In 1928, a year after collectivisation had begun, peasants throughout the Soviet Union were still resisting the reform and refusing to pool their labour, or even to sell exclusively to the state. In desperation, it was decreed that those who continued to disobey must now be severely dealt with. Stalin also brought the wealthier peasants, the Kulaks, into line by ordering them to surrender their property and equipment to the collectives. If they resisted, their land was to be seized;

they and their families were to be transported to Siberia and put to work in agricultural prison labour camps. When the time came to enforce the order, it was carried out with such inhumanity that one in five of the Kulaks, mainly the women and children, died on the journey – either in the cattle trucks or on forced marches. On arrival in Siberia, the working conditions were so barbarous that many more died. It is believed that 6 million of these uprooted farmers perished, a fact only discovered by the outside world on the collapse of Soviet Communism.

In spite of the human cost of Stalin's Five-Year Plan, completed in just four years as the regime proudly announced, it appeared at first sight to have worked. Agricultural and industrial production had increased significantly. But state interference had produced a distorted economy full of anomalies. With the emphasis on heavy industry, even fewer consumer goods were now available in the shops, which led to a further fall in the standard of living. Small wonder that in the years to come, vodka became the sole motivating force of Soviet industry, for there was little else to buy. Nor was the influx of people to the cities matched by a comparable increase in housing, medical facilities or schools. And although conditions were bad in the cities, they became disastrous in the country. Grain production actually declined between 1928 and 1932, causing the death from starvation of 7 million peasants. Livestock production also declined, and did not again reach its 1928 level until 1953. Matters were not helped by Stalin's callous order to hoard grain in order to buy foreign currency abroad.

News of these agrarian disasters were rigorously suppressed, a task made far easier by state control of information. The Five-Year Plan and collectivization were trumpeted to both the communist and capitalist worlds as major achievements of Soviet state planning. So it was understandable that a decade later, the Chinese leader Mao Tse-tung would assume that the way ahead for his country lay in the same economic model – namely, state ownership of industry and collective farms, both controlled by centralized economic planning.

As the Chinese economy was even more backward than that of Russia, Mao had first to rid the country of its historic feudalism that had remained virtually unchanged for a thousand years. His main proposal was a Development Plan, introduced in the autumn of 1949, which fundamentally challenged the traditional Chinese system based on close family ties and strong local and regional government. Mao's agrarian reform would require more modern methods of production, and the extension of the area of land under cultivation. China's vast human resources would be utilized by improving the outdated education system; the infrastructure would also be modernized with an improved road and rail network. This whole programme became known as the 'The Great Leap Forward'. Controversially, it depended upon deploying millions of farmers, in the Soviet manner, from agriculture to the construction of roads, dams, and the building of factories. The result was even more disastrous than Stalin's Five-Year Plan. A dramatic fall in food production initiated a famine that led to the death of approximately 30 million people. This was economic tyranny on a grand scale, putting Mao into the same league of life-wasting despotism as Hitler and Stalin – albeit without the concomitant brutality. 'The Great Leap Forward' proved to be a significant leap backwards for China, not only in its failure to meet self-imposed targets, but in terms of the human misery that resulted from it.

Although less costly in human lives, Chairman Mao's next great initiative was equally damaging to the culture and morale of the country. The Socialist Education Movement of the early 1960s was designed to restore ideological purity by increasing support for the on-going revolution and intensifying the class struggle. As with Pol Pot's later regime, intellectuals were especially targeted and forced out of schools, colleges and offices into the factories or the fields. An almost ceaseless barrage of propaganda was unleashed on them as they were urged to abandon individualism and subscribe to the party aims. Soon it was apparent both to his colleagues and the country as a whole that Mao's great initiatives were simply not working. As a result, he was forced to cede much of his power to other senior members of the party. Crucially, he managed to maintain the support of the People's Liberation Army, and in 1966 used it to launch the infamous Cultural Revolution. For the next decade the Chinese people witnessed the remains of their traditional culture being systematically assaulted by the Red Guards. A maelstrom of hatred and ignorance swept across the country, leading to the deaths of tens of thousands. Those perceived to be opponents of the Revolution were, if not murdered, then forced to give up their jobs. Once more China's economy suffered. Mao defended himself by saying 'A revolution is not the same as inviting people to dinner, or writing an essay, or painting a picture…A revolution is an insurrection, an act of violence by which one class overthrows another.' The cultural repression that followed was reminiscent of that visited on Germany by the Nazis. Book publication virtually ceased; liberal ideas were suppressed. Art schools were closed and the publication of art journals prohibited. As with all repressive and puritanical regimes, historic temples and monuments were smashed or vandalized. Finally the army had to intervene to restore order.

Mao's legacy was to prove as dire as that of Stalin. Their drive for efficiency came at a terrible human cost, and the results were questionable at best. Without their heavy-handed and despotic interventions, both China and Russia would have evolved more slowly but more solidly. It was the attempt to short-circuit genuine progress via unrealistic plans that had proved so disastrous.

While Stalin and Mao sought to improve national efficiency by grandiose and theoretical long-term plans, Hitler took a quicker and more pragmatic route. Essentially, what he did was to nationalize Germany's industry while allowing Germany's non-Jewish capitalists in the Nazi party to keep their factories and wealth – as long as they accepted that there was now only one customer: the German government. To further reduce unemployment and boost the status of the Nazi regime, Hitler eased credit restrictions and began commissioning large-scale public works, such as the new autobahn road network. The result was that entrepreneurship declined as Nazi Germany became almost a corporate state. The compensation was apparently spectacular growth in the early 1930s, which contrasted markedly with the slow but steady progress of the United States economy. Clearly Hitler had a great advantage over the other totalitarian dictators, because Germany had in 1933 a far more advanced industrial infrastructure than either the Soviet Union or China. Less concerned with updating antiquated technology, Hitler concentrated on reforming the labour laws and motivating the workforce. The programme began with an edict that brought the independent trade unions under state administration, while at the same time imposing strict controls on both wages and prices. In defiance of the Paris Peace Treaty that had ended the First World War, the Führer ordered Germany to commence rearming, thereby cutting unemployment at a stroke. This was essentially creating a military economy in peacetime; it involved large-scale spending that gave a temporary boost to the economy, but did little to increase the underlying need for creativity, innovation or greater economic flexibility. As the people flocked back to work they discovered the price they had paid for this apparent economic miracle – they no longer had the protection of independent trade unions, and wages were rigidly controlled.

Given the unrealistic nature of the Nazi regime, it was not surprising that Hitler had decided that rearmament would be paid for by the profits of future conquest. To solve his immediate cash flow problem, he ordered that the payment of German reparations to the Allies for the First World War should be suspended at once. But the long-term problem remained, in that by shackling the cost of rearmament to future military gains rather than future earnings, as is customary, Hitler was behaving like a gambler. Without territorial expansion the German economy would collapse; he appears to have had little alternative but to go to war. He had placed himself in the position of an armed robber who must rob the bank in order to get the money he owes on his gun. Hitler's reckless expenditure on armaments, along with the threat of inflation as a result of the expansion in money supply, caused explosive pressures.

As a result, he had to find a constant supply of new victims to pillage – Austria, Czechoslovakia, Poland and eventually the Rhineland. Then came the biggest gamble of all: his ill-judged invasion of the Soviet Union, which ensured his inevitable defeat. Hitler's move on Austria began in February 1938 when he invited the Austrian chancellor, Kurt von Schuschnigg, to join him at his Bavarian retreat, the Bertesgarden. By remorseless pressure, Hitler forced the Chancellor to sign an agreement that gave the Austrian Nazis a virtual free hand in deciding the destiny of their country. When Schuschnigg later attempted to repudiate the agreement by announcing a plebiscite on the question of an Anchluss with Germany, Hitler immediately ordered occupation by German troops. This operation would set the pattern for his next moves, as the enthusiastic reception that the Austrian people gave him, made Hitler decide to annex the nation. Returning in triumph to Vienna, the scene of his youthful humiliations and hardships, was perhaps the height of Hitler's personal triumph and equal to the capitulation of France. Having seen that there was no resistance forthcoming from either Britain or France, he now set his sights on Czechoslovakia. Konrad Henlein, leader of the German minority in Czechoslovakia, was instructed to agitate for the rights of Sudetenland Germans, making new demands that the Czechoslovakian government would find impossible to concede, and so making German annexation inevitable. The Slovak majority was provoked into open opposition to the German minority, so offering Hitler the excuse of intervening. On March 16, 1939, he proclaimed the dissolution of the Czechoslovakian state whose very existence he, as an Austrian, had always regarded as unnatural.

There now appeared to be nothing to stop Hitler achieving his next and even more important goal; the seizure of Poland. In this case, however, there was united hostility from the Poles and the risk of conflict with both Britain and France, who had treaty obligations to Poland. Before making his move Hitler strengthened his alliance with Italy by signing the Pact of Steel in May 1939 and negotiating a non-aggression pact with the Soviet Union that was completed on 23 August. With this done, he ordered German military forces to attack Poland on 1 September 1939. Having witnessed the supine attitude of the allies over his past annexations Hitler might well have believed that they would again refuse to act over Poland but it was a step too far and Britain and French regretfully declared war on Germany. Until this moment Hitler had unwaveringly pursued the objectives of his foreign policy clearly laid down in *Mein Kampf*. Moreover, he had shown astonishing skill in timing and in correctly judging the mood of the European democracies. Up to this point his every move had been successful; and even now any doubts about British and French military intervention were dispelled by the rapid triumph of the German army in

Poland. The result was to convince him of his own infallibility and to encourage him to push ahead with his plans for ultimate conquest in the Soviet Union.

Hitler's single-mindedness was to prove his downfall, however. While it drove his remorseless rise to power, it proved a liability when it came to developing a flexible economy. It could also be said to have fatally compromised his military decisions, as he often refused point-blank to allow his generals to retreat and regroup. In consequence, the German armies were condemned to a series of remorseless defeats. His economic management contrasts strongly with that of a far less significant despot, for although José Gaspar Rodríguez de Francia of Paraguay was a particularly bloody tyrant, he was also a gifted amateur economist. Ruling from 1814 until his death in 1840, Francia succeeded in building a strong, prosperous, secure and independent nation. He left Paraguay at peace, with government coffers full and with many infant industries flourishing. In person, Francia was honest, capable, diligent and unconcerned with personal aggrandisement, which made him popular with the lower classes. Like Hitler, he trampled on human rights and imposed an authoritarian police state on his people, but it was his peculiar theories that make him unique in the history of despotism. For the 26 years of his presidency, he ran the country with the aid of only three other people, aiming to establish a society on the principles of Rousseau's Social Contract, which maintained that people should give up some rights to a government in order to receive social order. To create his personal utopia, he imposed an extraordinary isolation on Paraguay – all external trade was forbidden, but industries were encouraged. His policies were a weird mixture of progression and repression. All opposition was outlawed, higher education was curtailed, but primary schools were developed. The interference in Paraguyan religious affairs by the Catholic Inquisition was abolished, but so too were newspapers and the postal service. In all, Francia produced a culture in which a high level of efficiency was combined with obscurantism – a unique society ruled by the strangest of despots.

CHAPTER 13

Despotic Groups

The despotism so far considered in this book has been that of a single man, king, tyrant or dictator who, often with the help of others, has either seized or inherited power over a subject people. He alone dictates the rules, targets his enemies and pursues a single vision that may or may not depend on some form of religious or ethical belief. But despotism may not always be the preserve of a single man. Occasionally despotism can be imposed by a group that lacks a single all-powerful leader but that unites in a common purpose. The group does not need to control the society as a whole to do this but just to dominate part of it. Criminals, for example, have done this for thousands of years combining in gangs to extort money from their neighbours and in the process terrorizing neighbourhoods, businesses and individuals. Such despotic groups have often evaded full retribution because they pose no threat to the nation as a whole and yet the misery they impose on people is often more brutal and persistent than that of any single despotic ruler. Psychological research has shown that the criminal mind has much in common with the despotic: both have their origin in a traumatic childhood lacking in positive experiences and conventional relationships. Studies of criminal psychology at UCLA (University of California, Los Angeles) have shown that the most important factors in the creation of an adult criminal are the absence of a father in childhood and a general lack of affection. Revealingly these are exactly the same early experiences suffered by Adolf Hitler, Joseph Stalin, Idi Amin, Saddam Hussein and many of the world's most despotic tyrants. The studies at UCLA have also shown that criminals share a common inability to form friendship when young: not only are they rejected by their family but also shunned by other 'normal' children in their neighbourhood or community. They become loners like Saddam Hussein, learning to depend on their own resources and never fully trusting anyone for the rest of their lives. As a response to rejection these children defend themselves by claiming that they find other children uninteresting and their more conventional lives boring. As a result, the potential young criminal gravitates towards those who are older and more adventurous than his contemporaries. When reading that young American delinquents consistently use the classroom as an arena for practising criminal activity by fighting, lying, stealing and engaging in power play against teachers and other pupils, Mussolini's hostility and aggression towards his teachers is recalled. Those in charge take the place of the parents who have rejected him and must suffer his frustration and revenge. So the early childhood of Idi Amin or Saddam Hussein, loveless, neglected and isolated, is almost identical to that of many criminals and serial killers today.

The second characteristic shared by despots and criminals alike is the incapacity to experience any form of empathy or to imagine themselves in the place of their victims. The cruel behaviour displayed towards their victims by criminal gang leaders, such as the Kray brothers in London in the 1960s, has a great similarity to the sadism of Caligula or Ivan the Terrible when terrorizing Roman Senators or Russian boyars. The only difference between them is that the despotic rulers of entire countries were able to indulge their perversions regardless of consequences whereas the Krays were always aware they if they went too far the full force of the British state would descend on them. For as they proved, as long as they reserved their despotic control to their own territory in the East End of London and tortured only their fellow criminals, the Krays were largely left alone to build their crime empire. Young criminals have always been attracted to ruthless gangs much as young German males in the 1930s were attracted to Hitler's SS or young Russians to Ivan the Terrible's Oprichniki in the 16th century. Belonging to such organizations offers power and excitement together with a spurious form of glamour. It also provides the added benefit to the loner of bonding with an existing group providing him with instant comradeship and purpose. Members of criminal gangs in California have frequently described that they came to sincerely love each other and the gang became the substitute for their real family. To receive such instant status and acceptance as part of the group is as compelling a reason for any misfit to join a Los Angeles street gang as it was for a disgruntled Haitian to join Papa Doc Duvalier's criminal band of Tonton Macoutes.

Like the single despot, criminal groups have always been with us bringing terror and oppression to their fellow citizens: ancient Egyptian literature describes bands of robbers who preyed upon merchants transporting goods along the caravan routes and Chinese historians wrote similar accounts of specialized gangs that committed robberies and kidnappings for profit. Often the criminals were successful in creating a myth that they were honourable men and that their activities were for the common good. The folklore myth of Robin Hood robbing the rich to give to the poor is the best-known example. Pirates too, who made their living by murder, robbery and kidnap, were successful in leading some to believe that theirs was an exciting and romantic business. What these romanticized legends ignored was the misery visited on their victims – ordinary people struggling to exist while having to pay tribute to these criminals.

By the 19th century, American law enforcement already had the problem of dealing with urban criminal gangs that had established themselves in every major city. All had their origin in the various ethnic communities that had migrated to America. One of the first began its activities in the Five Points District of New York City in the 1820s. Imaginatively named the Forty Thieves, it operated along the waterfront, engaging in such despotic actions as murder, robbery, assault and other violent crimes. Composed of recently arrived Irish immigrants, the Forty Thieves was so successful that it attracted a group of young imitators who called themselves the Forty Little Thieves. The real victims of these criminals were the ordinary people of the various ethnic communities forced to pay tribute or risk gang violence. Throughout the 19th century criminal gangs continued to flourish and their numbers increased with discharged out-of-work soldiers who appeared at the end of the Civil War in 1865. These war veterans had great difficulty returning to a peaceful society and formed well-armed gangs led by talented criminals such as the infamous brothers Frank and Jesse James who recruited men, often boyhood friends or relatives, in the manner of the Sicilian Mafia to assist them. By the 1920s, Chicago is reported to have had over 1,000 gangs and the introduction of prohibition only encouraged more to form. Over time, these gangsters expanded their operations and made agreements with each other over disputed territories. The problem of dealing effectively with them was never overcome as law enforcement concentrated on the crimes rather than the criminal organizations behind them and so little was achieved.

The American Civil War (1861–1865) had, in fact, brought about the end of perhaps the most despotic system in modern history that was carried out by supposedly respectable landowners, merchants and shipping companies. This was slavery, a system of bondage described by the Abolitionists as 'absolute despotism of the most pernicious and unmitigated form'. A quotation from the Bible became the Golden Rule of their movement, 'All things whatsoever ye would that men should do to you, do ye even so to them.' Abolitionist preachers urged their listeners to imagine themselves as the enslaved, a message that would surely have fallen on deaf ears given the slave owners complete lack of empathy with their victims. The arguments that were used to justify slavery were substantially the same as those used to defend despotism of any other kind. As Aristotle had written over 2,000 years earlier, 'The relationship of master and slave is based on force and being so based has no warrant in justice.' This was certainly true of any slave suspected of a crime by his master, as he could be examined under torture and a master could refuse to grant a slave a fair trial at which he could defend or justify himself. In most cases the master also had the power of life and death over the slave. He could banish a slave at any time without having to give an account to anybody and imprison him in the most appalling conditions. The mechanisms of slavery are well known. Slaves were bought in Africa then transported to America in what was called the 'middle passage' – an appalling confinement in chains, even more terrible than being lowered into one of Ivan the Terrible's dungeons. Many slaves died during the journey because of the unsanitary conditions, succumbing to contagious diseases such as dysentery, or suffering from scurvy, starvation or malnutrition, suffocation, and most poignant of all, despair. On reaching America, the majority of the survivors were sold, while still on board ship, to plantation owners or their agents. They then endured a lifetime of hard work without civil rights of any kind. Even the children of slaves were considered slaves at birth and few slaves in the colonial period were ever freed. Public opinion, however, had already begun to recognise the gross injustice and cruel despotism of the slavery business. On 14 June 1788 the Massachusetts *Sentinel* newspaper carried a leader highly critical of slavery and indignant that 'a man should be treated in the same manner as a beast, or a piece of household furniture, and bought and sold, and entirely subjected to the will of another, whose equal he is by nature, and all this for no crime on his part, but merely because he is of a certain colour, born in a certain country, or descended of certain parents'. In Britain the contemporary outcry against the slavers was even more profound and within ten years there was a dramatic change in public opinion. The Abolitionist message was so successful that a country that had been the leading slave trader on the Atlantic route became committed to not only banning the slave trade but to attempting to force the rest of the world to do the same. Royal Navy ships began policing the seas and harassing the vessels of other nations still involved in the trade, often stopping them and removing the slaves.

With the defeat of the Confederate States of America, a constitutional amendment banning slavery in the United States was introduced in January 1865, slavery ended but its bitter legacy remained in a white community that resented the removal of its supremacy. The establishment, by the Union government, of the Freeman's Bureau, an organisation designed to protect the interests of former slaves by helping them to find paid work or providing them with educational and health facilities, provoked the most hostility among the defeated Southerners. There was also the first Civil Rights Bill, vetoed by President Andrew Johnson in February 1866, which was designed to protect freed slaves from existing Southern laws that had placed severe restrictions on them, such as prohibiting their right to vote, forbidding them to sit on juries, limiting their right to testify against white men, carrying weapons in public places and working in certain occupations. That same year, a new Radical Republican majority in Congress passed a Reconstruction Act that divided the South into five military districts, each under a major general. New elections were to be held in each state with freed male slaves being allowed to vote. This development was too much for the diehard white supremacists who established their own despotic group, the Ku Klux Klan (KKK). The first branch was established in Pulaski, Tennessee, to be followed by many more during the following years. Most of the leaders were former members of the Confederate Army and the first Grand Wizard was Nathan Bedford Forrest, who had been an outstanding general for the Confederacy during the American Civil War. Soon the Klan members, wearing masks, white cardboard hats and draped in white sheets, were terrorising freed slaves, torturing and killing them, and persecuting those whites who sympathised with the blacks. Immigrants from Europe were also targeted as they were blamed for the success of the Radical Republicans in the national elections. The success of the Klan was initially impressive as they managed to restore white rule in North Carolina, Tennessee and Georgia. Other despotic white supremacy groups emerged, such as the White Brotherhood, the Men of Justice, the Constitutional Union Guards and the Knights of the White Camellia. All were united by an implacable determination to stop black people from voting. Successful black businessmen were attacked and attempts to form black protection groups, such as trade unions, were quickly stifled. These groups became such a danger to democracy that the new President, Ulysses S. Grant, took action against the KKK and in 1870 instigated an investigation into the organization. The following year, a Grand Jury reported that Klan members comprised a large proportion of the white population of every profession and class throughout the South. Each member was required to furnish himself with a pistol, a Ku Klux gown and a signal light. Their operations were conducted by night and were invariably directed against blacks and members of the Republican Party. The Klan was inflicting summary vengeance on black citizens, breaking into their houses at the dead of night, dragging them from their beds, torturing them in the most inhuman manner, and in many instances murdering them. One black American, Pauli Murray, wrote about the experiences of her grandparents after the American Civil War. Late at night her grandmother would be awakened by the thudding of horses' hooves as nightriders, brandishing torches and yelling like banshees, swept into the clearing and rode round and round her cabin, churning the earth outside her door. She never knew when they might set fire to the place, burning her to death inside, and some nights she was so terrified that she would get out of bed in the middle of the night, creep through the woods to the roadway, and trudge the 12 miles (19 km) to the nearest town, preferring the dark, lonely but open road to the risk of being trapped at the farm. Such events have an uncanny similarity to the way in which Ivan the Terrible's Oprichniki horsemen terrorised rural Russia in the 16th century.

In April 1871 Congress finally passed the *Ku Klux Act*, which gave the President the authority to suspend the writ of *habeas corpus* in areas where disturbances occurred. The power of the Klan was broken but it had achieved its main objective – the re-establishment of white supremacy in the South. The organization practically disappeared and did not emerge again as a major political force until the 1920s, when it spread its despotism and oppression throughout the South, gaining new members in Texas, Oklahoma, Indiana, Oregon and Maine. By 1925 the total membership numbered some 4 million white supremacists. Although the local activities of the Klan continued it was not until the 1950s, with the emergence of the Civil Rights Movement, that it became a national issue again. One of the worst atrocities occurred in September 1963 when a bomb placed under the steps of the 16th Street Baptist Church in Birmingham, Alabama, exploded, killing four young black children attending the Sunday school class. This outrage led to the formation of the Congress of Racial Equality and the Student Nonviolent Coordinating Committee, dedicated to ending the political disenfranchisement of African Americans in the Deep South. This, together with the introduction of more effective Civil Rights laws, meant that the power of the KKK was finally broken and America was rid of its most despotic and anachronistic group.

While slavery itself had been ended in America after the Civil War in 1865 it was to re-appear in the African Congo in an equally virulent form under Belgian rule. The Congo, a vast area of Western Africa, was rich in natural resources and was internationally recognized as the personal property of King Leopold II of Belgium (1835–1909; reigned 1865–1909), once described by the writer Mark Twain as a 'greedy, grasping, avaricious, cynical, bloodthirsty old goat'. Leopold's possession was a strange anomaly agreed upon by Britain and Germany, colonialist powers themselves, in order to deter further French territorial ambitions in Africa. Once Leopold's right to the Congo had been confirmed in February 1885 he set about making it pay by intensifying the mineral exploration and improving the infrastructure, constructing a railway line from the centre to the coast. His first problem was to rid the country of the hundreds of Arab slavers who were firmly entrenched there. Ironically one of the conditions of Leopold's tenure was to end the last remnants of slavery that still existed. However, all this cost large sums of money and in just 5 years Leopold had already spent some 20 million francs on his venture. Now he came under even more pressure to show a good return on this borrowed capital. So in 1889 he mortgaged the Congo, transferring his own personal empire to his country of Belgium, in return for another 25-million-franc loan. To service this enormous debt he then set about extracting the maximum profit from the Congo using the most despotic and ruthless methods. Mining and the harvesting of ivory and rubber promised a big return but they relied heavily on labour. Large work teams were needed but the native Congolese showed little interest in joining the foreigners in the exploitation of their forests and so Leopold hired a large number of agents and overseers to 'persuade' local men to work for them. The methods of recruitment were as ruthless as the work pattern imposed, as the unfortunate workers were brutally driven to meet and even exceed very high production targets. This arrangement quickly led to a localized despotism characterized by the utmost tyranny and barbarism. Entire villages were held responsible for meeting the rubber production quotas with wives and tribal chiefs held hostage until they were achieved. Discipline was enforced by the use of the chicotte, a hippo-hide whip. Often workers were whipped to death and 90 lashes were considered the standard punishment for slackers. Such beatings were just one of the many atrocities inflicted on the terrorized people. As dramatized by Polish-born novelist Joseph Conrad in his novel, *Heart of Darkness*, Leopold's agents and armed African soldiers would also set themselves up as local minor despots, killing and mutilating anyone who opposed them. Stories began reaching the outside world of soldiers returning from expeditions bearing strings of human ears or collections of amputated hands. When compared to the Nazi holocaust or the casualties that resulted from Stalin's collectivization policy the numbers killed in the Congo are still surprisingly high at an estimated 15 million dead. While these atrocities were taking place in a distant land Leopold stayed safely at home in Belgium much as Stalin had remained in Moscow while his secret police tyrannized the Siberian gulags 2,000 miles (3,219 km) away. Both men had also presided over an army of petty despots who carried out their orders without question; the Russians out of fear and the hope of political advancement, and the Belgians and their native allies purely for financial gain.

Another tyrannical group that has preyed on the people for centuries is the Italian Mafia. With its roots in rural Sicily, and with a spurious code of 'honour' and fanciful rites and mythology, it has ruthlessly enforced its extortion and kept a stranglehold on the Sicilian economy for centuries. The Mafia began in the 18th century when Sicilian nobles moved from their rural estates into the cities of Palermo, Catania and Messina leaving their estates in the control of local land agents. Without the constraints or the sense of responsibility traditionally associated with the old aristocracy these, often ruthless, men showed little concern for their tenants other than to make sure that they paid their rents on time. Any delays or evasions were dealt with by local thugs specifically recruited for the purpose. These 'Mafiosi' now posing as 'men of honour' rapidly established a network of mutual co-operation groups divided up on a territorial basis with a 'capo' or leader in each Sicilian town. The first to suffer their depredations were the peasants who were forced to submit to the local mafia's despotic rule by means of brutal assaults or being driven from their meagre land holdings. From their rural origins the Mafia then extended its activities to urban crime, imposing a toll on trade and offering businessmen 'protection' from their rivals. By 1900 the Sicilian economy was virtually controlled by the Mafia who then began exporting their criminality to the United States. It is a strange fact that the only real check suffered by the Sicilian Mafia was at the hands of one of the 20th century's most prominent despots: following a visit to Sicily in June 1923 Mussolini decided to extend his totalitarian control to the whole island and that involved crushing the Mafia. The man he chose to carry out his orders was the Prefect, Cesare Mori. Based at his headquarters, the Villa Mori on the Palermo seafront, Mori used Mussolini's fascist forces to ruthlessly attack the organization's long established structure throughout the island. Mori's approach was simple and direct. Anyone suspected of involvement in the criminal organization were promptly arrested, along with their wives, children and even parents, and then tortured into confession. The methods used were as brutal as any used by the Mafiosi on their victims. Those arrested could have the soles of their feet burned, be given painful electric shocks or forced to have seawater thrust down their throats until they revealed information. As brutal as the Mafia had always been to their own victims, they were astonished at Mori's ruthless tactics as the bullies themselves became the victims. The result of Mori's campaign of counter violence was the near destruction of the whole organization with many of the remnants fleeing to the United States. However with the fall of Mussolini the Mafia began to reassert its control over the people of Sicily. In 1944 they had a lucky break when the collaboration of Sicilian-born Salvatore 'Lucky' Luciano with the US Navy made the Allied invasion of Sicily easier than it otherwise would have been. Delighted to have seen the ignominious fall of Mussolini, the Mafia leaders did all they could to ingratiate themselves with the new American-controlled administration. Soon old Mafiosi posing as sincere anti-Fascists, such as Calogero Vizzini of Villalba, were being given mayorships and other sinecures that put them in an ideal position to restore the organization's despotic power over the Sicilian economy. Now fully back in business, the Mafia infiltrated the building trade and began buying their way into government-run agencies. In Palermo, control of the planning system alone allowed the Mafia and their friends to build some of the worst modern development in the whole of Italy. Today few areas of commercial activity escape Mafia corruption and even the administrator of Palermo's largest hospital has traditionally been a Mafioso. Why Sicilians continue to accept this economic tyranny by criminals remains a mystery rooted in their suspicion of outsiders and their acceptance of fate.

Yet the Italian ethos as a whole is almost as cynical and people presume that their political leaders are as greedy and dishonest as the country's businessmen. This national cynicism has also led to the resigned acceptance of another Southern Italian criminal organization that has an even more despotic effect on peoples lives than the Sicilian Mafia, the Neapolitan Camorra. Composed of a network of thugs, exploiters and killers, the Camorra runs the slums of the city of Naples and the nearby towns with particular brutality bringing fear and extortion to thousands. Divided into warring families, frequently in dispute with each other, the Camorra is the main reason why the Italian province of Campania has the highest murder rate in Europe. Its origins are even more historic than those of the Mafia for it is said to have originated with the Garduna of the late Middle Ages. This criminal group began operating in Seville and then moved to Naples when Spain took control of the region in the 15th century. The new Spanish rulers found Naples in such chaos and disorder that they allowed their own Spanish merchants to hire the imported criminals, now called the Camorra, to protect their trade. Over the years the organization established a network of both illegal and semi-legal activities that extended far beyond Naples. Today the Camorra, apart from terrorizing any outsiders who oppose its actions, remains in a state of constant feuding within itself. Criminal bosses are killed on the orders of other criminal bosses in what is, in reality, a war among gangs, and innocent people are often caught up in the ambushes. In recent years the Camorra has become best known for drug trafficking but the lucrative and clandestine trade in industrial waste disposal is its second largest source of revenue. The companies that manage rubbish collection and waste treatment centres in Naples and the surrounding Campania region are either infiltrated or directly controlled by the Camorra. Undercutting competitors' prices and ignoring the safety procedures that are observed throughout the rest of Europe, the Camorra have become so successful that they ship thousands of tons of industrial waste from the north of Italy. Without bothering with the relevant technology, their companies dump it illegally both in and around Naples in a business that has an estimated turnover of almost 4 billion dollars a year. Such is their control of local politics that they have been able to sabotage plans for new incinerators. Instead the waste continues to be buried or burned and poisoning the local environment so that people living in parts of the Campania region are three times more likely to get liver cancer than those living in the rest of the country. Other hazards for the local people include being caught up in the frequent drive-by shootings between various Camorra gangs. Many honest politicians have given up in despair when faced with attempting to control the endemic crime that contaminates the region. As the Italian Premier, Romano Prodi, said in 2007 'The Camorra is the greatest single obstacle to the development of Southern Italy.'

Less well known than either the Neapolitan Camorra or the Sicilian Mafia is the even more brutal, if that could be possible, 'Ndrangheta – the name derives from a Greek word meaning 'honour' – in Calabria. Originally a rural-based criminal organization it had until recently confined its activities to kidnappings in the remote rural South. In recent years it has extended its activities to the large industrial cities in the north of Italy where the 'Ndrangheta families control once legitimate banks, restaurants, shopping centres, construction companies, betting shops, luxury boutiques, supermarkets, night-clubs, discotheques and gaming arcades. Working through a network of accountants, lawyers and bank managers, the organization is estimated to include 10,000 members both in Italy and abroad. They control legal and illegal businesses with a turnover that amounts to 3.5 per cent of Italy's total GDP. The main business, however, remains drug dealing and from its home in Calabria the 'Ndrangheta now controls most of the drug trafficking in Europe and throughout the world. The 'Ndrangheta's move north has transformed the industrial city of Milan into the cocaine capital of Europe with three times as many drug users there as in the rest of Italy. New business activities include money laundering and online transactions at which its members are just as adept as they once were in the use of the sawn-off shotgun in the wilds of Calabria.

What makes the 'Ndrangheta a particular threat in the future is that although a third of its profits are ploughed back into crime, two thirds are clandestinely invested in legitimate businesses. So powerful has it become and so widespread its operations – six men were shot to death in Germany in 2007 during an 'Ndrangheta dispute – that many Italians suspect that its members will soon infiltrate the political system, much as the Sicilian Mafia had done in the past. Defeating this despotic organization is a difficult task, as criminal and family loyalties overlap making it almost impossible for any single member to turn against the whole. While new laws introduced in the early 1990s made it far easier for a Mafioso to turn state's evidence, it did nothing to break the 'Ndrangheta's close knit loyalty. Any member proposing to give information to the police would soon realize that he would be betraying perhaps 200 or more of his own relatives. Often this loyalty collapses within the family groups and turf wars and disputes break out. The late 1980s saw the violent deaths of over 800 people in the area of Reggio Calabria alone. Many of those killed were innocent bystanders caught up in the gangsters' crossfire. Nor is the danger posed by the 'Ndrangheta confined to Italy alone for like the Sicilians, the Calabrians have consistently emigrated abroad, mainly to Canada and Australia where they have created branches of the organization to distribute the illicit drugs. There are also large communities of Calabrian descent in Latin America who have helped the 'Ndrangheta become leading players in the global cocaine trade. There are even claims that 80 per cent of all cocaine entering Europe is brought in by these Calabrian mobsters. Due to the power of the Mafia, the Camorra and the 'Ndrangheta, one-third of Italy is in the grip of organized crime that keeps the region in a permanent state of neglect. So why do the Southern Italians tolerate this criminal despotism? Perhaps the answer lies in the innate character of the people, for while the democratic tradition flourishes in the North it has never fully taken root in the South. Northern Italians are used to co-operating with each other for the common good but in the South the people are more individualistic and mistrustful of each other, preferring vertical patronage systems that are deeply authoritarian.

These Italian-based criminal organizations have also made inroads into American organized crime. Some of their members came to the United States in the 1960s and were given permission by the boss of the largest Cosa Nostra family in New York to begin operating the newly established and highly lucrative heroin trade. Since then these groups have flourished and have taken over control of the criminal operations which once belonged exclusively to Cosa Nostra. This internationalism of organized crime poses an increasing threat for the future. A recent survey by the World Federation of United Nations Associations claims that the annual profits of criminal gangs around the world are roughly equivalent to the whole of Britain's GDP, of which half comes in the form of bribes. Contrary to the popular myth, only a small percentage goes to tyrants and corrupt officials of Third World Countries for, as the report states, the vast majority of bribes are paid to people in richer countries where bribery can influence far more lucrative projects. Much of the illicit income that flows through the world's black economy comes from the economic crimes of counterfeiting and piracy. In recent years human trafficking has grown dramatically providing a new form of slavery that is every bit as pernicious, if not as overtly brutal, as King Leopold's rule over the Congo. According to the United Nations an incredible 27 million people are still held in slavery throughout the world – far more than at the peak of the African slave trade.

CHAPTER 14

Are Despots Mad?

Anyone who has read an account of the horrors and atrocities inflicted by despots must ask this simple question: were these men insane? Not just obsessive in their behaviour, or sadistically cruel, or even deeply paranoid – but fundamentally and clinically insane? In an attempt to find an answer, the Italian writer Riccardo Orizio in 2004 interviewed six deposed dictators, and also the wife of Enver Hoxha of Albania. Each despot had enjoyed supreme power in his own country, but had been driven out and was now living in exile. All had different justifications for seizing power, ranging from fighting terrorists (Slobodan Milošević), to simply having been told by his father that he must inherit the family business (Jean-Claude Duvalier). All showed delusions of grandeur, and all appeared to Orizio to be completely divorced from reality. Duvalier was so caught up in the myth that he inherited from his father that he was convinced that one day he would be deified. He quoted a prayer that his father, Papa Doc, had decreed must be said by all Haitians. It began, 'Our Papa Doc, who art in the National Palace for life, hallowed be thy name by present and future generations.' The bloody ex-tyrant of Uganda, Idi Amin, who had taken refuge in Saudi Arabia, consistently referred to himself throughout the interview as 'the last king of Scotland'. Jean-Bédel Bokassa still insisted long after his removal by French paratroops that Pope Paul VI (1897–1978; in office 1963–1978) had nominated him as the '13th apostle of the Holy Mother Church', to set along-side his self-proclaimed title of 'Grand Master of the International Brotherhood of Knights Collectors of Postage Stamps.' All believed that they had been unfairly removed from power and considered they had a divine right to rule. Any accusations of tyranny or ethnic persecution were abruptly dismissed, with Mrs Hoxha being the most adamant defender of her late husband's rule. She dismissed proven cases of torture and murder in Albania as 'mere trifles not worth mentioning'. All were convinced that history would eventually absolve them, while feeling that they had been completely misunderstood by world opinion. Their self-justification was astonishing; they seemed to have no comprehension of the roles they had played in destroying or ruining vast numbers of lives. When asked by Orizio if he felt any remorse, Idi Amin replied, 'No, only nostalgia.' Although they could all be seen as living proof of the 'banality or evil', their self-delusion was so extreme and unusual that on this ground alone their sanity might well be doubted.

Anyone studying the reign of Ivan the Terrible 400 years ago would not find it difficult to believe that he was clinically insane, or at least drifted in and out of bouts of insanity throughout his life. There is consistent evidence of paranoia, expressed in his excessive anxiety about his own health and wellbeing. This was often taken to irrational excess; he was convinced that he was suffering persecution, and that all manner of conspiracies were in process, including attempts to poison him. Although never stable nor predictable, his mental health dramatically deteriorated in 1553 when he fell suddenly ill with a fever, perhaps caused by pneumonia or encephalitis. For several days he drifted in and out of consciousness in the Kremlin. His condition deteriorated, and he appeared about to die. Summoning his leading boyars he demanded they swear, in the likely event of his death, an oath of allegiance to his six-month-old son and heir, Dimitri. In the confusion that followed his order, some boyars obeyed, but others either ignored his request or left the palace – their behaviour intensifying Ivan's already acute suspicions as he lay recovering. Seven years later, his terror of poisoning was reawakened when his adored wife Anastasia was taken suddenly ill and died. As she was carried to the grave, Ivan followed her bier wailing and moaning, convinced that his enemies had used either magic or poison against her. Anastasia had been a loyal and simple creature, and her loss must have brought back the terrible sense of isolation that Ivan endured as a child surrounded by dangerous enemies. From the moment of her death, his cruel and erratic behaviour intensified, and he was said to have flown into sudden and inexplicable rages. Other disturbing symptoms accompanied these sudden mood swings, and he began indulging in wild bouts of drinking, fornication and sodomy. Great beakers of alcohol were said to have been forced on him by his cronies; he was encouraged to drink a toast to the devil. Wild dancing, dressing in masks and cavorting with the many clowns, minstrels and jugglers that he had encouraged into his palace all added to the Breugelian atmosphere of the court.

Shortly before Christmas 1564, Ivan suddenly announced his decision to abdicate. He quietly packed up his belongings and treasures and left Moscow. Given his paranoia and the boyars' hostility towards him, this seemed a dangerous move; it would leave the absent Tsar at the mercy of whoever chose to seize power. But his ploy was more carefully thought out than was at first realized. The people clamoured for his return, and after a month of careful negotiations, he agreed to return – on the understanding that he would now exercise absolute power, and have complete freedom to punish disloyalty and seize the states of recalcitrant boyars. What appeared an act of lunacy was in reality an astute gamble that convinced the people of his good intentions. From now on, he showed little compassion for his subjects; they were beaten up, robbed or raped just for his own sadistic entertainment. His personal friendships were of short duration and his 'friends' usually ended up dead. Yet Ivan was constantly afflicted with guilt – not for the atrocities that he had committed, but for the religious sins of blasphemy and fornication. These were all the more agonizing because he considered himself the sacred conduit between God and the Russian people. Consequently, most of the instructions he issued were couched in the religious or semi-apocryphal terms appropriate to someone who thought himself half-man, half-god. This semi-divine status, he believed, gave him the authority to act as he thought best and fully endorsed his use of 'divine violence'.

By 1571 Ivan the Terrible was almost 40 years old and fast declining into morbid paranoia. Both his second and third wives had died mysteriously; he was convinced that they, like Anastasia, had been poisoned by the enemies that surrounded him. For this reason he had suddenly ordered the arrest and execution of some of his most loyal servants in July 1570. His letters to his friend Prince Kurbsky, which attempted to justify his actions, show no pity for either the victims or the families that were executed alongside them. Ivan's pitiless ruthlessness was abnormal even for a despot – he claimed that he wanted no one left alive to pray for the souls of the dead. He was fascinated not only with religion, but with black magic, and had a primitive fear of the power of magicians. This was inherited from his parents – his father Vasily III and his mother Elena had once scoured Russia for a magician who could make Elena pregnant, their agents even going as far as Finland and Lapland in search of a fertility shaman. When on 11 November 1572 a brilliant supernova star appeared in the sky above Moscow, Ivan became terrified that it was an omen of disasters to come, and that he might be ousted from the throne of Russia.

One of the few people with whom the Tsar maintained a sane relationship was his eldest son and heir, the Tsarevitch. But on 19 November 1581, Ivan fell into a rage with his son's pregnant wife, screaming and shouting that the clothes she wore were immodest. He then proceeded to beat her until she miscarried her baby. When his son burst in and began protesting, Ivan raised the pointed iron staff he always carried and struck him a fatal blow to the head. The young man was fatally wounded, but lay in a coma for several days before succumbing to the injury. Once again Ivan was overcome with remorse, banging his head against his son's coffin as he was carried to his tomb. The following day he started taking liquid mercury to dull his grief, and soon became addicted to it. It is hard to imagine anything more physically devastating than this substance, which he kept bubbling in a cauldron beside his bed. Later, the exhumation of his body showed that he had suffered from advanced mercury poisoning, but also that his bones showed signs of syphilitic ostratis. As mercury was a long-established treatment for this venereal disease, this could also explain why he had taken it. However, the results of this autopsy, dramatic as they are, cannot fully explain Ivan's life-long mental instability, nor the crucifying paranoia that drove him to acts of the most appalling cruelty.

Mercury had also been involved in the death of Emperor Qin in ancient China, and may well explain why he lost his grip on reality in later years. He was said to have steadily increased the dose in his vain search for immortality, for liquid mercury was known to Chinese alchemists as the only substance that could dissolve eternal, incorruptible gold. To Qin, it must have seemed like a supernatural substance with magical powers – even the elixir of eternal life. Mercury cannot be absorbed directly by the body, however, so Chinese alchemists would have mixed it in soluble compounds that could be more easily digested. As absorption takes place, it begins to attack the nervous system, causing tremors that become steadily worse. But the greatest damage is done to the brain, making the victim unusually volatile, argumentative and finally aggressive; it is also known to provoke paranoia, as was observable in Emperor Qin. He once ordered that anyone who revealed his whereabouts was under instant sentence of death, along with their entire family. Seven years after the emperor had initiated his quest for immortality, the mercury began to poison his body as well as his mind, and his kidneys began to fail. Knowing that time was running out, he began to plan his own funeral and a magnificent tomb that would include an underground lake filled with liquid mercury.

The paranoia that underpinned much of Ivan the Terrible's cruel behaviour and the Emperor Qin's later tyranny was to be uncannily repeated in Stalin's rule of Soviet Russia. His surviving cronies later described the daily nightmare of dinners in the Kremlin. The macabre ceremony was repeated night after night; Stalin would sit at the head of the table, forcing his ministers and acolytes to drink while he plotted and probed and flattered and terrified them. As dawn approached, his unwilling guests awaited their fate, their brains befuddled with fear, vodka and confusion. Sometimes nothing happened, but occasionally the NKVD would suddenly enter and lead one or two of them away to be shot. Stalin had refracted violent fear through the alcohol, then presided over a bullying mind-game that often ended in death. According to the American psychiatrists Robins and Post, Stalin was a typically paranoid personality. One of the principal psychological mechanisms involved in his mental disorder was projection, in which he was unable to come to terms with his own 'badness', rage and hostility and therefore projected these qualities onto others. As Post wrote, 'Violently angry and afraid of their own aggression, paranoids defend against their rage by viewing themselves as the victims of persecutors. In effect, the paranoid's impulse to persecute and tyrannize others is denied and projected on to phantom enemies who then become imaginary persecutors who must be hunted down and either subjugated or destroyed.'

Stalin used any excuse to justify the elimination of even the most senior members of his government – men who had been his comrades in the early days of the Revolution, and often his closest supporters in his rise to power. The more loyal they appeared, the more he suspected them, for to Stalin's twisted mind, wouldn't a clever plotter give the impression of being wholeheartedly faithful? This perverse logic led him to murder many of Lenin's and his own most able colleagues, men such as Trotsky, Zinoviev, Kamenev, Radek and Rakovsky. The trial of the so-called 'Trotskyite-Zinovievite Terrorist Centre', was the first of the Moscow Show Trials. It set the tone for the subsequent charades in which thousands of innocents were tortured into confessing to increasingly unbelievable crimes, such as espionage, poisoning, sabotage, and so on.

As Stalin's paranoia raged on, it became clear that no one close to him was safe. Next it was the turn of the Red Army. In June 1937, documents were found that implicated the higher command, led by Marshal Tukhachevsky, in a conspiracy against Stalin. They were clearly Nazi forgeries. The only evidence produced at the trial was from forced confessions, and was used as an excuse to eliminate 3 of the 5 army marshals, 13 out of 15 army generals, 8 out of the 9 admirals as well as 50 out of 57 army corps commanders and all 16 army political commissars. In all, over 30,000 officers and men were executed, leaving the Red Army in chaos. Not only did the depleted army then suffer a humiliating defeat at the hands of tiny Finland in the Winter War of 1939, but it was also too weak to resist the German invasion two years later. Indeed, it was the chaotic state of the Red Army that encouraged Hitler to launch Operation Barbarossa in the first place. That Russia eventually prevailed and Stalin became an international hero is one of the great ironies of modern history, given his paranoid near-destruction of both his army and his administration. But even in the years following the war, when he was at the height of his celebrity, Stalin remained driven by these paranoid urges. In 1949, a group of local politicians organized a Leningrad Trade Fair. The idea was to boost the post-war economy and support the survivors of the siege of Leningrad with goods and services, but Stalin became suspicious. Convinced that they were setting up some form of competition to himself, he ordered an army of lawyers and secret agents to fabricate accusations against them. The following year Nikolai Voznesensky, Mikhail Rodionov, Aleksei Kuznetsov, Pyotr Popkov, Y. F. Kapustin and P. G. Lazutin were all found guilty of embezzling of the state budget for 'non-approved business purposes' and were summarily executed. This was only the beginning, for over 2,000 of Leningrad's most able civil servants were subsequently removed from their posts; 200 of them were sent to the gulags. Among these were some of the most respected scientists, writers and educators of the city, who all eventually perished in the wastes of Siberia. In their place Stalin ordered thousands of supposedly loyal bureaucrats and party officials to move from Moscow to Leningrad and take their place

After the destruction of the Leningrad bureaucrats, Stalin searched around for new victims and found them in Russia's Jewish community. In view of the Cold War, he concluded that as so many Jews had relatives in the United States, they were obviously spying for the CIA. So a new persecution began in the winter of 1952–1953, just before Stalin's death. The writer Samuel Kassow recalled that during that terrible winter, Jewish children came home from school bruised and beaten. Jews were assaulted on public buses; patients shunned their Jewish doctors. Rumours began to spread that the government had decided to deport all Jews to Birobidzhan, the Jewish autonomous region in the far east; there were reports of barracks and freight trains made ready for them. Jewish celebrities such as the violinist David Oistrakh and the ballerina Maya Plisetskaya were ordered to sign a letter of personal allegiance to Comrade Stalin, which implored him to protect their people from the wrath of angry Russians. This was to be Stalin's last monstrous persecution, for a month later, on 28 February 1953 he did not appear after a typical drinking session the night before. His guards and comrades were so terrified of his paranoid reactions that for hours, no one was brave enough to enter his bedroom. Eventually, an aide plucked up enough courage to approach the bed, but jumped back in alarm when one of Stalin's eyes opened briefly to deliver a last baleful stare.

Stalin's paranoia recalls in some respects that of Francia, the despot of Paraguay, who subjected his country to an extraordinary climate of fear in which no one could understand why arrests were made, or why so many were tortured and executed on the president's whim. As Francia's mental condition deteriorated he became increasingly eccentric; he appointed himself head of the Catholic Church in Paraguay, but immediately banned all religious procession and the use of churches at night, in case people were assembling to plot against him. When a real conspiracy was detected, led by his old colleague General Yegros, Francia became frantic, ordering that every hedge or wall near his palace be demolished so as not to provide assassins with cover. One old country woman who attempted to present a petition at the door was seized and thrown into prison for years. After that, Francia ordered his guards to fire on any one who even dared to look at his palace. Wherever he went, he was accompanied by a large escort of guards; the moment he stepped outside the palace, the bell of the cathedral opposite began tolling a warning to the citizens to stay inside their houses. Anyone who did meet him knew to avert their eyes and look at the ground as Francia passed. Ever more reclusive, he died in 1840 having taken to his room and forbidden anyone to enter. As he lay dying, he became consumed with rage at a doctor who was waiting outside, and in a last fit of irrational paranoia he seized a sword and rushed out to kill him – only to fall dead himself in a fit of apoplexy.

A more comprehensive form of madness, no less destructive than the paranoia already described, appears to have afflicted the Emperor Caligula in ancient Rome. His medical history is unusually well documented for the times, and reveals that as a child he suffered constant poor health. His conditions included epileptic fits; these so concerned his predecessor, Emperor Augustus, that he appointed two doctors to attend the child whenever he travelled. Even as a young adult, Caligula continued to have fainting fits and had difficulty keeping his balance, although this did not prevent him racing chariots and horses in the arena. But the most significant sign of disturbance was in his speech: whenever he had to address a public audience, he spoke in an excited torrent of words, shifting from one foot to the other, unable to keep still. When taking part in dramatic performances his excitement was again apparent. He often became obsessed with the part he was playing, adding impromptu words and phrases to his speeches. Being so highly strung, he had great difficulty sleeping; according to Suetonius, who knew him better than most, he often managed little more than three hours a night before being awakened by nightmares. Suetonius blamed Caligula's condition on a single event – a powerful aphrodisiac administered to him by his wife, Caesonia – and recalled that he would often hold conversations with the statue of Jupiter on the Capitoline Hill, or would shout out challenges to the gods while brandishing a spear. Other contemporaries such as Seneca and Jewish philosopher Philo of Alexandria (c.10 BC–AD 45) also cast doubt on the Emperor's sanity, and used words such as dementia to describe his condition. Philo became convinced that the emperor was insane, having endured a crazed verbal onslaught while being required to follow him from room to room. Modern historians and psychologists have speculated that Caligula was a schizophrenic or psychopath, although his malicious sense of humour could account for much of his behaviour. His cruel wit never left him; for example, a supposedly rich man was executed on Caligula's orders. On discovering that the unfortunate victim was penniless, Caligula exclaimed ironically, 'What a pity, he seems to have died in vain.'

Caligula was born into an illustrious Roman family. His father, Germanicus, was one of the most able and popular generals that Rome ever produced, who, before his early death, was seen as the natural successor to the reigning Emperor Augustus. Caligula became the darling of the army, and when the tyrannical Emperor Tiberius died he was elected unanimously to the throne. In the first years of his rule, Caligula was hugely popular – so much so that when he fell suddenly ill, soon after becoming Emperor in AD 37, the crowd slept in the open outside his palace waiting for hourly bulletins on his health. The cause of this illness remains a mystery, although Suetonius claimed that since childhood Caligula had suffered from epilepsy. This was known at the time as the 'parliamentary disease', since it was regarded as an especially bad omen if anyone had a fit while public business was being conducted. Caligula's distant relative, Julius Caesar, had also suffered occasional attacks. Philo, who was living in Rome at the time, states that the illness was caused by the stress of being emperor and by Caligula's increased bath-taking, drinking and sexual activity. His weakened constitution then led to a disease that resulted in some form of severe mental breakdown. Certainly, as Suetonius records, the new emperor showed little sexual restraint with either men or women; he was said to have engaged in homosexual relations, both active and passive, with Marcus Lepidus, Mnester the comedian and various foreign hostages. Another of his contemporaries, Valerius Catullus, a young man of a consular family, even boasted publicly that he had buggered the emperor and quite worn himself out in the process. Besides incest with his sisters and a notorious passion for the prostitute Pyrallis, Caligula was said to have made advances to almost every woman of rank in Rome. This sexual licence may have given him some form of venereal disease that affected his brain, but a modern diagnosis by the medical historian A. T. Sandison is probably more accurate: he suggests that Caligula was suffering from epidemic encephalitis, known to produce symptoms of mental derangement as well as paralysis of the eye muscles. This may explain Suetonius's claim that the emperor was constantly looking in a mirror and pulling faces. An alternative modern diagnosis by R. S. Katz suggests that the stress of becoming emperor had caused Caligula to develop an overactive thyroid gland, although no contemporary witnesses mention the bulging eyes characteristic of this condition.

Whatever the sickness was, it appears to have fundamentally altered his character. There was a marked change in his behaviour; Suetonius claims that he now developed a moon fetish, chronic insomnia and emotional fits as well as the most disgusting table manners. All this brought about the end of his honeymoon with the Roman people. Soon after his announced recovery, he began acting with unprovoked aggression. Turning on two prominent and respected citizens, Gemellus and Silanus, he forced them to commit suicide on suspicion of plotting against him. The following year saw the death of his sister Drusilla, with whom he had been having an incestuous relationship. Caligula's reaction was hysterical; in a bizarre show of grief, he refused to cut either his hair or beard and insisted that Drusilla be deified, so becoming the first mortal woman to be worshipped as a goddess in Rome. This interference with Rome's complicated religious system made him many enemies. More objectively, he began to waste large sums of public money on vast and senseless building projects such as the construction of a bridge from the Palatine Hill, where he resided, to the Capitoline Hill opposite, so that he could be closer to the statue of Jupiter. Driven, like so many despots after him, by a growing megalomania, he ordered that the Temple of Augustus and the Theatre of Pompey be completed and that the imperial palace be extended. His new aqueducts, the Aqua Claudia and Anio Novus, were considered by Pliny the Elder as engineering marvels; he even had a large Egyptian obelisk shipped from Alexandria and erected in what is now the square facing St Peters in Rome. Caligula's insane ambitions bore no relation to the resources needed to complete such projects; although he did raise new taxes by imposing a levy on taverns, artisans and even, irrationally, on slaves. All food sold in the city was now to be taxed, as were lawyers and the daily wages of porters; even the income of pimps and prostitutes was taxed. The burden of these new levies may well have been the last straw for a Rome shocked and baffled by their Emperor's eccentric behaviour. The general conviction that Caligula had gone mad seemed finally confirmed when he announced his proposal to dig a canal through the Isthmus in Greece, yet another hare-brained scheme that was soon abandoned. Then, in AD 39, rather than embark his army in ships, he ordered a pontoon bridge 3 miles (4.8 km) long to be built across over the Gulf of Baiae (part of the Bay of Naples), and then led his soldiers over it in a triumphal procession. By now, Caligula was behaving with increasing irrationality. Having decided to invade Britain, he prepared a large army for embarkation, only to suddenly and inexplicably order them to collect shells from the beach instead. These were to be carried at once to Rome as 'the spoils of the ocean'. To their astonishment, the senators were then directed to add the shells to the treasures of the Capitol. Descending further into irrationality he contemplated setting up his own image in the temple at Jerusalem and compelling the Jews to worship it. In the context of this strange behaviour, the well-known rumour that he nominated his favourite horse, Incitatus, as a Consul of Rome is totally believable.

Unfortunately, there was now no provision in Roman law for an emperor to be held responsible for his actions or removed from power. A despot such as Caligula could revel in cruelty or indulge in the wildest excesses without restraint. The only way to get rid of such a ruler was to kill him, which his Praetorians duly did in AD 41. The question of whether or not Caligula was clinically insane remains unanswered. Some of his contemporaries such as Philo thought him no more than a vicious prankster. Modern psychology would probably diagnose Caligula as delusional, and possibly suffering from antisocial personality disorder as a result of his traumatic upbringing. Certainly his behaviour was bizarre, as were the incestuous relationships that appeared to exist between Caligula and his sisters – particularly Drusilla – and his habit of watching executions over dinner. As his reign progressed he became ever more confused; Suetonius claimed that he often sent for men he had already secretly killed, as though they were still alive.

After Caligula's death, Rome did not have to wait long for another emperor of doubtful sanity to take the throne. The very name of Nero has become synonymous with sadism, and as the nephew of Caligula he may have inherited the mental instability of his uncle. Yet eyewitness accounts of his odd behaviour indicate that he was more likely to have been a masochist. The writer Petronius, a close witness of the emperor's lifestyle, mocked life at Nero's court in his famous work the *Satyricon*, claiming 'it was more useful to use one's genitals than one's genius'. According to Petronius, the whole court was suffused with sado-masochism. Nero was deferential to strong figures including his mother Agrippina and his tutor Seneca; he was even seen to be subservient on occasion to his guard commander, Burrus. He was known to go out at night dressed as a slave, and to return the following morning with his faced bruised. When he played stage roles, he often chose submissive characters – such as a man in chains – or roles that involved transvestism, such as a bride being made love to by her husband. In *De Vita Caesarum* (*Lives of the Caesars*), Suetonius claims that:

> He had the boy Sporus castrated and actually tried to make a woman of
> him; and he married him with all the usual ceremonies, including a dowry
> and a bridal veil, took him to his home attended by a great throng, and
> treated him as his wife. And the witty jest that someone made is still
> current, that it would have been well for the world if Nero's father
> Domitius had that kind of wife. This Sporus, decked out with the finery of
> the empresses and riding in a litter, he took with him to the courts and
> marts of Greece, and later at Rome through the Street of the Images,
> fondly kissing him from time to time.

Nero's obvious masochism may have prompted his strange behaviour in drama competitions, as he always pretended to be at the mercy of the judges, falling on his knees in supplication. Why an emperor would need to do this – particularly as he persistently bribed up to 5,000 people to come along and applaud him – remains a mystery.

In AD 68, Nero appears to have indulged in the ultimate act of masochism. When warned that his enemies were coming to kill him, he refused to escape or even summon his guards. Instead, he remained quietly at the palace and ordered his servants to dig him a grave in the grounds. When the assassins arrived, he asked his most trusted attendant to help him cut his own throat. Insane or not, Nero was certainly one of the most charismatic figures in the whole of Roman history. Long after he was declared dead the people refused to believe it, and at least three Nero impostors appeared, claiming to be the lost emperor. The most convincing not only looked like him but seemed to have all Nero's old skills such as a good singing voice and an ability to play the cithara. A decade later, another cithara-playing Nero emerged in Asia, and led a rebellion that was put down with some difficulty by the legions. Yet the cult of the lost emperor remained; in AD 422, almost 400 years after his death, St Augustine of Hippo, disgusted by Nero's lingering admirers, wrote that 'Some suppose that he is not even dead... that he now lives in concealment and will live until he is revealed in his own time and restored to his kingdom.'

What then of the sanity of Adolf Hitler? Could such a man really be classed as mentally normal, given the irrational and incandescent hatred that drove him to attempt to eliminate the Jews? Unlike other despots, particularly Stalin, he did not suffer from extreme paranoia; he appeared convinced of the loyalty of the SS and the great majority of the army. However, one intriguing episode did occur in 1938. Lieutenant Colonel Hans Oster of German Forces Intelligence organized a plot involving Generals Beck, Brauschitch, von Witzelben and Halder, together with Admiral Wilhelm Canaris. Their plan was to overthrow the Führer, have him declared insane and incarcerate him in a mental institution. To succeed, the plotters needed strong British opposition to Hitler's proposed takeover of the Czech Sudetenland; but when Neville Chamberlain (1867–1940; British prime minister 1937–1940) capitulated to Hitler's demands, making him the hero of the hour, they postponed the attempt. This well-documented event suggests that Hitler's sanity was being questioned, even at that time. One modern historian, Robert Waite, has no doubt that Hitler was both a psychopath and clinically insane; but a leading American psychiatrist, Dr Fritz Redlich, concludes that though Hitler exhibited many psychiatric symptoms, he was not truly mentally ill. He may have suffered some strange delusions – notably that the Jews were plotting to take over the world – but the rest of his personality functioned perfectly well; and although he was afflicted with a whole variety of physical ailments, both real and imaginary, these could not explain his criminal actions.

Nor, according to his personal physician Dr Morell, was the Führer the crazed drug addict depicted by Allied intelligence throughout the War. Morell admits prescribing amphetamines, but this was a common practice at the time, and Hitler certainly did not become addicted. It should also be remembered that he did not have an addictive personality, and was neither a drinker nor a smoker. Yet the Allies remained convinced that Hitler must be in some way insane, and that if they could discover the reason why, it could be used in some way to bring about his military defeat. The United States Government's Office of Strategic Services was therefore commissioned to produce a psychological profile of Hitler. What became apparent was that he had survived childhood, while three brothers had died; that he later escaped death on one of the most dangerous battlefields of the First World War; and that he had thus become convinced that he had been spared by God to complete some great messianic task. It was noted that he twice grew a Christ-like beard after the war. A detailed examination of his speeches revealed a frequent use of words such as 'dirt', 'filth', 'dung' and 'smell', which could be ascribed to poor toilet training and motherly neglect at an important period of his childhood. Similarly, the report suggested that Hitler might have developed an Oedipal complex about his mother and feared symbolic castration by his father as a punishment. This led in turn to a fear of syphilis and an aversion to physical contact; it was suspected that his relationship with Eva Braun was unconsummated. There was also the suggestion that Hitler enjoyed looking at other men's bodies, and had strong, if sublimated, homosexual tendencies. The report went on to thoroughly examine Hitler's career to date, and to explore the psychological reasons for his decisions. It concluded with fascinating predictions of what might occur when Hitler realized the war was lost, one of them being clinical insanity:

> He has many characteristics which border on the schizophrenic. It is
> possible that when faced with defeat his psychological structure may
> collapse and leave him at the mercy of his unconscious forces… this would
> not be an undesirable eventuality from our point of view since it would do
> much to undermine the Hitler legend in the minds of the German people.

The extensive research on Hitler's mental condition has encouraged psychiatrists to examine the sanity or insanity of other more recent depots. Before his downfall, two other researchers, Jerrold M. Post and Amatzia Baram, produced a psychological profile of Saddam Hussein for the US Air Force. Although they found him clinically sane, they suggested that he could be described as a malignant narcissist, a label that they also applied to Stalin and Hitler. Malignant narcissism is defined by psychiatrists as a severe form of narcissistic personality disorder. As such, Hussein would be grandiose, self-centred, oversensitive to criticism and unable to feel empathy for others, while disguising his deep insecurity by presenting an inflated self-image to the world. Malignant narcissists also tend to paranoia and aggression; they display an anti-social personality, including the absence of moral or ethical judgment. Hussein, far from appearing psychotic, was adept at charming and manipulating those around him and was able to take control because his narcissism was expressed in grandiosity, self-assurance and the conviction that he knew exactly what Iraq needed. Anyone who opposed him became the victim of his cruel and sadistic behaviour. Dr Post added that the bunker built beneath one of Hussein's palaces was a perfect metaphor for his personality. Under the grandiose palace with its inlaid woods and fine marbles lay a cellar of reinforced concrete and steel, '…a grandiose facade and under it a siege state, ready to be betrayed, to be attacked, to strike back'.

CHAPTER 15

The Future

In 2002, the Russian post office issued a new set of colourful postage stamps celebrating the 80th anniversary of the Soviet Counter-Intelligence Service and its so-called 'heroes': Artur Artuzov, Sergei Puzitsky, Vladimir Styrne and Vsevolod Balitsky. These men were not soldiers or astronauts, but four of Stalin's most brutal and ruthless torturers. As one of Stalin's many biographers, Donald Rayfield, remarked, 'Imagine the row if Germany issued stamps commemorating Reinhard Heydrich, Heinrich Himmler and Adolf Eichmann.' Rayfield also notes that although no one in Germany smokes 'Auschwitz' cigarettes, the Belomorkanal brand in Russia bears the same name as a camp where 100,000 people were exterminated. Equally surprising is that the town of Dzerzhinsk, the most polluted city in all Russia, still effectively bears the name of Feliks Dzerzhinsky, the monstrous head of the Soviet secret police. For although Germany went through a period of national confession and recognition of the crimes committed under Hitler, Russia has never fully recognized the terror visited on its people by its cruellest despot, Stalin. Instead, his crimes are generally ignored; he is remembered and cherished as the leader of the Russian people in the Great Patriotic War. American philosopher and poet George Santayana has warned, 'Those who do not remember their past are condemned to repeat their mistakes.' Yet in recent years, there have been signs that Stalin is undergoing a form of rehabilitation, and that many elderly Russians, when faced with the challenges of an open society and a free enterprise economy, look back on his reign with nostalgia. Whatever his faults, they argue, those were the days when Russia was a great military nation which, at enormous cost to itself, defeated the German invaders. The argument is understandable, for never having known freedom under a succession of Tsars or under the communist regimes of Lenin and Stalin, Russia lacks any long-term experience of traditional democracy.

There are also ominous signs that Vladimir Putin (b.1952; Russian president 1999–2008) is beginning to establish himself in the manner of a traditional Russian despot. Opposition politicians are harried, laws changed to favour his continued rule and dissidents murdered by his secret service in either Moscow or London. Business booms, but the clear message from the Russian leader is that to remain and prosper, the new oligarchs must keep their noses out of politics. Putin appears to have little time for the messy interchange of democratic politics as he steadily accrues power to the central authority, nationalizes the independent television channel NTV and uses vote rigging to ensure a landslide victory for himself and his party in presidential elections. The most worrying aspect of his rule, however, is his undoubted popularity, which has increased in direct proportion to his power. He is steadily building a personality cult in a way that is eerily reminiscent of past despots. His determined stride, firm yet menacing smile and no-nonsense manner declare him a man on a mission for change. His image is everywhere as his slick publicity machine, using state resources, moves into gear. When shown stripped to the waist in his karate outfit he appears disturbingly like the half-naked Mussolini helping to drain the Pontine Marches in the 1930s. Increasingly backed by Russia's vast reserves of oil and gas, Putin has the economic weapons that today are more effective than guns and bombs. With these strategic resources behind him, Putin could make Russia a truly international power again. Significantly, he has withdrawn from arms limitation agreements and is devoting more resources to rebuilding the run-down military. Perhaps fears that Vladimir Putin will become the world's next powerful despot will not be realized, but he stands suspiciously close to a direct line of tyranny that leads from Ivan the Terrible to Joseph Stalin.

With the forced departure of Saddam Hussein, Kim Jong-Il has moved up to the top of the list of the world's worst despots still in power. In spite of constant skirmishes with the United States, Kim appears under little pressure internally. There is no perceivable opposition to his rule and he continues, in the Ceausescu manner, to live in great luxury in palaces staffed by his country's most beautiful women. Meanwhile, the people of North Korea continue to endure a grim existence of near starvation and political repression. It has been claimed that over 2 million of his subjects have starved to death as a result of mismanagement; at one point the steel mills shut down, the trains stopped running, there was no electricity for days and even the hospitals ran out of medicine. Yet Kim survived the crisis and maintains total control over the national media – every radio and TV set is neutered, its tuning dial soldered in one position, so that it can only receive transmissions from the state broadcasting system. Access to the Internet is generally banned; cell phones are confiscated from visitors to the country on arrival. Daily newspapers are dominated by accounts of The Dear Leader's doings, the full text of his interminable speeches only supplemented by mundane accounts of the few local events permitted. Kim is protected by the growing might of China and by the strategic importance of North Korea, particularly to the United

States. Successive American regimes have condemned his tyranny, but have hesitated to bring about his downfall for fear of provoking an increasingly powerful China. Diplomatically, Kim has proved himself a master strategist, particularly when dealing with the United States over North Korea's possession of nuclear weapons. His ability to taunt and tease the world's most powerful military machine is legendary. A few years ago he ordered the test firing of a new long-range missile as his own contribution to the Independence Day celebrations. Yet within a month, he had signed a secret agreement with the United States promising to be less provocative; in return, the Bush administration quietly lifted many economic sanctions. Then, having expelled UN nuclear inspectors so that he could test more atomic weapons and missiles, Kim allowed them back in again and received the thanks of the United States government. In frustration, the United States has showered insults on him, accusing him of everything from provoking a new arms race to money laundering.

Threats of war by the United States have only served to bolster Kim's regime and earn him kudos for standing up to a superpower, thus enabling him to develop a personality cult similar to that of Stalin. Few would wager on Kim Jong-Il losing power in the near future, and he appears confident enough to start grooming one of his two sons to take over. If this occurs, Kim Jong-Choi will be the third generation of his family to exercise despotic rule. Yet this may not happen. Given the increasing involvement of South Korea in the North, the Korean people may assert themselves in the manner of the Romanians in 1989. Kim's regime may suffer a similar fate to his architectural monument in the centre of Pyongyang – a vast glass walled pyramid standing 1,000 feet (305 m) high, by far the highest building in the city. But like Kim's diplomacy, it has never been completed. It was apparently intended to be a hotel, but something mysterious went wrong with the construction and it is now crumbling slowly away. The building is clearly an embarrassment to the regime, for curious visitors are discouraged from asking about it; it is never mentioned by guides, appears in no official publication and there no pictures of it. At night it remains unlit, and is the only high building in Pyongyang with no aircraft warning lights. One rare visitor, an American journalist, noted that it is almost exactly the same height and shape as the Ministry of Truth in George Orwell's *1984*.

In recent years, Robert Mugabe has joined the exclusive club of modern despots still in power. Once a positive symbol of the new independent Africa, Mugabe has presided over an increasingly repressive regime that has brought about a dramatic fall in the health and wellbeing of the Zimbabwean people – both black and white. According to the World Health Organization (WHO), his country now has the world's shortest life expectancy – 37 years for men and 34 for women – and the highest percentage of orphans, at 25 per cent of all born. Moreover, Zimbabwe's rate of inflation – well over 1000 per cent – represents the largest peacetime collapse of any economy since the disintegration of the German Weimar Republic in 1933. In some ways, Mugabe resembles 'Papa Doc' Duvalier of Haiti, having spent a similar childhood as a loner – refusing to join other boys in group activities, and preferring to trap animals alone than hunt them in groups. Today Mugabe appears a typical African dictator with his histrionic gestures, attempts at shallow popularism and constant verbal attacks on his political rivals. He also has his loyal support group of secret police, the much-feared Central Intelligence Organisation, that rules the townships with an iron hand. So self-confident is Robert Mugabe that he allows the police to beat up the Zimbabwe opposition leaders in public, and remains unconcerned at the intense condemnation it provokes. If public representatives can suffer such treatment in front of the world's media, what can ordinary people expect at Mugabe's hands? While Mugabe was careful not to mistreat Ian Smith, the leader of the old white regime, he was more brutal with his black opponents, once boasting that in addition to his seven academic degrees, he held a 'degree in violence'. When Mugabe first came to power, several of his ex-colleagues (his potential rivals) died mysteriously – one in a car crash, others found riddled with bullets. Opposition newspaper offices were blown up and journalists tortured. To this day, anyone showing opposition to the regime is dragged to prison camps where women are raped and men are beaten.

An embarrassment to Africa, Mugabe remains in power because of his anti-colonial credentials. Conscious of world condemnation for supporting Mugabe's regime, the president of South Africa, Thabo Mbeki, has repeatedly tried to broker talks between the opposition and the ruling party on some form of power-sharing in Zimbabwe, but this has always been rejected. Some observers see a perverse connection between events in Zimbabwe and those in South Africa, pointing out that the start of Mugabe's misrule coincided with the release of Nelson Mandela, who then took over the mantle of great independence hero of Africa. While Mandela was in prison, Mugabe could do no wrong; he was feted as the anti-apartheid leader of Africa, while presiding over national reconciliation of different races and a buoyant economy. Then Mandela arrived on the scene to spoil the party. South Africa's economy was far larger and began drawing international investment; Mandela himself stole the press coverage and the limelight. To Mugabe's chagrin, Zimbabwe was cast into the shade. When the two met, Mugabe was seen to be twitching with distaste and annoyance.

Many modern despots have thankfully departed the scene. Although Idi Amin did not enjoy the sanctuary of Saudi Arabia long, his predecessor Milton Obote, only marginally less brutal than Amin himself, lives happily in Zambia. Haiti's Jean-

Claude Duvalier found refuge in France and Mengistu Haile Mariam (b.1937; head of state 1974–91), whose 'Red Terror' campaign in Ethiopia led to the persecution of tens of thousands of political opponents, enjoys the protection of President Robert Mugabe of Zimbabwe. Paraguay's Alfredo Stroessner (1912–2006; president of Paraguay 1954–1989), who used torture and repression to maintain his rule for over three decades, retired to Brazil, where he died in 2006.

Yet other despotic regimes continue to flourish unchecked. In Uzbekistan, Islam Karimov (b.1938; President from 1990) presides over one of the most repressive regimes in the whole of central Asia. In April 2002, a special UN report concluded that torture in the country was 'pervasive and persistent... throughout the investigation process'. In the same year, Muzafar Avazov, an opposition leader, was boiled alive for refusing to abandon his religious convictions in prison. In 2003, Bush granted a waiver to Uzbekistan, when its failure to improve its human rights record should have led to its aid being slashed. In February 2004 the US secretary of defence, Donald Rumsfeld, visited Islam Karimov and said, 'The relationship between our countries is strong and growing stronger. We look forward to strengthening our political and economic relations comprehension.'

It is possible that the events of 21 December 1989 marked a turning point in the long history of despotism. The moment when Nicolae Ceausescu looked up from his speech and realized that it was all over was witnessed around the world. The petty if powerful dictator was suddenly transformed into a frightened old man who knew that his time was up. His subsequent attempt to escape, his capture and summary execution showed how just how easy it could be to get rid of a tyrant once the spell was broken. Perhaps this event had a cathartic effect on the conscience of the democratic world, for within four years of Ceausescu's fall the World Court at the Hague had established the International Criminal Court (ICC). Its function is to investigate and try cases of genocide, war crimes and crimes against humanity anywhere in the world, and as such is the most important advance in combating despotism since the Nuremberg War Crimes trials of 1945–1946. Whereas the previously established World Court could hear only lawsuits between governments, the ICC has the express power to prosecute individuals, although initially only for crimes committed outside the offender's own country. For this reason, Slobodan Milošević of Serbia could only be charged with offences committed against the Kosovo Albanians. Pol Pot could not be tried for killing his own Cambodians, nor General Pinochet for the thousands of 'disappeared' in Chile. Yet the potential political significance of the ICC, when it expands its remit, will be dramatic; it will be a major deterrent to anyone attempting to inflict terror and persecution on a people. Milošević was the first former head of state to be tried before any international criminal court since Admiral Karl Dönitz (1891–1980), who took over from Hitler in the closing days of the Second World War and stood with the other Nazis accused at Nuremberg. The offences that Milošević was charged with, apart from the 8,000 slain in Sbrenica (the worst atrocity on European soil since the Second World War) were a familiar litany of misdeeds: genocide or complicity in genocide; persecutions; extermination, murder and wilful killing; unlawful confinement, imprisonment, torture, wilfully causing great suffering, other inhumane acts; deportation and inhumane acts such as forcible transfers; wanton destruction, plunder of public or private property; cruel treatment and attacks on civilians. But in reality, Milošević was not a despot but a traditional Balkans warlord, ruthlessly defending what he saw as the best interests of his people. Found unanimously guilty by the ICC, he died soon after his conviction; but his trial had served as a warning to others.

There are encouraging signs that countries around the world are prepared to arrest and try mass murderers and despots outside their own domain, provided there is sufficient evidence to charge them. The arrest in Britain in 1998 of the former Chilean dictator, Augusto Pinochet, led to court decisions that were seen as a landmark in the development of a universal jurisdiction. Spain had requested his extradition to face charges over alleged human rights abuses during his time in power and Britain placed him under house arrest. Although Pinochet was eventually freed on grounds of ill health, his case showed that tyrants might be held accountable by the international community, even if granted immunity in their own country. Mexico also agreed to extradite to Spain the notorious Argentine naval officer, Ricardo Miguel Cavallo. He was wanted for the alleged torture and 'disappearance' of a Spanish citizen during Argentina's 'dirty war', which ended in 1983. Also under threat is Hissène Habré (b.1930; in power 1982–1990), the former despot of Chad. Habré, who has taken refuge in Senegal, was indicted by a Chadian court on charges of crimes against humanity. Although Senegalese courts ruled that they did not have the power to extradite him, they are still holding him until he can be deported to stand trial in Belgium. A Belgian judge has formally visited Chad to investigate the charges, and the current Chadian government has waived Habré's immunity. There is also the case of Sebastien Nzapali, once known in the Congo as 'the King of the Beasts', who has been brought to trial in a Dutch court for the crimes of torture, rape and extreme cruelty committed in his own country. Nzapali was not a bandit, but a colonel in the Democratic Republic of the Congo's civil guard; his arrest, on the basis of charges filed against him by three Congolese nationals, implicated the regime of the ex-president, Mobutu Sese Seko. Clearly the Dutch mean to send out a signal that there is no refuge for war criminals in the Netherlands; five years ago, they also established a special genocide and war crimes investigation team to seek out suspects hiding in the country and try them under Dutch law. The same mechanism might well be used to bring to justice the perpetrators of the Rwanda massacre, or those controlling the militias that have ravaged Darfur. Perhaps Robert Mugabe will one day face prosecution for overseeing the massacre of thousands of villagers by North Korean-trained soldiers in Matabeleland, in the southwest of Zimbabwe, in the early 1980s.

But caution is needed if trials are to be effective. The Human Rights Watch (HRW) group said that Saddam Hussein's trial was among the most important war tribunals since the Nazi trials in Nuremberg, stating that it 'represents the first opportunity to create a historical record concerning some of the worst cases of human rights violations, and to begin the process of a methodical accounting of the policies and decisions that give rise to these events'. Unfortunately, many international commentators saw the trial as unsatisfactory: the HRW condemned its many 'serious administrative, procedural and substantive legal defects'. The 5 November trial for crimes against humanity was not fair; even Hussein's right to lodge an appeal was dismissed, by an Iraqi government that seemed determined to get rid of the despot as soon as possible, regardless of legal niceties. Trials such as this may also raise another problem: what tyrant, seeing the imprisonment of Miloševic, the execution of Hussein and the treatment of Pinochet, would be stupid enough to abandon his sovereign immunity and risk this treatment?

All these attempts to impose international justice on crimes of national despotism show how important the modern nation-state has become in protecting the people from abuse. The great philosopher Jean-Jacques Rousseau had, in the early 18th century, anticipated an age of liberation in which the state would destroy all social ties, releasing the individual from loyalty to anything except the state itself. Rousseau wrote, 'Each citizen would then be completely independent of all his fellow men but absolutely dependent on the state.' Rousseau's concept of the state as a liberator was a revolutionary idea. It implied that politics could be the means not only of creating a just society, but of actually transforming human nature and creating respect for the principles of democracy, human rights and freedom of speech. But it does not account for the people: in a tyranny, it is public opinion that can often bring about the downfall of the tyrant. It was public opinion that brought the end of the Ceausescus' regime in Romania, and the downfall of Trujillo in the Dominican Republic. In Trujillo's case, the murder of three young women proved his undoing, rather than the nameless thousands he had slaughtered on the Haitian border. The Mirabal sisters – Patria, Minerva, and María Teresa – came from a wealthy and privileged background and might well have been the beneficiaries of his dictatorial government. Yet during the 1950s the three young women joined an underground movement opposed to Trujillo. Gradually each became involved in the resistance; the sisters, known as 'Las Mariposas', the butterflies, became its best known and most inspirational leaders. On the evening of 25 November 1960, as the Mirabal sisters returned home from visiting their husbands in the Puerto Plata prison, Trujillo's soldiers ambushed their jeep. The three women and their driver were either strangled or beaten to death and their bodies placed in the jeep and pushed off a cliff.

Their deaths caused an extraordinary outburst of popular anger. The Dominican people refused to believe the government version of events, and the Catholic Church became openly critical of the regime. This marked a turning point for Trujillo. The resistance gained momentum, and six months later, on 30 May 1961, his car was ambushed in the street. He was assassinated with guns supplied by the American CIA. The sisters' home became a shrine to democracy and the day of their assassination was sanctioned by the UN as a day of remembrance for women who have been the victims of tyranny.

Significantly, it was America's decision to oust him that led to the removal of Trujillo. Dominican public opinion alone would not have been sufficient. A similar problem faces the people of Burma if they are ever to remove their own despotic military regime, which has China as a patron and main trading partner, and the diplomatic support of another notorious despotism, North Korea. The Burmese military rulers achieved power in 1988, beginning with the massacre of 3,000 students in the streets. The junta then overturned a democratically elected government in 1990 and imprisoned its leader, Aung San Suu Kyi (b.1945), who has had her activities severely restricted and been placed under house arrest for a great deal of time since the late 1980s. The regime sealed its power through the repression of ethnic minorities, the use of slave labour and involvement in the global drug trade. When Buddhist monks marched peacefully through the streets in protest, they were dragged under the canopy of jungle, where satellites are unable to record their massacre. Burma continues to be ruled by a violent military regime that cares little for world opinion, and with the powerful international protection of China it can expect to get away with it for years to come.

World opinion appears to mean little to the rulers of the Sudan either, which continues to deny providing money and assistance to the Janjaweed militia that has been persecuting tens of thousands of refugees in Darfur. The refugees are black Africans, classic scapegoats subjected to persecution by an Arab majority. The UN estimates that the conflict has left 450,000 dead from violence and disease, while as many as 2.5 million people have been displaced from their homes, with around 200,000 seeking refuge in neighbouring Chad. The Sudanese government's actions include the suppression of information, imprisonment and killing witnesses; to hinder international inquiries, evidence has been destroyed and journalists have been arrested. The crisis in Darfur should, in theory, be relatively easy to deal with, as the Sudan has no powerful international protectors, but little is done. The genocide is attributed to the brutal plan of three men in the Sudanese national government – President Bashir, Vice-President Taha and Security Chief Gosh, who have spread their system of persecution to other African countries including Chad and the Central African Republic. The powerlessness of the international community to deal with the crisis is mystifying. It can only be explained by Western democracies' hesitation to offend Arab opinion, in the same way that they have been reluctant to interfere in Mugabe's Zimbabwe.

Although mechanisms now exist to bring despots to trial, the causes of tyranny still exist. While Marxism is a spent force and Fascism is looked upon as a transitory aberration, religious tyrannies are more active than ever. Their appeal is in the moral certitude they express, unconditioned by reason, debate or simple humanity. Combined with nationalism, they make a formidable challenge to the Western tradition of democracy. The danger is that the leaders of this bitterly anti-Western and anti-liberal fundamentalism are not the poor, illiterate and isolated, but wealthy and well-educated intellectuals who are familiar with the West. It hardly needs mentioning that Osama Bin Laden and his supporters in Al Qaeda are from this background, and it can only be imagined what kind of theocratic despotism would be imposed if they gained power.

There is also a growing irrationalism in the liberal democracies of the West, and a tendency to embrace pseudo-science, which makes them vulnerable to religious fundamentalism. The problem is that democracy, however desirable it may be, is the most inefficient form of government. In order to change a government or decide a referendum, the people must go to the polls. Opinions have to be listened to, groups must meet and talk, representatives have to be briefed. Bills in a typically democratic parliament need to go through three readings before being voted on and becoming law. They are only effective because they reflect the will of people. They execute the will of the majority, protect the rights of minorities and, most importantly, the majority and minorities are not fixed entities. In a democracy their roles can change and even be reversed, which could never happen in a despotism. In over 2,000 years, nothing has been devised that can substitute for this unwieldly system; and although despots have come and gone, democracy, with all its faults and weaknesses, still remains our proven defence against tyranny.

CHAPTER 16

Exceptions That Prove the Rule

Almost every despot described in this book has been a man. The aggression, ruthlessness and single-mindedness needed to seize power and to dominate a country are traditionally seen as male characteristics. But in nature it is often the female that exhibits these traits. Among meerkats, for instance, the lead female is the despot of the group. She is a serial killer who will even eat her own grandchildren to keep control. So powerful is her social position that only she and her chosen mate reproduce. Any animal that challenges her right to dominate is instantly attacked. In human history, any female exhibiting such despotic characteristics has usually been a consort, for example Elena Ceausescu or Nexhmije Hoxha.

The most famous dominant wife was the Empress Theodora of Byzantium (c.AD 500–548; Empress AD 527–548) who married the Emperor Justinian I (c.AD 482–565; Emperor 527–565) in AD 527. Theodora was the daughter of the bear-keeper at the circus in Constantinople. When still a young girl, she became one of the most famous prostitutes in the city with a reputation for inventiveness and insatiability. Her extraordinary rise from a woman of the streets to empress of the most powerful Christian state in Europe was well documented by the Byzantine historian Procopius (c.AD 499–565), who was highly honoured by Justinian I. He claims that Justinian became so infatuated with her that he treated her as his intellectual equal, and allowed her to participate in the political decisions of the empire. Justinian himself stated that he always consulted Theodora before he promulgated any new law. Although she encouraged many of the great achievements in Byzantine art and architecture that marked their joint rule, Theodora showed a ruthless and despotic capacity to protect her status as empress, and every court official had to take an oath of allegiance to her as well as to the emperor. Suspicious of everyone, she placed her spies everywhere in the city and ordered them to watch for any sign of dissent. Anyone suspected of sedition was locked away in one of her private prisons and left there to rot. Theodora became so powerful that she even corresponded directly with foreign ambassadors. In character, she seems to have been harsh and ill-tempered, with a tendency to take offence easily and to seize the property of anyone who displeased her.

There is only one female despot in history to rival the dozens of male tyrants who have seized and abused power. This was Ranavalona, queen of the island of Madagascar in the early 19th century. Ranavalona was the adopted daughter of the dynasty-founding king, and became the wife of his son and heir Radama. When King Radama died, she found herself in great danger, because the rightful heir to the throne was the eldest son of Radama's eldest sister, Prince Rakatobe. Fearing that she would be disposed of, Ranavalona had already established a secret network of supporters who, like her, were opposed to the Christian missionaries that her late husband had allowed into the country. This made her the natural leader of opposition to the growing Western influence on the island, and united the priests and supporters of the old religion behind her. This traditional belief system, the *ombiasy,* involved the conviction that there were close ties between the living and the dead. With the help of two court officials, Ranavalona organized a palace coup and proclaimed herself Queen of Madagascar on 1 August 1828. Displaying a ruthlessness worthy of any male despot, she then turned on the royal family and slaughtered every potential claimant to the throne. Her sister-in-law was starved to death. Then, in a manner worthy of the Emperor Caligula, Ranavalona installed herself on a throne overlooking the sea, from where she watched as prisoners were thrown to their deaths. One of the first to die was Andrianmihaja, the lover who had helped her seize power. He was now the commander of the army, but his sympathy to Europeans had made him enemies among his own people. When accused of treason, he refused to attend the hearing; so Ranavalona sent an executioner to despatch him in the traditional Madagascan manner – by stabbing a knife through his throat.

Ruling alone, Ranavalona introduced a reign of sadistic terror to Madagascar. Torture, crucifixions and beheadings became commonplace; anyone suspected of disloyalty was flayed alive or sawn in half. The appalling atrocities she condoned are as bad as anything ordered by either Vlad Tepes or Ivan the Terrible. Guilt was decided at trials by whether or not the accused responded to a poisonous local shrub – in other words, trial by ordeal, which had been used on suspected witches in medieval Europe. In a ritual unique to the island, the accuser paid a deposit of money that was returned if the accused was found guilty. Even more bizarre was the traditional Madagascan practice, enthusiastically endorsed by Ranavalona, of progressive amputation. First the fingers were cut off one at a time; then the toes; and finally the limbs. At each stage, the accused was invited to confess his guilt. If he did, he was instantly executed; if not, he simply bled to death, but his relatives were comforted by the knowledge that he was an innocent man.

Many of these strange and sadistic rituals might be discounted as little more than horror stories had not a reliable French traveller been present to witness them. Jean Laborde, the son of a blacksmith, had made a small fortune by trading in Bombay, but had lost it all in a mad quest for shipwrecked gold on the shores of Madagascar. He found favour at Ranavalona's court and records that as her reign progressed, the Queen became ever more paranoid. Thousands of citizens suspected of treason were put to death every year. Anyone accused of Christian sympathies also became a victim and was forced to lick the Queen's bare feet, which were covered with a bright pink poison. A refusal meant instant execution, but it was a pointless exercise that only served to satisfy Ranavalona's perverted sadism. Together with this addiction to cruelty the queen had a taste for sex and, like the Empress Theodora, selected lovers at random. In everything she did, Ranavalona behaved exactly like the worst male tyrants in history. When she died in 1861, she departed like so many of her kind, totally at peace and lying quietly in her bed.

Bibliography

ABBOTT, ELIZABETH, HAITI, *The Duvaliers and Their Legacy*, Simon and Schuster, New York, 1988.

ABZUG, ROBERT H., *Inside the Vicious Heart*, Oxford University Press, 1985.

ADORNO, THEODOR W., *The Authoritarian Personality*, W. W. Norton, New York, 1993.

ANTONOV-OVSEYENKO, ANTON, *The Times of Stalin: Portrait Of a Tyranny*, translated by GEORGE SAUNDERS, Harper & Rose, New York, 1981.

ARENDT, HANNAH, *The Origins of Totalitarianism*, Andre Deutsche, London, 1986.

– *Eichmann in Jerusalem*, Penguin Books, London, 1971.

– *On Revolution*, Penguin Books, London, 2006.

– *On Violence*, Harcourt Brace & World, New York, 1969.

Aristotle's Politics, translated by BENJAMIN JOWETT, Clarendon Press, Oxford, 1945.

AXELROD, ALAN and PHILLIPS, CHARLES, *Absolute Rulers and Would-Be Rulers in World History*, Facts on File, New York, 1995.

AYLING, S. E., *Portraits of Power*, Barnes & Noble, New York, 1963

BECKER, ELIZABETH, *When the War Was Over: The Voices of Cambodia's Revolution and its People*, Simon and Schuster, New York, 1986.

BECKER, JASPER, *Hungry Ghosts: Mao's Secret Famine*, John Murray, London, 1996,

BEHR, EDWARD, *Kiss the Hand You Cannot Bite*, Penguin Books, London, 1992.

BETHELL, NICHOLAS, *Betrayed*, Times Books, New York, 1984.

BOUC, ALAIN, *Mao Tse-tung, A Guide to His Thoughts*, translated by PAUL AUSTER and LYDIA DAVIS, St. Martin's Press, New York, 1977.

BOSWORTH, R. J. B., *Mussolini's Italy*, Penguin Books, London, 2005

BULLOCK, ALAN, *Hitler and Stalin, Parallel Lives*, HarperCollins. London, 1991.

– *Hitler, A Study in Tyranny*, Penguin Books, London, 1969.

CHAN, STEPHEN, *Robert Mugabe: A Life of Power and Violence*, I. B. Tauris, London, 2002.

CHANDLER, DAVID, *The Tragedy of Cambodian History: Politics, War, and Revolution Since 1945*, Yale University Press, 1991.

CHIROT, DANIEL, *Modern Tyrants: The Power and Prevalence of Evil in Our Age*, Princeton University Press, 1996.

CLEMENTS, JONATHAN, *The First Emperor of China*, Sutton Publishing, Gloucestershire, 2007.

COLLIER, BASIL, *Barren Victories: Versailles to Suez*, Doubleday & Co., New York, 1964.

COLLIER, RICHARD, *Duce!: A Biography of Benito Mussolini*, Fontana, London, 1972.

CONSTABLE, PAMELA and VALENQUELA, ARTURO, *A Nation of Enemies*, W. W. Norton & Company, London, 1991.

COUSINS, NORMAN, *The Pathology of Power*, W. W. Norton & Company, New York, London, 1987.

CRANKSHAW, EDWARD, *Gestapo, Instrument of Tyranny*, Viking Press, New York, 1956.

DARWISH, ADEL and ALEXANDER, GREGORY, *Unholy Babylon: The Secret History of Saddam's War*, Gollancz, London, 1991.

DAVIDSON, EUGENE, *The Making of Adolf Hitler*, Macmillan Publishing, New York, 1977.

DICKIE, JOHN, *Cosa Nostra: A History of the Sicilian Mafia*, Hodder Paperback, London, 2007.

DIEDERICH, BERNARD, *Papa Doc: The Truth About Haiti Today*, Penguin Books, London, 1972.

DUNLOP, IAN, *Louis XIV*, Sinclair-Stevenson, London, 1999.

DWYER, PHILIP, *Napoleon: The Path to Power 1769–1799*, Bloomsbury, London, 2007.

EAGAN, JAMES, *Maximilien Robespierre: Nationalist Dictator*, Octagon Books, London, 1978.

ENGLUND, S, *Napoleon: A Political Life*, Harvard University Press, 2005.

EVERITT, ANTHONY, *The First Emperor: Caesar Augustus and the Triumph of Rome*, John Murray, London, 2007.

FALASCA, SIMONETTA, *Fascist Spectacle*, University of California Press, 2000.

FERGUSON, JAMES, *Papa Doc: Baby Doc*, Blackwood Publishers, Oxford, 1988.

FITZGERALD, C. P., *Mao Tse-tung and China*, Penguin Books, London, 1977.

FOLEY, MARTIN, *Trujillo: Death at a Distance*, Washington House, USA, 2005

FRASER, SIR ALAN, *Frederick The Great*, Allen Lane, London, 2000.

FRIEDLANDER, SAUL, *Nazi Germany and the Jews*, Phoenix, London, 1998

FROMM, ERIC, *The Anatomy of Human Destructiveness*, Jonathan Cape, London, 1974.

GARNIER, CHRISTINE, *Salazar*, Farrar, Strauss & Young, New York, 1954.

GLASS, JAMES, *Psychosis and Power*, Cornell University Press, 1986.

GOLDING, CARL, *Speaking With the Devil: A Dialogue With Evil*, Viking, New York, 1996.

GWYN, DAVID, *Idi Amin – Death-Light of Africa*, Little Brown, New York, 1977.

HALLIDAY, JON, *The Memoirs of Enver Hoxha*, Chatto & Windus, London, 1986.

HERTLAND, W. E., *A Short History of the Roman Republic*, Cambridge University Press, 1929.

HIBBERT, CHRISTOPHER, *Il Duce, The Life of Benito Mussolini*, Penguin Books, London, 1965.

HUNTER, EDWARD, *Brainwashing: The Study of the Men Who Defied it*. Farrar, Strauss & Giroux, New York, 1956.

JOHNSON, A. H., *The Age of the Enlightened Despot 1660–1789*, Methuen, London, 1936.

KARSH, EFRAIN and RANTSI, INARI, *Saddam Hussein, A Political Biography*, The Free Press, New York, 1991.

KAY, HUGH, *Salazar and Modern Portugal*, Eyre & Spottiswood, London, 1970.

KIERNAN, BEN, *How Pol Pot Came to Power*, Verso, London, 1985.

KLONSKY, MILTON, *The Fabulous Ego*, New York Times Books, 1974

KUBIZEK, AUGUST, *The Young Hitler I Knew*, translated by E.V., ANDERSON, Greenhill Books, UK, 2006.

KUPER, LEO, *Genocide: Its Political Use in the Twentieth Century*, Penguin Books, London, 1981.

LAIDLER, KEITH, *Female Caligula*, Wiley, Chichester, 2005.

LAQUEUR, WALTER, *Fascism, Past, Present, Future*, Oxford University Press, 1996.

LE BON, GUSTAV, *The Crowd*, Fisher Unwin, London, 1909

LEE, STEPHEN, *European Dictatorships 1918–45*, Routledge, London, 2000.

LEWIS, PAUL, *Authoritarian Regimes in Latin America*, Rowman & Littlefield, Maryland, 2006.

LI ZHISUI, *The Private Life of Chairman Mao*, translated by TAI HUNG-CHAO, Random House, New York, 1994.

LUDWIG, EMIL, *Three Portraits: Hitler, Mussolini, Stalin*, Longmans Green, New York, 1940.

MACDONOUGH, GILES, *Frederick The Great*, Weidenfeld & Nicholson, London, 1999.

MA'OZ, MOSHE, *Asad, The Sphinx of Damascus*, Weidenfeld & Nicolson, London, 1988.

MACHIAVELLI, NICCOLÒ, *The Prince*, translated by G. BULL, Penguin Books, London, 1970.

MADRIAGA, IRIS DE, *Ivan the Terrible*, Yale University Press, 2006.

MASSIE, ALAN, *Nero's Heirs*, Hodder & Stoughton, London, 1999.

MASSIE, ALAN, *Caligula*, Sceptre, London. 2004.

MILLER, ALICE, *For Your Own Good: Hidden Cruelty in Child-rearing and the Roots of Violence*, Virago, London, 1983.

– *Though Shalt Not Be Aware: Society's Betrayal of the Child*, Farrar, Strauss and Giroux, New York, 1984.

OPPENHEIM, WALTER, *Europe and the Enlightened Despots*, Hodder Arnold, London, 1990.

ORNES, GERMAN E., *Trujillo: Little Caesar of the Caribbean*, Thomas Nelson, Nashville, 1958.

OVERY, RICHARD, *The Dictators*, BCA, London, 2004.

– *Goering: The Iron Man*, Weidenfeld & Nicholson, London, 2000.

PAYNE, STANLEY, *History of Fascism, 1914–1945*, Routledge, London, 1996.

PERRIE, MAUREEN, *Ivan the Terrible*, Longmans, London, 2003.

PLATT, RICHARD, *Julius Caesar: Great Dictator*, Dorling Kindersley, London, 2003

PRESTON, PAUL, *Franco: A Biography*, Fontana, London, 1995.

RENGGER, JOHAN, *The Reign of Doctor Joseph Gaspard Roderick de Francia of Paraguay*, Kennikat Press, USA,.

REPPETTO, THOMAS, *American Mafia: A History of its Rise to Power*, Owl Books, USA, 2005.

RICHARDSON, ROSAMOND, *Stalin's Shadow: Inside the Family of One of the World's Greatest Tyrants*, St. Martin's Press, New York, 1994.

ROBERTS M., *Gustavus Adolphus*, Longmans, London, 1992.

Ross, Terrill, *Mao: A Biography*, Harper & Row, New York, 1980.

Rounding, Virginia, *Catherine The Great: Love, Sex and Power*, Hutchinson, London, 2006.

Shirer, William, *Rise and Fall of the Third Reich*, Simon & Schuster, New York, 1962.

Smith, Edward Ellis, *The Young Stalin*, Cassell, London, 1968.

Snow, Edgar, *Red Star Over China*, Penguin Books, London, 1972

Spooner, Mary Helen, *Soldiers in a Narrow Land: The Pinochet Regime in Chile*, University of California Press, Berkeley, 1994.

Stefoff, Rebecca, *Pol Pot*, Chelsea House Publishers, New York, 1991.

Suetonius, *The Twelve Caesars*, translated by Robert Graves, Penguin Classics, London, 2003.

Thomas, Hugh, *The Spanish Civil War*, Penguin Books, 2003.

Toland, John, *Adolf Hitler, Vols I, II*, Doubleday & Company, New York, 1976.

Trevor-Roper, Hugh, *The Last Days of Hitler*, Macmillan, London, 1947.

Trow, M. J., *Vlad the Impaler*, The History Press, London, 2003.

Troyat, Henri, *Catherine The Great*, Penguin Books, London, 1994.

Tucker, Robert C., *Political Culture and Leadership in Soviet Russia From Lenin to Gorbachev*, W. W. Norton, New York, 1988.

Tucker, Robert C., *Stalin in Power: The Revolution From Above, 1928–1941*, W. W. Norton, New York, 1992.

Waite, Robert G. L., *The Psychopathic God*, Basic Books, New York, 1977.

Wilkinson, Richard, *France and Louis XIV, 1661–1715*, Hodder Arnold, London, 1993.

Wilson, Edward Osborne, *On Human Nature*, Penguin Books, London, 2001.

TIMELINE

Dates given represent period in power.

336–323 BC Alexander the Great, King of Macedonia

221–210 BC Qin Shi Huang, Emperor of China

AD 14–37 Tiberius, Roman Emperor

AD 37–41 Caligula, Roman Emperor

AD 54–68 Nero, Roman Emperor

1206–1227 Genghis Khan, Warrior-ruler of Mongolia

1456–1462 and **1476** Vlad the Impaler, Ruler of Walachia

1547–1584 Ivan the Terrible, Tsar of Russia

1625–1649 Charles I, King of Great Britain and Ireland

1643–1715 Louis XIV, King of France

1740–1780 Maria Theresa of Austria, Archduchess of Austria, Queen of Hungary and Bohemia

1740–1786 Frederick II (Frederick the Great), King of Prussia

1762–1796 Catherine II, Empress of Russia

1771–1792 Gustavus III, King of Sweden

1774–1792 Louis XVI, King of France

1793–1794 Maximilien Robespierre, ruled France

1804–1815 Napoleon Bonaparte, Emperor

1814–1840 José Gaspar Rodriguez de Francia, dictator of Paraguay

1816–1828 Shaka, Zulu King

1856–1884 Mutesa I, King of Buganda

1862–1870 Francisco Solano López, dictator of Paraguay

1865–1909 Leopold II, King of the Belgians

1922–1943 Benito Mussolini, Italian dictator

1923–1930 Miguel Primo de Rivera, dictator of Spain

1924–1953 Joseph Stalin, Russian dictator

1930–1961 Rafael Leónidas Trujillo, Dominican Republic dictator

1931–1976 Mao Tse-tung, Chairman of Chinese Communist Party, **1949–1959** Chairman of People's Republic of China

1932–1968 António de Oliveira Salazar, Portuguese dictator

1933–1945 Adolf Hitler, German dictator

1939–1975 Francisco Franco, Head of government of Spain

1944–1985 Enver Hoxha, Albanian leader

1948–1994 Kim Il Sung, Communist leader of North Korea

1954–1989 Alfredo Stroessner, President of Paraguay

1957–1971 François 'Papa Doc' Duvalier, President of Haiti

1958–1963 Abdul Karim Kassem,

Premier of new republic of Iraq

1964–1974 Constantine II, King of Greece

1966–1971 and **1980–1985** Milton Obote, President of Uganda

1966–1977 Jean-Bédel Bokassa, President of Central African Republic, **1977–1979** Emperor of Central African Republic

1971–1979 Idi Amin, President of Uganda

1971–1986 Jean-Claude 'Baby Doc' Duvalier, President of Haiti

1974–1989 Nicolae Ceausescu, President of Romania

1974–1990 Augusto Ugarte Pinochet, Chilean dictator

From **1977** Muammar Gaddafi, President of Libya

1979–2003 Saddam Hussein, President of Iraq

From **1987** Robert Mugabe, Executive President of Zimbabwe

1990–2006 Saparmurat Atayevich Niyazov, President of Turkmenistan

From **1994** Kim Jong-Il, leader of North Korea

1997–2000 Slobodan Milosevic, President of Yugoslavia

1997–2003 Charles Taylor, President of Liberia

From **1998** Hugo Rafael Chávez, President of Venezuela

1999–2008 Vladimir Putin, Russian president

ACKNOWLEDGEMENTS

The author would like to acknowledge the influence on this work of the ideas of the great philosopher Karl Popper who left us a timely warning that the enemies of the Open Society come not only from the extreme Right or extreme Left.

PICTURE CREDITS

1. © Bettmann/Corbis
2. © Bettmann/Corbis
3. © Corbis,
4. © Hulton-Deutsch Collection/Corbis
5. ILN Photos
6. ILN Photos
7. ILN Photos
8. © Bernard Bisson/Sygma/Corbis
9. © Geneviève Chauvel /Sygma/Corbis
10. © PEER GRIMM/epa/Corbis
11. © Handout/CNP/Corbis
12. © Corbis
13. ILN Photos
14. © Bettmann/Corbis
15. © Alain Nogues/Alain Nogues/Corbis
16. © Bettmann/Corbis
17. © Bettmann/Corbis
18. © William Campbell/Sygma/Corbis
19. © Richard Melloul/SygmaCorbis
20. © epa/Corbis

Index